Globalization/Anti-Globalization

Second edition

Globalization/Anti-Globalization

Beyond the Great Divide

Second edition

David Held and Anthony McGrew

polity

First published in 2007 by Polity Press
Reprinted in 2011

Polity Press
65 Bridge Street
Cambridge CB2 1UR, UK

Polity Press
350 Main Street
Malden, MA 02148, USA

ISBN-13: 978-07456-3910-9
ISBN-13: 978-07456-3911-6 (pb)

A catalogue record for this book is available from the British Library.

Typeset in 11 on 13 pt Sabon
by Servis Filmsetting Ltd, Manchester
Printed and bound in the United States by Odyssey Press Inc., Gonic, New Hampshire

For further information on Polity, visit our website: www.politybooks.com

Contents

Contents

Figures and Tables

Figures

List of Figures and Tables

List of Figures and Tables

Preface to the Second Edition

In the aftermath of 9/11 and the war in Iraq, there has been much talk of the end of globalization. These post-mortems for globalization, we argue, are entirely premature. We evaluate the claims of those who dismiss the continuing significance of globalization through a comprehensive assessment of contemporary global trends. This thematic exploration focuses on the primary structures of world order: patterns of governance, organized violence, and cultural, ecological and economic exchange, with particular emphasis given to global patterns of inequality, exclusion and domination. Each chapter discusses and evaluates the contending claims and counterclaims of the principal antagonists in the globalization debate: the globalists and sceptics. Building on this analysis we present the case for continuing to take globalization seriously as both a description and an explanation of our current global predicament. Indeed, globalization remains, we argue, a fundamental source of both intense controversy and conflict within and more significantly beyond the academy. For it resurrects, albeit in a new context, some foundational questions of political life: who rules, in whose interests, to what ends, according to what ethical principles, and by what means? In this respect it engages one of the most important ethical and political debates of our times: can globalization be tamed? Whether a more just and stable world order is either desirable or feasible is explored in the concluding chapters, which present an alternative ethical and political agenda for the twenty-first century – a global covenant of cosmopolitan social democracy.

Globalization/Anti-Globalization was first published in 2002 when these terms had a slightly different meaning than today. Since its initial publication the globalization debate has matured and altered. This second edition reflects this development both substantively and intellectually. Substantively it has involved the addition of many new chapters and much new material to take account of the enormous literature which now exists, as well as the changed global context. Intellectually it has involved engaging with much more sophisticated critiques of globalization and responses to them, as well as with the blurring of the boundaries between these positions. In particular the distinction between globalizers and anti-globalizers has become less sharp as the political emphasis has shifted towards the shared ground of alternative forms of globalization – that of the 'alt-globalizers'. Nevertheless, the political significance of the debate remains as crucial as it was in 2002, if not more so. What we believe has not changed fundamentally. The debate is still about how far, and to what extent, the world we live in is being reshaped by global forces and processes, that is, by what is commonly called 'globalization', and the implications of all this for the quality of people's lives.

The second edition, as with the first, distinguishes two different senses of the terms globalization and anti-globalization. In the first instance, it explores whether globalization is a 'really existing condition'. It sets out the academic debate between those who think it is – we call them the *globalists* – and those who believe it has never been a useful description of the principal trends in the global political economy – the *sceptics*. The latter have become more vociferous in the wake of 9/11 and the war in Iraq, arguing that world politics is returning to normality, that is, to geopolitics and imperialism. By contrast, the globalists consider current developments as indicative of the enduring nature of globalization, its militarization and the growing 'clash of globalizations'. Secondly, the volume also examines the contemporary politics of globalization, setting out the key political positions in favour of, and against, globalization in its current or alternative forms. The complex politics being pursued in relation to globalization in Washington, Mumbai, Hong Kong, Genoa, Porto Alegre and elsewhere is mapped. This exercise embraces the more popular understandings of the globalization/ anti-globalization debate.

Chapter 1 clarifies the concept of globalization, while in part I, 'The Globalization Controversy', chapters 2 to 7 examine the evidence for and against globalization in each of the key areas in the public and academic debate: the role of the state, the fate of national culture, the problems of global violence and security, the nature of the world economy, patterns of global inequality and development, and the role of global governance. Part II, 'Remaking Globalization', discusses, in chapters 8 to 12, the current state of the academic debate on globalization, the ethical foundations of political community and global order, the contentious politics of globalization (explaining what is at stake, and why it matters), and the way to move beyond (in both theoretical and political terms) the antithesis between globalization and anti-globalization. Accordingly, the last two chapters examine cosmopolitan social democracy and set out the political implications of this project in the current global context. Of course, it is too much to hope that all parties to these hugely important discussions will agree with us. But at the very least, the chapters in part II show a shared conviction that there is a compelling intellectual and political argument for moving beyond the antinomies of globalization/ anti-globalization.

This book draws on two decades of thinking and writing about globalization but it has remained, as with the first edition, a novel and intellectually engaging exercise for us: an attempt to state briefly and succinctly the key questions in this field and how they might be addressed. (Our previous attempts run to many hundreds of pages: see *Global Transformations, The Global Transformations Reader, Governing Globalization* and *Theories of Globalization*.) We would like to thank John Thompson for encouraging us to develop both the original text and also this second edition; Sue Pope for much assistance in preparing it for publication; Emma Hutchinson as our editor; Kevin Young and Jo Stone for invaluable research assistance; and Gill Motley, Neil de Cort, Ann Bone and Breffni O'Connor for extraordinarily professional help at all stages of production and marketing.

Acknowledgements

The authors and publisher are grateful to the following for permission to reproduce copyright material:

Blackwell Publishing for figures 4.1 and 4.3 from M. Sarkees, F. Wayman and J. D. Singer, 'Inter-state, intra-state and extra-state war', *International Studies Quarterly* 47(1) (2003): 49–79, and figure 5.15 from C. Hay, 'What's globalization got to do with it?', *Government and Opposition* 41(1) (2006): 1–22;

   Cambridge University Press for figure 5.1 from D. Irwin, 'Long run trends in world income and trade', *World Trade Review* 1(1) (2002): 89–100, and figure 5.16 from M. Obstfeld and A. M. Taylor, *Global Capital Markets: Integration, Crisis and Growth* (Cambridge University Press, 2004);

   Grahame Thompson for the use of figure 5.4 and for agreeing to the adapted version of this;

   National Bureau of Economic Research for figures 6.4 and 6.5 from Xavier Sala-i-Martin, 'The disturbing "rise" of global income inequality', NBER Working Paper 8904, April 2002;

   Oxford University Press for figure 7.4 from H. Anheier, M. Glasius, and M. Kalder (eds), *Global Civil Society 2001* (Oxford University Press, 2001);

   Pluto Press for figure 7.3 from P. Kennedy, D. Messner and F. Nuscheler, *Global Trends and Global Governance*. (Pluto Press, 2002);

   Polity Press for figure 7.1 from M. Koenig-Archibugi, 'Mapping global governance', in D. Held and A. McGrew (eds), *Governing Globalization: Power, Authority and Global Governance* (Polity, 2002);

Acknowledgements

Princeton University Press for table 6.1 from B. Milanovic, *Worlds Apart: Measuring International and Global Inequality* (Princeton University Press, 2005);

UNCTAD for figures 5.8 and 5.10 from *World Investment Report* (2006);

University of Chicago Press for figures 5.9 and 5.12 from M. Obstfeld and A. M. Taylor, 'The Great Depression as a watershed', in M. D. Bordo, C. Goldin and E. White (eds), *The Defining Moment* (University of Chicago Press, 1998), and tables 5.3, 6.2 and 6.3 from P. H. Lindert and J. G. Williamson, 'Does globalization make the world more unequal?', in M. D. Bordo, A. M. Taylor and J. G. Williamson (eds), *Globalization in Historical Perspective* (University of Chicago Press, 2003);

UNU-WIDER for table 6.5 from J. B. Davies et al., 'The world distribution of household wealth', WIDER Research Paper, 5 Dec. 2006, table 8, p. 45;

Worldwatch Institute for table 12.1 from *State of the World 2004: Consumption by the Number* (Worldwatch Institute, www.worldwatch.org, 2004).

Every effort has been made to contact copyright holders, but if any have been omitted, the publishers will be pleased to make the necessary arrangements at the first opportunity.

Abbreviations

APEC   Asia-Pacific Economic Cooperation
ARF   ASEAN Regional Forum
ASEAN   Association of South East Asian Nations
BIS   Bank for International Settlements
EU   European Union
FATF   Financial Action Task Force
FDI   foreign direct investment
G7   Group of Seven (leading industrial countries):
            Canada, France, Germany, Italy, Japan, UK, USA
G8   Group of Eight: G7 plus Russia and EU
G15   Group of Fifteen: leading developing and non-
            aligned states
G20   Group of Twenty: G7 plus countries regarded as
            'emerging markets'
G22   Group of Twenty-Two: emerging economies from
            each world region
G77   Group of Seventy-Seven: developing countries
GDP   gross domestic product
IASB   International Accounting Standards Board
IGO   intergovernmental organization
IMF   International Monetary Fund
INGO   international non-government organization
IOSCO   International Organization of Securities
            Commissions
IPCC   Intergovernmental Panel on Climate Change
LDC   less developed countries

Abbreviations

MERCOSUR	Southern Cone Common Market (in Latin America)
NAFTA	North American Free Trade Agreement
NATO	North Atlantic Treaty Organization
NGO	non-governmental organization
NIE	newly industrializing economy
OECD	Organization for Economic Cooperation and Development
PBEC	Pacific Basin Economic Council
PPP	purchasing power parity (a meaasure of what one unit of a given currency actually purchases in another currency)
RMA	revolution in military affairs
TNC	transnational corporation
UN	United Nations
UNDP	United Nations Development Programme
UNICEF	United Nations Children's Fund
WIDER	World Institute for Development and Economic Research
WTO	World Trade Organization

1

Introduction: Current Controversies about the Demise of Globalization

Obituaries for globalization – simply understood as the widening, deepening and speeding up of worldwide interconnectedness – have become numerous in the wake of 9/11 and the resurgence of American unilateralism. Among others, the historian Ferguson writes of 'sinking globalization', Wolf asks 'Will globalization survive?', Gray states that 'the era of globalization is over', Milanovic discusses 'why globalization is in trouble', Saul predicts 'the end of globalism' and Rosenberg observes that 'the age of globalization is unexpectedly over' (Ferguson 2005; Wolf 2006; Gray quoted in Naimi 2002; Milanovic 2006a; Saul 2005; Rosenberg 2005). This 'post-globalist' turn connects with the popular belief that the catastrophic events of 9/11 proved a historical watershed in global politics (Kennedy-Pipe and Rengger 2006). For those of a sceptical disposition, world politics after 9/11 appears to be returning to 'normality', as geopolitics, violence and imperialism – following the dashed hopes for a new internationalism in the 1990s – reassert themselves with a vengeance. By contrast, for those of a globalist persuasion, the war on terror and the war in Iraq are evidence of an enduring and pervasive 'clash of globalizations' rather than the demise of globalism (Hoffmann 2002). Globalization, both as an idea and a political project, thus continues to incite controversy within and beyond the academy. This chapter seeks to map the intellectual terrain of this debate, explaining why globalization remains such a fiercely defended and contested, not to mention detested, idea among academics and activists alike.

Within the academy, opinion divides over the evidence for, as well as the explanatory significance of, contemporary globalization. In

1

the political sphere, globalization elicits sharply divergent responses and fuels radically different projects, from the globaphobia of the extreme right to the globaphilia of neoliberals. Both the academic and the political controversies are interrelated, connecting how the contemporary world order is best understood and explained to the issue of what values and ethical principles should inform its future development. Among the most critical questions posed by these controversies are the following:

- Is globalization being eclipsed by a resurgent geopolitics or are we witnessing the militarization of globalization?
- Empire or globalization: are these complementary or contradictory explanations of the current conjuncture?
- Is globalization at risk or can it be tamed?
- What alternative global worlds are imaginable and possible?

Such questions dominate the current controversy about globalization and are indicative of why it is likely to remain of such fundamental concern to social scientists and social activists well into this century.

Making sense of globalization

Globalization denotes the intensification of worldwide social relations and interactions such that distant events acquire very localized impacts and vice versa. It involves a rescaling of social relations, from the economic sphere to the security sphere, beyond the national to the transnational, transcontinental and transworld. It can be understood as a historical process characterized by

- a *stretching* of social, political and economic activities across political frontiers so that events, decisions and activities in one region of the world come to have significance for individuals and communities in distant regions of the globe. Civil wars and conflict in the world's poorest regions, for example, increase the flow of asylum seekers and illegal migrants into the world's affluent countries;

- the intensification, or the growing *magnitude*, of interconnectedness, in almost every sphere of social existence from the economic to the ecological, from the activities of Microsoft to the spread of harmful microbes, such as the SARS virus, from the intensification of world trade to the spread of weapons of mass destruction;
- the *accelerating pace* of transborder interactions and processes as the evolution of worldwide systems of transport and communication increases the rapidity or velocity with which ideas, news, goods, information, capital and technology move around the world. Routine telephone banking transactions in the UK are dealt with by call centres in India in real time;
- this growing *extensity, intensity* and *velocity* of global interactions is associated with a *deepening* enmeshment of the local and global in so far as local events may come to have profound global consequences and global events can have serious local consequences, creating a growing collective awareness or consciousness of the world as a shared social space, that is, globality or globalism. This is expressed, among other ways, in the worldwide diffusion of the very idea of globalization itself as it becomes incorporated into the world's many languages, from Mandarin to Gaelic.

Rather than growing interdependence between discrete bounded national states, or internationalization, the concept of globalization describes a structural shift underway in the organization of human affairs: from a world of discrete but interdependent national states to the world as a shared social space. Central to this structural change are contemporary informatics technologies and infrastructures of communication and transportation. These have greatly facilitated new forms and possibilities of virtual real-time worldwide organization and coordination, from the operations of multinational corporations to the worldwide mobilization and demonstrations of the anti-globalization movement. Although place and distance still matter, globalization is synonymous with a process of time-space compression – literally a shrinking world – in which the sources of even very local developments, from unemployment to ethnic conflict, may be traced to distant conditions or actions. In this respect globalization embodies a process of relative deterritorialization: as social, political and economic activities are increasingly 'stretched' across the globe, they become in a significant sense no longer organized solely according to a strictly territorial logic. Terrorist and criminal networks, for instance, operate both locally and globally. National economic space, under conditions of globalization, is no longer coterminous with national territorial space; for example, many domestic companies have their headquarters abroad, while many national companies now outsource their production to China and East Asia among other locations. This is not to argue that territory and borders are now irrelevant, but rather to acknowledge that under conditions of globalization their *relative significance*, as determinants of, or constraints on, social action and the exercise of power, is declining (in comparison with the past). In an era of instantaneous real-time global communication and organization, the distinction between the domestic and the international, between inside and outside the state, breaks down. Territorial borders no longer demarcate the boundaries of national economic or political space.

A 'shrinking world' implies that sites of power and the subjects of power quite literally may be continents apart. Under these conditions, the location of power cannot be disclosed simply by reference to local circumstances. As the East Asian economic collapse of 1997–8 demonstrated, key sites of global power, such as the International Monetary Fund and the World Bank, are quite literally oceans apart from the communities whose destiny they help shape. In this regard, globalization involves the idea that power, whether 'hard' (economic or military) or 'soft' (political and cultural), is often organized and exercised at a distance. As such, the concept of globalization implies the relative denationalization of power in so far as, in an increasingly interconnected global system, it is organized and exercised on a transregional, transnational or transcontinental basis, while many other actors, from international organizations to criminal networks, exercise power within, across, and against states. Whether globalization, either as an idea or a political project, advances or impairs genuine understanding of the actual historical forces shaping the current world order has become the source of intense academic and political controversy.

Making sense of the globalization controversy: the key sources of contention

Controversies about globalization are shaped by two principal axes of disagreement. The first concerns the contested intellectual hegemony of the concept of globalization in the social sciences: its descriptive, analytical and theoretical purchase. The second concerns values and normative attachments: whether on ethical grounds globalization as a political project or ideal is to be defended, transformed, resisted or rejected. Combined, these two axes define a conceptual space for thinking about what distinguishes the plurality of voices in the debate. Figure 1.1 attempts a mapping of this space. The vertical scale represents the contest over the intellectual hegemony of globalization characterized by either a privileging of globalist forms of analysis (the globalists) or alternatively statist or societal forms of analysis (the sceptics). The horizontal scale represents the normative domain differentiating

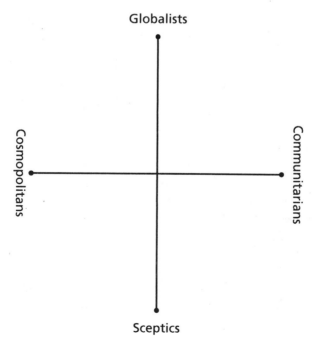

Figure 1.1 The great globalization controversy

between cosmopolitan and communitarian forms of ethical reasoning: that is, in rough terms, an attachment to making the world a singular 'good global community', on the one hand, as opposed to a world of coexisting 'good national or local communities', on the other. This figure constitutes a heuristic device for identifying, mapping and differentiating the intellectual and ethical contours of the great globalization controversy. As with any device like this it is neither definitive nor exhaustive but rather a tool for comparative enquiry.

The demise of globalism: the sceptical analysis

Since 9/11, the limits to globalization have become apparent, while the geopolitical conditions which underwrote it appear to have dissipated. For the first time in almost a decade, the simultaneous growth of trade, capital flows and foreign investment turned significantly negative: by 2002, global trade had fallen by a huge 4 per cent; capital flows by 19 per cent (2001) and a further 67 per cent (2002); and foreign direct investment collapsed by 41 per cent in 2001 and a further 21 per cent in 2002 (BIS 2003; WTO 2002; UNCTAD 2003). This reversal of economic flows also endured for much longer than previous global economic downturns. Furthermore, this slowing of economic globalization was accompanied by dramatic changes in the global political context, evidenced in shifts from multilateralism to unilateralism, stability to insecurity, cooperation to geopolitical competition, and soft power to hard power. For sceptics these shifts represent the erosion of the liberal global order which underwrote the intensification of globalization, and the continuing primacy of the state, territorial power, geopolitics and even empire.

Globalization, so the critics suggest, is increasingly in jeopardy. It is no longer, if it ever was, a useful description of the current world order, nor does it provide a cogent explanation of the social forces shaping it. Furthermore, globalism as a political and economic project has been replaced by a new imperialism as humanity adjusts to the realities of the unipolar moment and violent reassertion of geopolitical competition. In short, the world is witnessing the demise of globalization as description, explanation and ideology.

Introduction

Today borders and boundaries, nationalism and protectionism, localism and ethnicity define an epoch, the sceptics argue, of radical de-globalization: the disintegration and demise of globalism. In the wake of the Iraq war, the rapidity of the return to 'normality' in geopolitics demonstrates the intellectual bankruptcy of 'globalization' as a description, explanation and ideology of world order. The many contemporary obituaries for globalization appear to affirm Stiglitz's quip that 'globalization today has been oversold' (2005: 229). Sceptics argue that it has been oversold in at least three senses: as a description of social reality, as an explanation of social change and as an ideology of social progress (a political project). These contemporary critiques of globalization have inherited a theoretically informed and empirically rich scepticism from the work of, among others, Hirst and Thompson (1999), Hay (2005), Gilpin (2002b) and Rugman (2000). Though their analyses differ in significant ways, their studies concur that contemporary globalization is far from historically unprecedented, that the dominant economic trends are towards internationalization or regionalization, and that the discourse of globalization has greater significance than does the concept's descriptive or explanatory value. In effect, they argue that globalization scholarship exaggerates its historical and theoretical significance, since the world remains principally one of discrete and competitive national states.

Furthermore, it is contended, many accounts of globalization confuse cause and effect, that is, whether it is the phenomenon doing the work of explanation (the explanans), or alternatively whether it is being done by the object of explanation (the explanandum) (Rosenberg 2000). Eliding the two, such that the social effects to which globalization refers become effectively its causes, is clearly problematic. However, for many critics it is not so much this inversion of explanans and explanandum which undermines the intellectual coherence of much globalist scholarship, but rather a failure to recognize that globalization is essentially *epiphenomenal*. If, as historical materialists argue, globalization is principally the consequence of an inherent expansionary logic of capitalist societies, then it has no independent causal powers, that is, it is epiphenomenal. Some therefore consider the 'globalization turn' as simply the folly of so much contemporary liberal and radical social science in which advocacy has displaced scepticism or 'balanced social scientific reflection' (Rosenberg 2005: 66). What is principally at stake here is the explanatory purchase of the very concept of globalization itself. This strikes at the very raison d'être of globalization studies, since, as Rosenberg argues, if the concept provides no convincing 'guide to the interpretation of empirical events' it must in any meaningful sense be analytically redundant (Rosenberg 2005: 1; Hay 2005). In short, globalization is both bad empirics and bad theory.

Qualifying such scepticism, Hay argues that there is one sense in which globalization remains absolutely central to any account of the current global condition: as an idea or discourse which provides social meaning by framing, as well as legitimating, social and political change (Hay 2005). As an idea or discourse, globalization finds expression almost everywhere in the rhetoric of politicians and social movements as a rationale for social and political action (see, for example, Wolf 2004). 'Globalization', as the discursive construction of the social world, may be essential to understanding the contemporary epoch. But even this is becoming increasingly problematic as vociferous opposition to the project of globalism has become both more widespread and more socially entrenched.

Embedded globalization: the globalist analysis

Rather than the demise of globalization, current trends, the globalists suggest, indicate that it has proved much more resilient or socially embedded than sceptics believed or desired. There is little evidence to suggest that those domestic and transnational social forces on which the advance of economic globalization is contingent have lost their ardour for it. Furthermore, as the worldwide economic and distributional impacts of slowing globalization became increasingly apparent in 2001–2, those social forces which are its main beneficiaries strongly reasserted their domestic and transnational influence, especially in the wake of the failed summit of the World Trade Organization at Cancún, to advance the globalization project, albeit in a slightly modified form. As Harold James explains in his analysis of the collapse of a previous era of globalization, the belle époque (1880–1914), 'the pendulum is so slow in swinging back from globality' today both because of its global institutional and social embeddness, and because of the absence of any viable political alternative to an open world economy (James 2001: 224). Globalization, in its multiple forms, remains far more socially and institutionally entrenched than its critics have recognized.

Despite a record contraction, globalization in this decade remains on almost all measures more intensive and extensive than a decade ago (A.T. Kearney/Foreign Policy 2003). Where trade was concerned, 2004 witnessed the strongest growth in a decade and trade reached historic levels of world GDP; flows of foreign direct investment (FDI) also rebounded to the levels of the early 1990s, while flows to less developed countries (LDCs) accelerated much faster than to industrialized economies; and in addition, financial flows increased and foreign exchange transactions reached a historic $1.9 trillion per day (WTO 2005; UNCTAD 2005; BIS 2004). Measured in terms of migration, communication, or even the arms trade, there is little evidence of a rush to autarky or de-globalization (A.T. Kearney/Foreign Policy 2005, 2006). Given the scale of the 2001 global economic downturn, endemic political instability, and global insecurity, a much greater and more sustained contraction might have been expected. Overall the empirical evidence is indicative of recovery from a cyclical downturn which began well before 9/11, and as world growth prospects have improved so have the prospects for economic globalization. Beyond the economic domain, most especially in the military and security domains, there has been little diminution, but rather an acceleration, of the militarization of globalism.

Underpinning the nature and pace of contemporary globalization, there are, moreover, a number of 'deep drivers' which are likely to be operative for the foreseeable future, irrespective of the exact institutional form taken. Among these drivers are the changing infrastructure of communications linked to the IT revolution; the expansionary logic of capitalism and the development of global markets in goods and services, connected to the worldwide distribution of information; the new global division of labour driven by multinational corporations; the end of the Cold War, and the diffusion of democratic and consumer values across many of the world's regions (alongside some marked reactions to this); and the growth of migration and the movement of peoples, linked to shifts in patterns of economic demand, demography and environmental degradation. These deeply structured processes generate dense patterns of global interconnectedness, real and virtual. As a result, political communities can no longer be considered (if they ever could be with any validity) simply as 'discrete worlds'; they are enmeshed in complex structures of overlapping forces, relations and networks. Clearly, these are structured by inequality and hierarchy. However, even the most powerful among them – including the most powerful states – do not remain unaffected by the changing conditions and processes of the many different forms of regional and global entrenchment. States remain important, but they share the global stage with a diversity of agencies and are enmeshed in systems of transnational, regional and global governance which circumscribe notions of state power and territoriality. In this new world order, states, though still dominant agents, are very much disaggregated players rather than coherent geopolitical entities (Slaughter 2004). Obituaries for globalization – as description, explanation and ideology – are therefore somewhat premature, the globalists retort.

Part I

The Globalization Controversy

2

The Reconfiguration of Political Power?

There is no doubt that contemporary social life is associated in many respects with the modern state, which specifies the proper form of nearly all types of human activity. The state appears to be omnipresent, regulating the conditions of life from birth registration to death certification. From the policing of everyday activities to the provision of education and the promotion of health care, the steady expansion of state power appears beyond question. Quantitatively, the growth of the state, from the size of its budget to the scope of its jurisdiction, is one of the few really uncontested facts of the last century. On many fundamental measures of political power (for example, the capacity to raise taxes and revenues, the ability to produce weapons of mass destruction) states are, at least throughout most of the OECD world (the states belonging to the Organization for Economic Cooperation and Development), as powerful as if not more powerful than their predecessors (Mann 1997). The sceptics make a great deal of this, as they do of the rise and dominance of the modern state in general. It is useful to rehearse this position, especially its many implications for the form and organization of political power, before examining the alternative globalist account.

The formation and rule of the modern state

The claim of the modern state to an overarching role is a relatively novel one in human history, even in the place that gave birth to it – Western Europe. A thousand years ago, for example, inhabitants

13

of an English village knew little of life beyond it; the village was the beginning and practically the end of their world. Villagers might have visited the nearest market town but would scarcely have ventured further. They would probably have recognized the name of the king, although they would rarely, if ever, have seen him; and they might well have had more contact with representatives of the church than with any 'political' or military leaders (Lacey and Danziger 1999). And while 500 years later two forms of political regime – absolute and constitutional monarchies – were beginning to crystallize across the European continent, Europe resembled more a mosaic of powers, with overlapping political claims and jurisdictions (Tilly 1975; Poggi 1978). No ruler or state was yet sovereign in the sense of being able to claim supremacy over a bounded territory and population.

Modern states emerged in Western Europe and its colonial territories in the eighteenth and nineteenth centuries, although their origins date back to the late sixteenth century (Skinner 1978; Held 1995: chs 2–3). They distinguished themselves initially from earlier forms of political rule by claiming a distinctive symmetry and correspondence between sovereignty, territory and legitimacy. The promotion of the concept of sovereignty was pivotal to this development, for it lodged a special claim to the rightful exercise of political power over a circumscribed realm – an entitlement to exclusive rule over a bounded territory (see Skinner 1978). Modern states developed as nation-states – political bodies, separate from both ruler and ruled, with supreme jurisdiction over a demarcated territorial area, backed by a claim to a monopoly of coercive power, and enjoying legitimacy as a result of the loyalty or consent of their citizens. The major innovations of the modern nation-state – territoriality that fixes exact borders, monopolistic control of violence, an impersonal structure of political power and a distinctive claim to legitimacy based on representation – marked out its defining (and sometimes fragile) features. The regulatory power of such states expanded throughout the modern period, creating (albeit with significant national differences) systems of unified rule across demarcated territories, centralized administration, concentrated mechanisms of fiscal management and resource distribution, new types of lawmaking and law enforcement, professional standing armies, a concentrated war-making capacity and, concomitantly, elaborate formal relations among states through the development of diplomacy and diplomatic institutions (P. Anderson 1974; Giddens 1985).

The consolidation of the power of leading European nation-states was part of a process in which an international society of states was created, first in Europe itself, and then, as Europe expanded across the globe, in diverse regions as Europe's demands on its colonies were pressed and resisted (Ferro 1997). This 'society of states' laid down the formal rules which all sovereign and autonomous states would, in principle, have to adopt if they were to become full and equal members of the international order of states. The origins of this order are often traced to the Peace of Westphalia of 1648, the treaties which concluded the Thirty Years' War (see Falk 1969; Krasner 1995; Keohane 1995). But the rule system codified at Westphalia is best understood as having created a *normative trajectory* in international law, which did not receive its fullest articulation until the late eighteenth and early nineteenth century. It was during this time that territorial sovereignty, the formal equality of states, non-intervention in the internal affairs of other recognized states, and state consent as the foundation stone of international legal agreement became the core principles of the modern international order (see Crawford and Marks 1998). Of course, the consolidation of this order across the world, paradoxically, would have to wait until the decline of its earliest protagonists – the European powers – and the formal process of decolonization after the Second World War. But it is perhaps fair to say that it was not until the late twentieth century that the modern international order of states became truly global; for it was only with the end of all the great empires – European, American and finally Soviet – that many peoples could finally join the society of states as independent political communities.* The number of internationally recognized states more than doubled between 1945 and 2005. There are now 202 sovereign states (192 are member states of the United Nations, nine are not UN members but are recognized under the Montevideo Convention, and one is generally recognized internationally (Vatican City)). The high point of the

---

* Whether the US today seeks a return to imperial status is a question returned to later.

modern nation-state system was reached at the end of the twentieth century, and it was buttressed and supported by the spread of
new multilateral forms of international coordination and cooperation, in international organizations like the UN, and new international regulatory mechanisms, such as the universal human
rights regime.

Not only has the modern nation-state become the principal type
of political rule across the globe, but it has also increasingly
assumed, since decolonization and the collapse of the Soviet
empire, a particular political form; that is, it has crystallized as representative or liberal democracy (Potter et al. 1997). Several distinctive waves of democratization have brought particular
countries in Europe, such as Portugal and Spain, into the democratic fold, and brought numerous others closer to democracy in
Latin America, Asia, Africa and Eastern Europe. Of course, there
is no necessary evolutionary path to consolidated liberal democracy; the path is fragile and littered with obstacles – the hold of
liberal democracy on diverse political communities is still tentative
and open to serious challenge.

Surveying the political scene in the first decade of the twenty-first
century there are good reasons, argue the sceptics, for thinking of
this period as the age of the modern state. For states in many places
have increasingly claimed a monopoly of the legitimate use of force
and judicial regulation, established permanent military forces as a
symbol of statehood as well as a means of ensuring national security, consolidated tax-raising and redistributive mechanisms, established nationwide communication infrastructures, sought to
systematize a national or official language, raised literacy levels and
created a national schooling system, promulgated a national identity, and built up a diverse array of national political, economic and
cultural institutions. In addition, many states, west and east, have
sought to create elaborate welfare institutions, partly as a means to
promote and reinforce national solidarity, involving public health
provision and social security (Ashford 1986; Esping-Anderson
1990, and cf. 2002). Moreover, OECD states have pursued macroeconomic management strategies, shifting from Keynesian demand
management in the 1950s to 1970s, to extensive supply-side measures from the early 1980s, in order to help sustain economic
growth and widespread employment. While success in these

domains has sometimes been hard to maintain, the economic strategies and policies of Western nation-states have been emulated in many regions of the world.

It certainly can be argued that much of this 'emulation' has been more the result of necessity than of choice. Decolonization clearly did not create a world of equally free states. The influence of Western commerce, trade and political organization outlived direct rule. Powerful national economic interests have often been able to sustain hegemonic positions over former colonial territories through the replacement of 'a visible presence of rule' with the 'invisible government' of corporations, banks and international organizations (the International Monetary Fund and the World Bank, for example) (Ferro 1997: 349–50). Furthermore, interlaced with this have been the sedimented interests and machinations of the major powers, jostling with each other for advantage, if not hegemonic status (Bull 1977; Buzan, Little and Jones 1993). The geopolitical roles of individual states may have changed (for example, the shifts in the relative position of the UK and France during the twentieth century from global empires to middle-ranking powers), but these changes have been accommodated within the prevailing structures of world order – the modern state system and capitalist economic relations – which have governed the strategic choices open to political communities. The restricted nature of these choices for many countries has become clearer with the collapse of Soviet communism and the bipolar division of the world established during the Cold War. Accordingly, the development programmes of states in sub-Saharan Africa, Latin America and the ex-Soviet territories have tended to acquire a uniform shape – market liberalization, welfare restrictions, minimal regulation of private capital flows, deregulation of labour markets – and to be governed by political and economic necessity rather than by public design.*

Yet, however limited the actual control states possess over their territories, they generally fiercely protect their sovereignty – their entitlement to rule – and their autonomy – their capacity to choose

---

* This pattern does not, of course, apply to all states. It has been resisted successfully where countries have benefited from strong leadership and robust political institutions, for example in China (see chapters 10 and 12).

appropriate forms of political, economic and social development. The distinctive 'bargains' governments create with their citizens remain fundamental to their legitimacy. The effective choices of states vary dramatically according to their location in the hierarchy of states, but, in the age of nation-states, the independence bestowed by sovereignty, in principle, still matters greatly to all states. Modern states are political communities which create the conditions for establishing national communities of fate; and few, if any, are willing to give this up. Although national political choices are constrained, they still count, and remain the focus of intense public debate. According to the sceptics, national political traditions are still vibrant; distinctive political bargains can still be struck between governments and electorates; and states continue, given the political will, to rule. The business of national politics is as important as, if not more important than, it was during the period in which modern states were first formed. The competence with which this business is performed is of great significance to all who live in a bounded community. Building strong state capacities in developed countries, and nurturing these capacities where they are fragile or non-existent in many developing countries, is the primary domestic challenge in contemporary politics if competence – in economic, social and welfare policies – is to be attained, and national objectives met (see chapter 10 for an elaboration of this theme).

The implications for international affairs of thinking about the state as the primary unit of politics have been explored most systematically by 'realism' within international relations theory (see Morgenthau 1948; Wight 1986; S. Smith 1987). In the context of a global states system, realism conceives of the state as a unified entity whose primary purpose is to promote and defend its national interest. At its simplest, the realist position views the state as a vehicle for securing national and international order through the exercise of national power. In order to survive and develop, states must pursue their aims in a highly uncertain and competitive political environment. Accordingly, realism posits that the system of sovereign states is inescapably anarchic in character; and that this anarchy forces all states, in the inevitable absence of any supreme arbiter to enforce moral behaviour and agreed international codes, to pursue power politics in order to secure their vital interests.

This realpolitik view of states has had a significant influence on both the analysis and practice of international relations in recent times, for it offers a clear prima facie explanation of the chaos and disorder of interstate affairs, particularly in the twentieth century. On this account, the modern system of states is a 'limiting factor' which will always thwart any attempt to conduct international relations in a manner which transcends power politics. In this regard, the reassertion of the might of American military power after the attacks of 9/11 is the inevitable result of both the provocation constituted by the attack on the US and the power logic of international affairs, which requires that such threats to national security be met with decisive retaliation. A powerful state, in this case a hegemonic power, must act to sustain its primacy and defend its national interest. International norms and institutions will be of little relevance under these circumstances.

Realism questions the idea that the construction or maintenance of international order can transcend the logic of power politics (geopolitics). International order is the order produced by the most powerful states. This understanding reinforces a sceptical attitude towards the claim that genuine global cooperation and robust international agreements could ever exist in a system of sovereign states. This scepticism is supported by the state-centric conception of order as interstate order: states are the primary actors in world affairs. To the extent that other actors have an impact on global political and economic conditions, this occurs within a framework constituted and dominated by states and military power (Waltz 1979: 94; Gilpin 1981: 18). In addition, international institutions are interpreted either as ineffectual or as largely epiphenomenal, that is, devoid of autonomous causal power (Strange 1983; Mearsheimer 1994). Accordingly, the susceptibility of the United Nations to the agendas of the most powerful states, the weaknesses of many of its enforcement operations (or lack of them altogether), the underfunding of its organizations, the continued dependency of its programmes on the financial support of a few countries, and the inadequacies of the policing of many environmental regimes (regional and global) are neither surprising nor unexpected. States matter, above all other political entities, and world order is decisively shaped by the most powerful states. To date, the continuity in these structures is much more significant than any contemporary political developments.

Towards a global politics

Globalists would generally contest many aspects of the above account. Their argument runs as follows. The traditional conception of the state, in which it is posited as the fundamental unit of world order, presupposes its relative homogeneity, that is, that it is a unitary phenomenon with a set of singular purposes (Young 1972: 36). But the growth of international and transnational organizations and collectivities, from the United Nations and its specialized agencies to international pressure groups and social movements, has altered the form and dynamics of both state and civil society. The state has become a fragmented policy-making arena, permeated by transnational networks (governmental and non-governmental) as well as by domestic agencies and forces (Slaughter 2004). Likewise, the extensive penetration of civil society by transnational forces has altered its form and dynamics (Kaldor 2003).

There has been a shift in the nature and form of political life. The distinctive form this has taken in the contemporary period is the emergence of 'global politics' – the increasingly extensive form of political networks, interaction and rule-making activity. Political decisions and actions in one part of the world can rapidly acquire worldwide ramifications. Sites of political action and/or decision-making can become linked through rapid communications into complex networks of political interaction. Associated with this 'stretching' of politics is an intensification or deepening of global processes such that 'action at a distance' permeates the social conditions and cognitive worlds of specific places or communities (Giddens 1990: ch. 2). As a consequence, developments at the global level – whether economic, social or environmental – can acquire almost instantaneous local consequences, and vice versa.

The idea of global politics challenges the traditional distinctions between the domestic/international, territorial/non-territorial, inside/outside, as embedded in conventional conceptions of inter-state politics and 'the political' (see Held et al. 1999: chs 1, 2 and 9). It also highlights the richness and complexity of the inter-connections which transcend states and societies in the global order. Moreover, global politics today is anchored not just in trad-itional geopolitical concerns but also in a large diversity of eco-nomic, social and ecological questions. Pollution, drugs, human rights and terrorism are among an increasing number of transna-tional policy issues which cut across territorial jurisdictions and existing political alignments, and which require international cooperation for their effective resolution.

Nations, peoples and organizations are linked, in addition, by many new forms of communication which range across borders. The digital revolution in microelectronics, in information technol-ogy and in computers has established virtually instantaneous worldwide links which, when combined with the technologies of the telephone, television, cable, satellite and jet transportation, have dramatically altered the nature of political communication. The intimate connection between 'physical setting', 'social situ-ation' and politics which distinguished most political associations from premodern to modern times has been ruptured. The speed with which the events of 11 September 2001 reverberated across the world and made mass terrorism a global issue is one poignant example.

The development of new communication systems generates a world in which the particularities of place and individuality are constantly represented and reinterpreted through regional and global communication networks. But the relevance of these systems goes far beyond this, for they are fundamental to the possibility of organizing political action and exercising political power across vast distances (see Deibert 1997). For example, the expansion of international and transnational organizations, the extension of international rules and legal mechanisms – their construction and monitoring – have all received an impetus from these new communication systems and all depend on them as a means to further their aims. The present era of global politics marks a shift towards a system of multilayered regional and global governance (see chapter 7).

This can be illustrated by a number of developments, including, most obviously, the rapid emergence of multilateral agencies and organizations. New forms of multilateral and global politics have

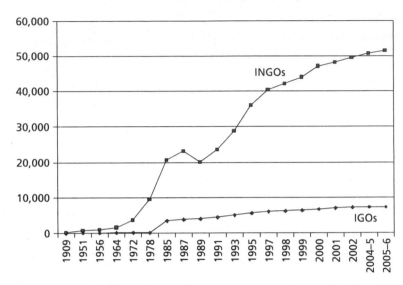

Figure 2.1 Recorded numbers of intergovernmental organizations (IGOs) and international non-governmental organizations (INGOs) 1909–2006

Source: Union of International Associations, *Yearbook of International Organizations*, annual; see www.uia.org.

been established involving governments, intergovernmental organizations (IGOs) and a wide variety of transnational pressure groups and international non-government organizations (INGOs). At the beginning of the twentieth century there were just 36 IGOs and 176 INGOs, while in 2000 there were 7,350 IGOs and 51,509 INGOs (UIA 2001).* Figure 2.1 illustrates the dramatic increase in these two types of international organization over the course of almost a century. What is particularly striking is the increase in INGO activity very recently. Since 1989, the number of INGOs has increased by more than 150 per cent.

In addition, there has been a very substantial development in the number of international treaties in force, as well as in the number of international regimes, altering the situational context of states (Held et al. 1999: chs 1–2). According to Ku (2001: 23), in the

---

* An organization is intergovernmental if it is created by the signature of an agreement between (at least three) governments engendering obligations among them. The numbers for IGOs and INGOs have to be treated with some caution because they include inactive or redundant organizations. See UIA 2001: app. 3.

period 1648 to 1750 there were 86 multilateral treaties, whereas in the years 1976 to 1995 there were over 1,600 treaties, of which 100 created international organizations.

To this pattern of extensive political interconnectedness can be added the dense web of activity of the key international policy-making forums, including the summits of the UN, G7 (Group of Seven leading industrialized countries), International Monetary Fund (IMF), World Trade Organization (WTO), European Union (EU), Asia-Pacific Economic Cooperation (APEC) and MERCOSUR (the Southern Cone Common Market – in Latin America) and many other official and unofficial meetings. In the middle of the nineteenth century there were two or three interstate conferences or congresses per annum; today the number totals over 9,000 annually (UIA 2000). National government is increasingly locked into an array of global, regional and multilayered systems of governance – and can barely monitor it all, let alone stay in command. Foreign policy and domestic policy have become chronically intermeshed, making the coordination and control of government policy increasingly complex.

At the regional level, the EU has, in remarkably little time, taken Europe from the disarray of the Second World War to a world in which sovereignty is pooled across a growing number of areas of common concern. Judged in the context of state history, it is, for all its flaws, a remarkable political formation. In addition, there has been a significant acceleration in regional relations beyond Europe: in the Americas, Asia-Pacific and, to a lesser degree, in Africa. While the form taken by this type of regionalism is very different from the model of the EU, it has nonetheless had significant consequences for political power, particularly in the Asia-Pacific, which has seen the formation of the Association of South East Asian Nations (ASEAN), APEC, the ASEAN Regional Forum (ARF), the Pacific Basin Economic Council (PBEC) and many other groupings. Furthermore, as regionalism has deepened, so interregional diplomacy has intensified as old and new regional groups seek to consolidate their relations with each other. In this respect, regionalism has not been a barrier to political globalization but, on the contrary, has been a building block for it (see Hettne 1998).

There has, moreover, been an important change in the scope and content of international law. Twentieth-century forms of international law – from the law governing war, to that concerning crimes against humanity, environmental issues and human rights – have created components of what can be thought of as an emerging framework of 'cosmopolitan law', law which circumscribes and delimits the political power of individual states (Held 2002b). In principle, states are no longer able to treat their citizens as they think fit. Although, in practice, many states will violate these standards, nearly all now accept general duties of protection and provision in their own practices and procedures (Beetham 1998).

Another notable trend is the growing enmeshment of public and private agencies in the making of rules, the setting of codes and the establishment of standards. Many new sites of rule-making and lawmaking have emerged, creating a multitude of 'decentred lawmaking processes' in various sectors of the global order (Teubner 1997: xiii). Many of these have come into existence through processes of self-validation in relation to technical standardization, professional rule production and transnational regulation of multinational corporations, and through business contracting, arbitration and other elements of *lex mercatoria* (the global framework of commercial law) (see Teubner 1997). Global public policy networks involving public and private actors are reshaping the basis on which national and international rules are made and regulatory systems operate; and the results cannot easily be fitted into the traditional distinction between national and international law (Jayasuriya 1999; Reinicke 1999; Slaughter 2000). There is no longer a strict separation between public and private, domestic and international legal procedures and mechanisms – models of lawmaking and enforcement no longer simply fit the logic of the states system.

Interlaced with these political and legal transformations are changes in the world military order (see chapter 4). Few states, except perhaps for the US and China, can now solely contemplate unilateralism or neutrality as a credible defence strategy. Global and regional security institutions have become more salient as a collectivization of national security has evolved (Clark 2001). The paradox and novelty of the globalization of organized violence is that national security today is becoming a collective or multilateral affair. Moreover, states no longer have a monopoly of force, as the growth of transnational terrorism and the events of 9/11 demonstrate. Private military groups, private armies and the private provision of security play a significant role in many regions of the globe. The one thing that did most to give modern nation-states a focus and a purpose, that is, national security, which has been at the very heart of modern statehood, can now be realized effectively only if nation-states come together and pool resources, technology, intelligence, power and authority. Even in the sphere of defence and arms production and manufacture, the notion of a singular, discrete and delimited political community appears problematic. This poses many fundamental questions about how to think about political community and governance in our increasingly global age.

With the increase in global interconnectedness, the scope of strategic policy choices available to individual governments and the effectiveness of many traditional policy instruments tend to decline (see Keohane and Nye 1972: 392–5; Cooper 1986: 1–22). This tendency occurs, in the first instance, because of the growing irrelevance of many border controls – whether formal or informal – which traditionally served to restrict transactions in goods and services, and because of production factors and technology, and ideas and cultural interchange (see Morse 1976: chs 2–3). The result is a shift in the relative costs and benefits of pursuing different policy options. States suffer a further diminution in power because the expansion of transnational forces reduces the control individual governments can exercise over the activities of their citizens and other peoples. For example, the increased mobility of capital, induced by the development of global financial markets, shifts the balance of power between markets and states and generates powerful pressures on states to develop market-friendly policies, including restricted public deficits and curbs on expenditure, especially on social goods; lower levels of direct taxation that are internationally competitive; and privatization and labour market deregulation. The decisions of private investors to move private capital across borders can threaten welfare budgets, taxation levels and other government policies. In effect, the autonomy of states is compromised as governments find it increasingly difficult to pursue their domestic agendas without cooperating with other agencies, political and economic, above and beyond the state.

In this context, many of the traditional domains of state activity and responsibility (defence, economic management, health, and law and order) can no longer be served without institutionalizing multilateral forms of collaboration. As demands on the state have increased in the postwar years, the state has been faced with a whole series of policy problems that cannot be adequately resolved without cooperating with other states and non-state actors (Keohane 1984; McGrew 1992). Accordingly, individual states on their own can no longer be conceived of as the appropriate political units for either resolving many key policy problems or managing effectively a broad range of public functions.

None of this is to deny, globalists would concede, the resurgence of American power since 9/11, its attempt to construct a 'coalition of the willing' (more successful in Afghanistan than Iraq), and the pursuit under George W. Bush of unilateral strategies. The US can resist temporarily the collective security trends discussed above, and it is clearly the only great power (at present) able to project massive military power globally. Yet even so, it can mount no more than one and a half major military campaigns simultaneously. Nor can it easily win the peace unilaterally, for unilateralism proves a weak basis for winning the hearts and minds of people. Without widespread cooperation with other powerful states, and without the widespread cooperation of the peoples of countries such as Afghanistan and Iraq, unilateral military power is vulnerable to defeat. History shows that great powers can be humbled under these conditions, forcing them back to cooperative and collaborative solutions. In a democratic and global age, when dealing with international and transnational questions, acting alone will not be the way to generate either success or legitimacy.

It is for these reasons too that America's current position in the world should not, despite what some critics claim, be called an 'empire' (see Hardt and Negri 2000), or the re-emergence of an imperial order (cf. Held and Koenig-Archibugi 2004). The United States lacks the military capacity to dominate the world and deliver pacification (see Mann 2004). There is a huge gap between the destructive capacity of the American military machine and what this can achieve politically. American power is much less effective than is generally assumed, not least because today military force is largely unsuitable to achieve many political goals (see Kaldor 2004). Wider access to increasingly lethal weapons means that it is more difficult for 'the strong' to prevail as a result of technological superiority alone. Even military command of the air does not confer the actual capacity to control territory. Asymmetrical warfare, as in Iraq between 2003 and 2007, shows that military occupation of territory is politically very costly for great powers. This cost may well be too great for democratic states, making military victory almost impossible to realize.

These arguments suggest that the modern state is increasingly embedded in webs of regional and global interconnectedness permeated by supranational, intergovernmental and transnational forces, and unable to determine its own fate. Such developments, it is also contended, challenge both the sovereignty and legitimacy of states. Sovereignty is challenged because the political authority of states is displaced and compromised by regional and global power systems (political, economic and cultural). State legitimacy is at issue because, with greater regional and global interdependence, states cannot deliver fundamental goods and services to their citizens without international cooperation, and even the latter can be quite inadequate in the face of global problems – from global warming to the challenges posed by AIDS/HIV – which can escape national political regulation. To the extent that political legitimacy depends on competence and the ability to 'deliver the goods' to citizens, it is under increasing strain. Globalization, conclude the globalists, is eroding the capacity of nation-states to act unilaterally in the articulation and pursuit of domestic and international policy objectives: the power and role of the territorial nation-state is being transformed. Despite what the sceptics claim, political power is being reconfigured.

3

The Fate of National Culture

For long periods of human history most people have lived out their lives in a web of local cultures. While the formation and expansion of the great world religions and premodern empires carried ideas and beliefs across frontiers with decisive social impacts, the most important vehicle for this, in the absence of direct military and political intervention, was the development of networks of ruling class culture (Mann 1986). At points these bit deeply into the fragmented mosaic of local cultures, but for most people, most of the time, their daily lives and routines persisted largely unchanged. Before the emergence of nations and nation-states, most cultural communication and interaction occurred either between elites or at very local and restricted levels. Little interaction took place between the court and the village. It was not until the eighteenth century that a new form of cultural identity coalesced between these two extremes.

The story of national culture: the sceptic's resource

The rise of the modern nation-state and nationalist movements altered the landscape of political identity. The conditions involved in the creation of the modern state were often also the conditions which generated a sense of nationhood. As state-makers sought to centralize and reorder political power in circumscribed territories, and to secure and strengthen their power base, they came to depend on cooperative forms of social relations with their subjects (Giddens 1985; Mann 1986). The centralization of power spawned the dependence of rulers on the ruled for resources, human and financial. Greater reciprocity was created between governors and governed and the terms of their 'exchange' became contested. In particular, the military and administrative requirements of the modern state 'politicized' social relations and day-to-day activities. Gradually, people became aware of their membership in a shared political community, with a common fate. Although the nature of this emergent identity was initially often vague, it grew more definite and precise over time (Therborn 1977; Turner 1986; Mann 1987).

The consolidation of the ideas and narratives of the nation and nationhood has been linked to many factors, including:

- the attempt by ruling elites and governments to create a new identity that would legitimize the enhancement of state power and the coordination of public policy (Breuilly 1992);
- the creation, through a mass education system, of a common framework of understanding – ideas, meanings, practices – to enhance the process of state-coordinated modernization (Gellner 1983);
- the emergence of novel communication systems – particularly new media (such as printing and the telegraph), independent publishers and a free market for printed material – which facilitated interclass communication and the diffusion of national histories, myths and rituals, that is, a new imagined community (B. Anderson 1983);
- and, building on a historic sense of homeland and deeply rooted memories, the consolidation of ethnic communities through a common public culture, shared legal rights and duties, and an economy creating social mobility for its members within a bounded territory (A. Smith 1986, 1995).

Even where the establishment of a national identity was an explicit political project pursued by elites, it was rarely their complete invention. That elites actively sought to generate a sense of nationality and a commitment to the nation – a 'national community of fate' – is well documented. But 'it does not follow', as one observer aptly noted, that such elites 'invented nations where none existed' (A. Smith 1990: 180–1). The 'nation-to-be' was not just any large social or cultural entity; rather, it was a 'community of history and culture', occupying a particular territory, and often laying claim to a distinctive tradition of common rights and duties for its members. Accordingly, many nations were 'built up on the basis of pre-modern "ethnic cores" whose myths and memories, values and symbols shaped the culture and boundaries of the nation that modern elites managed to forge' (A. Smith 1990: 180; and see A. Smith 1986). The identity that nationalists strove to uphold depended, in significant part, on uncovering and exploiting a community's 'ethno-history' and on highlighting its distinctiveness in the world of competing political and cultural values (cf. Hall 1992).

Of course, the construction of nations, national identities and nation-states has always been harshly contested and the conditions for the successful development of each never fully overlapped with those of the others (see Held et al. 1999: 48–9, 336–40). States are, as noted previously, complex webs of institutions, laws and practices, the spatial reach of which has often been difficult to secure and stabilize over fixed territories. Nations are cross-class collectivities which share a sense of identity and collective political fate. Their basis in real and imagined cultural, linguistic and historical commonalties is highly malleable and fluid, often giving rise to diverse expressions and ambiguous relationships to states. Nationalism is the force which links states to nations: it describes both the complex cultural and psychological allegiance of individuals to particular national identities and communities, and the project of establishing a state in which a given nation is dominant. The fixed borders of the modern state have generally embraced a diversity of ethnic, cultural and linguistic groups with mixed leanings and allegiances. The relationships between these groups, and between such groups and states, have been chequered and often a source of bitter conflict. In the late nineteenth and twentieth centuries, nationalism became a force which supported and buttressed state formation in certain places (for example, in France) and challenged or refashioned it elsewhere (for instance, in multi-ethnic states such as Spain or the United Kingdom) (see Held et al. 1999: 337–8; Appadurai 1990; Guibernau 1995).

However, despite the diversity of nationalisms and their political aims, and the fact that most national cultures are less than two hundred years old, these new political forces created fundamentally novel terms of political reference in the modern world – terms of reference which appear so well rooted today that many, if not the overwhelming majority of, peoples take them as given and practically natural (cf. Barry 1998a). While earlier epochs witnessed cultural institutions that either stretched across many societies (world religions) or were highly localized in their form, the rise of nations, nationalism and nation-states led to the organization of cultural life along national and territorial lines. In Europe this assisted the consolidation of some older states, the creation of a plethora of new nation-states and, eventually, the fragmentation of multinational empires (such as the Austro-Hungarian Empire). The potency of the idea of the 'nation' was not lost on the rest of the world and notions of national culture and nationalism spread – partly as a result of the expansion of European empires themselves – to the Americas, Asia, Africa and the Middle East. This helped fuel independence movements, cementing once again a particular link between culture, geography and political freedom.

The struggle for national identity and nationhood has been so extensive that the sceptics doubt the latter can be eroded by transnational forces and, in particular, by the development of a so-called global mass culture. In fact, advocates of the primacy of national identity emphasize its enduring qualities and the deep appeal of national cultures compared to the ephemeral and ersatz qualities of the products of the transnational media corporations – hamburgers, coke and pop idols (see A. Smith 1990; Brown 1995). Since national cultures have been centrally concerned with consolidating the relationships between political identity, self-determination and the powers of the state, they are, and will remain, formidably important sources of ethical and political motivation (see chapter 9). Moreover, the new electronic networks of communication and information technology which now straddle the world help intensify and rekindle traditional forms and sources of national life, reinforcing their influence and impact. These networks, it has been aptly noted, 'make possible a denser, more intense interaction between members of communities who share common cultural characteristics, notably language'; and this provides a renewed impetus to the re-emergence of 'ethnic communities and their nationalisms' (A. Smith 1990: 175).

Furthermore, while new communication systems can create access to distant others, they also generate an awareness of difference; that is, of the incredible diversity in lifestyles and value orientations (see Gilroy 1987; Robins 1991; Massey and Jess 1995). Although this awareness may enhance cultural understanding, it often leads to an accentuation of what is distinctive and idiosyncratic, further fragmenting cultural life. Awareness of 'the other' by no means guarantees intersubjective agreement, as shown only too clearly by the Salman Rushdie affair and the Danish 'cartoon war', instances in which publications in Europe provoked an angry response from Muslims across the globe. Moreover, although the new communication industries may generate a language of their own, a particular set of values and consumption patterns, they confront a multiplicity of languages and discourses through which people make sense of their lives and cultures (J. B. Thompson 1990: 313ff.). The vast majority of the products of mass-market cultural corporations which flood across borders originate from Western societies. But the available evidence, according to the sceptics, suggests that national (and local) cultures remain robust; national institutions continue in many states to have a central impact on public life; national television and radio broadcasting continue to enjoy substantial audiences; the organization of the press and news coverage retains strong national roots; and foreign cultural products are constantly read and reinterpreted in novel ways by national audiences (Appadurai 1990; Miller 1992; Liebes and Katz 1993; J. B. Thompson 1995; Hafez 2007).

Defenders of the vitality and continuing significance of national culture point out that there is no common global pool of memories; no common global way of thinking; and no 'universal history' in and through which people can unite. There is only a manifold set of political meanings and systems through which any new global awareness must struggle for survival (see Bozeman 1984). Given the deep roots of ethno-histories, and the many ways they are often refashioned, this can hardly be a surprise. Despite the vast flows of information, imagery and people around the world, there are few signs of a universal or global culture in the making, and few signs of a decline in the political salience of nationalism.

Finally, thinking about the future of political cooperation across borders in the early years of the twenty-first century does not suggest there is a reservoir of common ground – of ideas and values – among humankind. From 9/11 to the 2006 war in the Lebanon, terrorism, conflict, territorial struggle and the clash of identities appear to define the moment. The contemporary drivers of political (and ethno-) nationalism – self-determination, secure borders, core values, geopolitical and geoeconomic advantage – place an emphasis on the pursuit of the national interest and geopolitics above concerns with what it is that human beings might have in common. Moreover, the new divisions in the world community arising in the post-Cold War era are not phenomena based on new sources of conflict; rather, they are typically mediated by ancient fault lines between different religious groupings and civilizations (Huntington 1996). This gives rise to divisive fundamentalisms, calling for a return to doctrines and standards from basic scriptures or texts, and for their application to social, economic and political life (Giddens 1999a: 48). Accordingly, renewed importance is given to tradition and its guardians, emphasizing unchallengeable borders between 'insiders' and 'outsiders'. Exclusivity is championed over universalist humanist aspirations. Complex and combustible mixes of nationalism and fundamentalism jostle for recognition, and seek a world order that accommodates their ideologies.

Communication and cultural globalization

Globalists take issue with most of the above, although they by no means dismiss the significance of 'the national question' or the challenge of fundamentalism. Starting with the national question, globalists often stress the *constructed* nature of national cultures: if these cultures were created more recently than many are willing to recognize, and elaborated for a world in which nation-states were being forged, then they are neither immutable nor inevitable in a global age. Nationalism may have been functional, perhaps even essential, for the consolidation and development of the modern state, but it is today at odds with a world in which economic, social and many political forces escape the jurisdiction of the nation-state.

Given how slow many people's identities often are to change, and the strong desire many people feel to (re)assert control over the forces which shape their lives, the complexities of national identity politics are, globalists concede, likely to persist. But such politics will not deliver political control and accountability over regional and global phenomena unless a distinction is made between cultural nationalism – the conceptual, discursive and symbolic resources that are fundamental to people's lives – and political nationalism, the assertion of the exclusive political priority of national identity and national interests. The latter cannot deliver many sought-after public goods and values without regional and global collaboration. Only a global political outlook can ultimately accommodate itself to the political challenges of a more global era, marked by overlapping communities of fate and multilayered (local, national, regional and global) politics. Is there any reason to believe that such an outlook might emerge? Not only are there many sources for such an outlook in the present period but, globalists would argue, there are precedents to be found in the history of the modern state itself.

While the rise of nation-states and nationalist projects intensified cultural formation and interaction within circumscribed borders, the expansion of European powers overseas helped entrench new forms of cultural globalization with innovations in transport and communications, notably regularized mechanical transport and the telegraph. These technological advances helped the West to expand and enabled the secular philosophies which emerged in the late eighteenth and nineteenth centuries – especially science, liberalism and socialism – to diffuse and transform the cultural context of almost every society on the planet.

Contemporary popular culture may not yet have had a social impact to match this but, globalists argue, the sheer scale, intensity, speed and diversity of global cultural communications today are unsurpassed. For instance, the value of cultural exports and imports has increased many times over the last few decades; there has been a huge expansion in the trade in television, film, music and radio products; national broadcasting systems are subject to intensifying international competition and declining audience shares; and the figures for connections and users of the internet are growing exponentially as communication patterns increasingly transcend national borders. Figures 3.1–3.5 and table 3.1 illustrate the spread of communication infrastructures, their usage and the

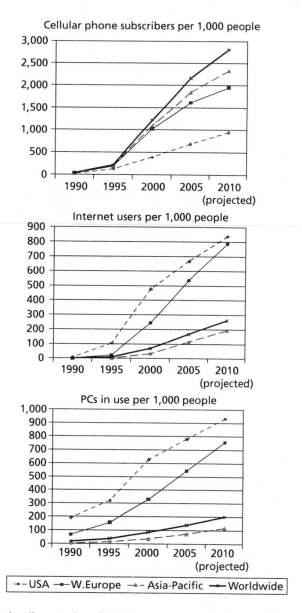

Cellular phone subscriber numbers for many countries using GSM technology are inflated because of the use of multiple SIM cards.

Figure 3.1 Comparisons of information communication technology use in different regions 1990–2005, with projected figures to 2010

Source: Calculated from data in the Computer Industry Almanac, at www.c-i-a.com/ pr0206.htm (accessed Aug. 2006).

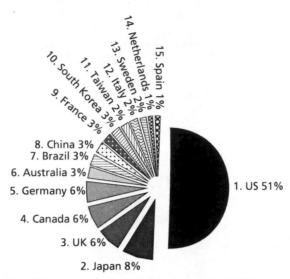

Figure 3.2 Top fifteen countries in internet use in 2000

Source: Calculated from data in the Computer Industry Almanac, at www.c-i-a.com/
pr1199.htm (accessed Aug. 2006).

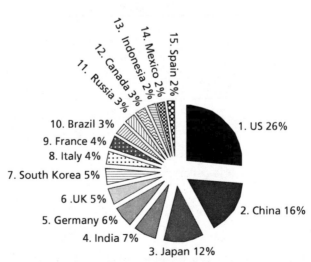

Figure 3.3 Top fifteen countries in internet use in 2006

Source: Calculated from data in the Computer Industry Almanac, at www.c-i-a.com/
pr1199.htm (accessed Aug. 2006).

Table 3.1 Cellular phone usage ranked worldwide, and penetration per 100 inhabitants, 2005

	Total subscribers (millions)	Penetration (per 100 inhabitants)
1 China	334.8	25.5
2 United States	181.1	61.0
3 Japan	91.5	71.6
4 Russia	74.4	51.6
5 Germany	71.3	86.4
6 Brazil	65.6	36.3
7 Italy	62.8	109.4
8 United Kingdom	61.1	102.8
9 India	47.3	4.4
10 France	44.6	73.7
11 Spain	38.6	93.9
12 Mexico	38.5	36.6
13 Korea (Rep.)	36.6	76.1
14 Turkey	34.7	48.0
15 Philippines	32.9	39.9
16 Indonesia	30.0	13.5
17 Thailand	28.0	44.1
18 Poland	23.1	59.9
19 Taiwan, China	22.8	100.0
20 South Africa	19.5	43.1
World	**1,751.9**	**38.8**

Note that many countries using the GSM technology have inflated subscriber numbers because of the use of multiple SIM cards.
Source: ITU 2005, p. 14.

growth of trade in major cultural products. They also highlight the uneven distribution of use and access across countries, although figures 3.2 and 3.3 show rapid changes in country positions (note the explosive development of internet use in China, India and Japan). The accelerating diffusion of radio, television, the internet, and satellite and digital technologies in general has made instant communication possible across large parts of the world. As a result, national controls over information have become ineffective in many countries. China has sought to maintain tight regulation over the internet, and yet even this can be circumvented by knowledgeable users. In addition, the spread of satellite television, mobile phone technology, and the cultural products of other countries (film, music, advertising and so on) exposes the Chinese, especially their young people, to new ideas, images and symbols. People everywhere are exposed to the values of other cultures as never

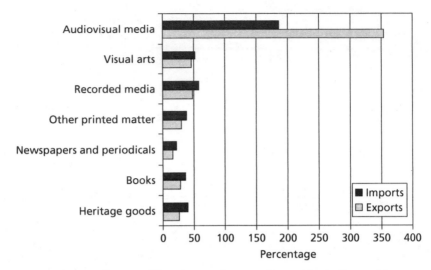

Import and export figures will not be equal as not all countries in the world are included in the UNESCO data from which these calculations are drawn.

Figure 3.4 Increases of imports and exports by cultural product category, 1994–2002

Source: UNESCO Institute for Statistics 2005: 68, 69.

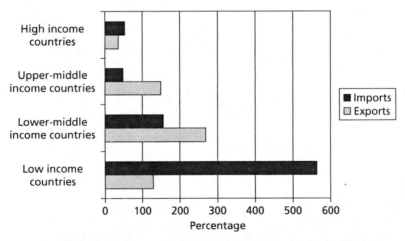

Import and export figures will not be equal as not all countries in the world are included in the UNESCO data from which these calculations are drawn.

Figure 3.5 Increases of imports and exports of cultural products by country income-quartile, 1994–2002

Source: UNESCO Institute for Statistics 2005: 68, 69.

before (Silverstone 2001: 15–17). While linguistic differences continue to be a barrier to the spread of TV programmes and other cultural commodities, the global dominance of English provides a linguistic infrastructure (especially in business, politics, administration, science, academia, computing and popular music) as powerful as any technological system for transmitting ideas and cultures.

Beyond their scale, what is striking about today's patterns of communication and cultural globalization is that they are driven by companies, not countries. Corporations, argue the globalists, have replaced states and theocracies as the central producers and distributors of cultural globalization. Private international companies are not new, but their mass impact is. News agencies and publishing houses in previous eras had a much more limited impact on local and national cultures than the consumer goods and cultural products of today's global corporations.

For the globalists the existence of new global communication systems is transforming relations between physical locales and social circumstances, and altering the 'situational geography' of political and social life (Meyrowitz 1985). In these circumstances, the traditional link between 'physical setting' and 'social situation' is broken. Geographical boundaries are overcome as individuals and collectivities experience events and developments far afield. Moreover, new understandings, commonalities and frames of meaning are elaborated without direct contact between people. As such, they can serve to detach, or disembed, identities from particular times, places and traditions, and can have a 'pluralizing impact' on identity formation, producing a variety of hyphenated identities which are 'less fixed or unified' (Hall 1992: 303, 309). While everyone has a local life, the ways people make sense of the world are now increasingly interpenetrated by ideas and values from many diverse settings. Hybrid cultures and transnational media corporations have made significant inroads into national cultures and traditional identities. The cultural position of the state is transformed as a result (cf. McLuhan 1964; Rheingold 1995).

Yet these developments have both negative and positive sides. On the negative side, the rise of contemporary fundamentalism can be closely linked to transnational phenomena and, in particular, to the spread of information technology and the expansion of the mass media (Ahmed and Donnan 1994). In fact, fundamentalism can be thought of as 'a child of globalization', which it both utilizes and responds to (Giddens 1999a: 50). Fundamentalist groupings, from Shia Muslims to Christian militants, have made extensive use of new communication technology to help establish transnational solidarity among diasporas and sympathizers. Moreover, they often manipulate the 24-hour global news networks by staging violent acts to spread their messages. Without these communication infrastructures, they could not be agents with global impacts. At the same time, leading symbols and elements of globalization are often the target of their hostility, as they juxtapose 'Western globalization' with their own standards and ideologies.

On the more positive side, those groups and states which seek to pursue rigid closed-door policies on information and culture are certainly under threat from these very same communication processes, and it is likely that aspects of the conduct of socio-economic life everywhere will be transformed by them as well. Cultural flows are transforming the politics of national identity and the politics of identity more generally. These developments have been interpreted, by some global theorists, as creating a new sense of global belonging and vulnerability which transcends loyalties to the nation-state, that is, to 'my country right or wrong' (see, for instance, Falk 1995b). The warrant for this latter claim can be found, it has been argued, in a number of processes and forces, including the development of transnational social movements with clear regional or global objectives, such as the protection of natural resources and the environment, and the alleviation of disease, ill-health and poverty (Ekins 1992). Organizations like Oxfam, Friends of the Earth and Greenpeace, and groupings like the Global Justice movement, have derived some of their success precisely from their ability to show the interconnectedness across nations and regions of the problems they seek to tackle. In addition, the constellation of actors, agencies and institutions – from regional political organizations to the UN – oriented towards international and transnational issues is cited as further evidence of a growing global political awareness. Finally, a commitment to human rights as indispensable to the dignity and integrity of all peoples – rights entrenched in international law and championed by transnational groups such as Amnesty International – is held to be additional support for an emerging 'global consciousness'. These factors, it is also maintained, represent the cultural foundations of an incipient global civil society (Falk 1995b; Kaldor 1998; Edwards 2003; and see chapter 10).

Some globalists interpret these developments as the beginnings of the formation of a cultural cosmopolitanism. What is involved in this notion? In the first instance, it is important to stress that cultural cosmopolitanism does not deny cultural differences or the enduring significance of national traditions. It is not against cultural diversity. Few, if any, contemporary cosmopolitans hold such views (see, e.g., Waldron 1999; Barry 1999; Held 2004: appendix). Rather, cultural cosmopolitans emphasize the possible fluidity of individual identity – 'people's remarkable capacity to forge new identities using materials from diverse cultural sources, and to flourish while so doing' (Scheffler 1999: 257). It celebrates, as Rushdie put it, 'hybridity, impurity, intermingling, the transformation that comes of new and unexpected combinations of human beings, cultures, ideas, politics, movies, songs' (quoted in Waldron 1992: 751). But it is *the ability to stand outside a singular location (the location of one's birth, land, upbringing, conversion) and to mediate traditions* that lies at its core. Political agents who can 'reason from the point of view of others' are better equipped to resolve, and resolve fairly, the challenging transboundary issues that create overlapping communities of fate. The development of this kind of cultural cosmopolitanism depends on the recognition by growing numbers of peoples of the increasing interconnectedness of political communities in diverse domains, and the development of an understanding of overlapping 'collective fortunes' that require collective solutions – locally, nationally, regionally and globally.

However, there are no guarantees that such a cultural outlook is sustainable or will even prevail. For it has to survive and jostle for recognition alongside deeply held national, ethnic and religious traditions. It is a cultural and cognitive orientation, not an inevitability of history. The core requirements of cultural cosmopolitanism include:

1 recognition of the increasing interconnectedness of political communities in diverse domains, including the social, economic and environmental;

2 development of an understanding of overlapping 'collective for-tunes' that require collective solutions – locally, nationally, regionally and globally; and
3 the celebration of difference, diversity and hybridity, while learning how to 'reason from the point of view of others' and mediate traditions.

Like national culture, cultural cosmopolitanism is a cultural project, but with one difference: it is better adapted and suited, so some globalists argue, to our regional and global age. It may also be essential for survival since intolerance and fundamentalism are a growing source of global insecurity and violence, from the resurgence of geopolitics to transnational terrorism.

4

Global Insecurities: Military Threats and Environmental Catastrophe

During 'Operation Allied Force' in 1999 bombers left their bases in Missouri before dawn, conducted their sorties over Kosovo, and returned to base by evening in time for their crews to have dinner (Ferguson and Mansbach 2004: 252). A century earlier the reinforcement of British forces fighting the Boers in South Africa took many weeks. In the intervening century technological change has enabled – for those with access to the relevant capabilities – the rapid projection of enormous destructive power over vast distances. During the Cold War global nuclear catastrophe was never much more than 30 minutes away. By the same token, the death of distance transforms far-off conflicts and threats into proximate dangers, as the events of 9/11 cruelly demonstrated. In military and geopolitical terms the present age is marked by globalized insecurity. Moreover it is no longer simply military threats which constitute this global insecurity since, among other things, environmental degradation, microbes and viruses do not recognize national borders. Climate change, for instance, connects individual household energy use decisions in the UK, industrial pollution in China and deforestation in Brazil to the long-term viability of human communities and countries across the globe. As Ulrich Beck has argued, a world risk society is in the making (Beck 1999b). This chapter reviews the competing arguments concerning two of the most urgent and grave dimensions of this global risk society: the dangers associated with organized violence, and environmental catastrophe.

With the end of the Cold War in 1990 there was a general presumption that it represented the demise of 'strategic globality' – the

43

military-strategic integration of the world. Nye and Donahue comment that 'in the context of superpower bipolarity, the end of the Cold War represented military deglobalization' (Donahue and Nye 2001). Regional rivalries reasserted themselves and the world appeared increasingly bifurcated into a zone of democratic peace – broadly the West – and a pre-Hobbesian zone of state collapse and endemic violence – broadly the Rest (Goldeier and McFaul 1992; Kaplan 1994; Keohane 1995). War, at least within the Western core, appeared, as Mueller argued, virtually obsolete, but beyond, in the borderlands or what Barnett refers to as 'the Gap' of exclusion and poverty, collective violence appeared an almost natural state of affairs (Mueller 1989; T. Barnett 2004; Keohane 1995). For Kaplan, and van Creveld, among others, the world is on the brink of a new dark ages in so far as traditional interstate war is in decline but the deployment of organized violence, in the context of trans-state, intrastate and low intensity conflicts, has reached historic levels (Kaplan 1994; Creveld 1991; Kaldor 1998). As van Creveld presciently observed in the early 1990s, 'as war between states exits through one side of history's revolving door, low intensity conflict among different organizations will enter through the other. Present day low intensity conflict is overwhelmingly confined to the so-called developing world. However, to think this will be so for ever or even for very long is almost certainly a great illusion' (Creveld 1991: 224). In the context of intensifying transregional flows of people, goods, arms and cultures, the notion that local conflicts or intrastate wars could simply be contained geographically has proved illusory, as Kaldor argued, and as the tragic events of 9/11 and 7/7 confirm (Kaldor 1998). Rather than the emergence of a strategically bifurcated or regionalized world, the post-Cold War era has been associated with the reassertion of a new narrative of strategic globality – in the form of the global war on terror – as well as an awareness of global vulnerability.

Yet another century of war: the sceptics' analysis

In his study of the rise of the modern state, Charles Tilly observes that 'war made the state, and the state made war' (Tilly 1990). Territory, military power and national security were fused together by the rise of the modern state. Within the system of states, peace and stability were always contingent since, in the absence of any global authority, national military power was the only means to ensure state survival and state security (see chapter 2). Interstate war, though not a normal state of affairs, was certainly a frequent occurrence. Modern European history is a history of great power competition, the balance of power and, when it failed, the prosecution of war. If organized violence had been central to the construction of the European state system, it was also the case, by the early twentieth century, that interstate war came to encompass the world.

Commenting on the history of organized violence, Tilly remarks that the twentieth century 'visited more collective violence on the world than any century of the previous 10,000 years' (2003: 55). From 1914, observes Hobsbawm, humankind has 'lived and thought in terms of world war, even when the guns were silent and the bombs were not exploding'. Industrial war and geopolitical competition fuelled an unprecedented internationalization of interstate violence which claimed in excess of 187 million fatalities worldwide (Hobsbawm 1994: 12). Modern warfare required permanent national preparation for hostilities and the mobilization of entire empires and societies.

The First World War demonstrated that war between great powers in the industrial age could no longer be confined exclusively to the combatants on the battlefield. As Klein remarks, 'war, once conducted by military geniuses on a battlefield of limited scope, had come to embrace whole continents and to involve citizens at the home front in the era of total warfare' (B. Klein 1994: 55). Total war, even more so in the case of the Second World War, rapidly became a 'global human catastrophe' (Hobsbawm 1994: 52). Hostilities raged across almost every continent and ocean, while few states could effectively remain neutral, since supplying the war effort of both the Axis (Germany, Italy and Japan) and the Allied powers (Britain, France, United States) required extensive worldwide sourcing. As McNeill confirms, 'transnational organization for war . . . achieved a fuller and far more effective expression during World War II than ever before' (1982: 356). Undoubtedly, the most profound consequence of this war for global hegemony was the demise of Europe's power as the US and the Soviet Union asserted their global superpower status.

For nearly five decades following the end of the Second World War, international politics was dominated by the political and military rivalry between these two superpowers. World politics was fractured into two rival blocs, each organized through competing systems of military alliances and regional security pacts. While the nuclear arms race made war between the two superpowers rationally unthinkable (but not necessarily improbable), East–West rivalry was displaced into Africa, Asia and Latin America. In turn, the process of decolonization and the struggle for national liberation became imbued with a Cold War military dynamic. Where direct intervention was eschewed, war by proxy ensued. As Europe's foreign military presence was reduced, that of the two superpowers expanded (see Harkavy 1989). Even outer space and the underwater world of the oceans began to be colonized for military purposes. Technological advances in military, logistics and communications systems delivered the possibility of the rapid worldwide projection of enormous destructive power. Intercontinental missiles collapsed military decision times because war could be launched in hours rather than weeks or months. The Cold War constituted a unique system of global power relations which, paradoxically, both divided the globe into rival camps and yet unified it within a singular world military order. This involved extensive and intensive regional and global networks of military relations, surveillance and, for the superpowers at least, geographically extensive military infrastructures to project unparalleled destructive power across the globe. At the height of the Cold War, in the mid-1980s, world military expenditure (in constant 1987 US dollars) approached $1,000 billion per annum (almost $190 for every individual on the planet); spending on military hardware exceeded $290 billion, while the trade in arms amounted to over $48 billion (see Krause 1992: 93; Sivard 1991: 499). If the twentieth century marked the end of formal empires, it was in no sense associated with the demise of geopolitics or the balance of power as enduring realities of world politics. To argue, as do many globalists, that war has been transformed in the twenty-first century is to ignore the history of warfare, which is one of continuous technical change, and the permanency of geopolitics, which makes the absence of great power war or even interstate war that much more historically contingent. War and preparation for war are endemic

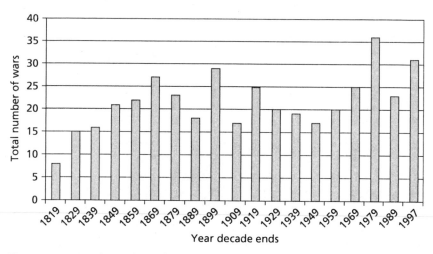

Figure 4.1 Total number of war onsets per decade (1819 and 1997 data normalized for ten years)

Source: Sarkees, Wayman and Singer 2003.

features of the modern states system, especially today. As figure 4.1 indicates, 'the long peace' since 1945 is largely a myth, for the incidence of warfare is little different than at the beginning of the twentieth century. There has been no secular shift to a more peaceful world. On the contrary, war remains very much an enduring aspect of world politics. What has changed is that old wars – interstate war – appear to have given way to new wars – intrastate warfare – while the location of war has shifted from the affluent North to the impoverished South. For sceptics this may be militarily significant but it does not amount to a transformation of war. As Colin Gray observes, 'although most of war's contexts are constantly changing . . . much of what is most important about war and warfare does not change at all' (C. Gray 2005).

Writing about the New Imperialism of the late nineteenth century, Karl Marx commented that 'in actual historical conquest, enslavement, robbery, murder, in brief violence, notoriously play the greater part' (Keane 2004: 10). Classical theories of state expansionism or imperialism, whether realist or historical materialist, have a great deal to say about the centrality of organized violence to the making of the modern global order. The current militarization of globalization is no surprise to these sceptics since the present conjuncture can be much more readily explained through the lexicons of Western imperialism, US hegemony, geopolitics and the inevitability of intercapitalist conflicts. For the sceptics, the apparent obsolescence of major power war, as with the belle époque (1880–1914), is likely to prove ephemeral, while the notion that globalization has transformed warfare, not to mention the erosion of the state's monopoly of legitimate violence, is 'another transformational fallacy' (C. Gray 2005).

Paradoxically it was the reassertion of US unilateral power, in the wake of 9/11, that brought greater awareness of the limits to globalization and of the historical primacy of geopolitics (Rosenberg 2005; and see table 4.1, which shows that US defence spending, however measured, far outstrips that of its nearest rivals). There are interesting parallels with the geopolitics of the early twentieth century in so far as the competition between the world's great powers for privileged access to, or control over, resources, markets and vital regions has acquired greater intensity in recent years. For Harvey (2003), this is evidence of a renewed imperialism, especially in the wake of the invasion of Iraq and the various humanitarian interventions in the 1990s. Neither globalization nor 9/11 and the responses to it has fundamentally altered the laws of geopolitics. 'Taken in the round . . . world politics does not seem to have been radically altered by 9/11' (Kennedy-Pipe and Rengger 2006).

Classical accounts of imperialism sought to explain the global social relations of organized violence. Hobson, Lenin and Bukharin identified monopoly capitalism as the principal source of imperialism, emphasizing the inevitability of great power rivalry and war (Brewer 1980). These analyses, sceptics maintain, have a continuing relevance, as do realist and neorealist accounts of geopolitics and hegemony. What they have in common is an emphasis on the enduring importance of territorial and military power, geopolitics, and the relations of domination and subordination which define each epoch (Mastanduno 1999; Mearsheimer 2001; Harvey 2003; Callinicos 2007). These are just as much in evidence today as at the beginning of the last century although the historical configuration of power relations is very different. The reassertion of US super-hegemony, the rivalry between China and the US in East Asia, the war in Iraq and numerous humanitarian

Table 4.1   The ten countries with the highest military expenditure in 2005 in market exchange rate terms and purchasing power parity terms

Military expenditure in MER dollar terms					Military expenditure in PPP dollar terms[a]		
			World share (%)				
Rank	Country	Spending ($bn)	Spending	Popul.	Rank	Country	Spending ($bn)
1	USA	478.2	48	5	1	USA	478.2
2	UK	48.3	5	1	2	China	[188.4]
3	France	46.2	5	1	3	India	105.8
4	Japan	42.1	4	2	4	Russia	[64.4]
5	China	[41.0]	[4]	20	5	France	45.4
Subtotal top 5		655.8	65	29	Subtotal top 5		882.2
6	Germany	33.2	3	1	6	UK	42.3
7	Italy	27.2	3	1	7	Saudi Arabia[b]	35.0
8	Saudi Arabia[b]	25.2	3	0	8	Japan	34.9
9	Russia	[21.0]	[2]	2	9	Germany	32.7
10	India	20.4	2	17	10	Italy	30.1
Subtotal top 10		782.8	78	51	Subtotal top 10		1,057.2
World		**1,001**	**100**	**100**			

MER = Market exchange rate (i.e. based on exchange rate in force); PPP = Purchasing power parity (see p. xvii); [ ] = Estimated.
Spending figures are in US$, at constant (2003) prices and exchange rates.
[a] The figures in PPP dollar terms are converted at PPP rates (for 2003), calculated by the World Bank, based on comparisons of gross national product.
[b] Data for Saudi Arabia include expenditure for public order and safety and might be a slight overestimate; the population of Saudi Arabia constitutes less than 0.5% of the total world population.
Source: SIPRI 2006.

interventions in the borderlands of the liberal peace demonstrate that geopolitics and imperialism remain the primary forces shaping world order. It is the struggle for power and hegemony between states and between national capitalists that best describes the current epoch – not globalization.

Given this enduring struggle for power there is little reason to presume that war, even between major powers, is likely to become obsolescent, as is evident in recent large increases in global military expenditure (see Hirst 2001 and figure 4.2). On the contrary, as Gray argues, 'One should not be confused by . . . globalization . . . and the prolonged relative rarity of inter-state warfare, into believing that the future political context is going to be vastly

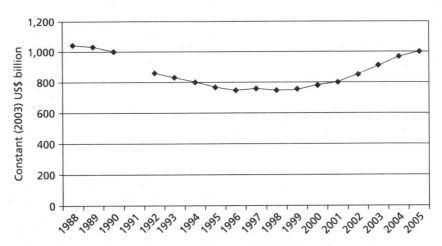

Figure 4.2   World military expenditure, 1988–2005

Source: SIPRI 2006.

different from the past' (C. Gray 2005). As neorealists emphasize, the apparent liberal peace is a product of US hegemony, and to the extent that it is challenged in the future, and historically no great power has gone unchallenged, the liberal peace remains a contingent rather than permanent feature of world order (Gilpin 1981; Mearsheimer 2001). Nor is it the case, as recent studies indicate, that the global incidence of war has declined substantially since the end of the Cold War (Sarkees, Wayman and Singer 2003; and see figure 4.1 on p. 47).Contrary to the death of distance too, empirical studies over recent years emphasize that territory and borders remain crucial factors in defining the pattern of contemporary conflicts (Buhaug and Gleditsch 2006; D. Newman 2006). The impact of globalization on both the scale and scope of contemporary warfare has been considerably exaggerated. Place and space still matter. Most conflicts are between geographically contiguous combatants, while most intrastate wars remain localized (Sarkees, Wayman and Singer 2003; Buhaug and Gleditsch 2006). Nor does transnational terrorism change this, since by almost all measures it has declined in recent years (Enders and Sandler 2006).

If the death of distance has been exaggerated, so too has the emergence of new wars and the revolution in military affairs.

Most victims of conflict are still the victims of Kalashnikovs not precision-guided munitions. According to Gray, 'Most of the military mayhem in the world of the future will be caused by organizations and people who are militarily modern only in a few respects' (C. Gray 2005). Asymmetric warfare and the internationalization of domestic conflicts would be very familiar to almost any eighteenth-century statesman. Along with fourth generation (network) warfare (see the next section), 'new wars' and irregular warfare have a long history such that their novelty and contemporary significance is greatly inflated (C. Gray 2005). To argue that war is undergoing a great transformation is simply to ignore the history of warfare and strategic thinking (McNeill 1982; Parker 1988; Hirst 2001; C. Gray 2005). Strategic globality was well understood in the seventeenth century (Bayly 2004). Even Napoleon recognized that 'the Battle of Waterloo had been lost in India' following the British defeat of the French forces (Bayly 2004: 86); while geopolitics was invented in the late nineteenth century in response to the 'first age of globalization'.

Furthermore, there is little evidence to suggest an erosion in the state's monopoly of legitimate violence, or in its monopoly of the production of means of destruction. The global diffusion of nuclear and missile technology is in fact evidence of the increasing nationalization of military technology as states everywhere seek to enhance their national military capabilities in an uncertain world; while the domination of multilateral security institutions, from the UN Security Council to the North Atlantic Treaty Organization (NATO), by the most powerful states suggests these are little more than instruments for the pursuit of national interests rather than effective constraints on the most powerful or belligerent states.

Finally, sceptics question the popular notion of a new security agenda. Environmental security, human security and economic security are important, but they remain effectively subordinate to the project of national security, without which the former are unrealizable. As Gray notes, 'The grand narrative of the new security agenda does not really explain what happens to old-fashioned inter-state rivalries' (C. Gray 2005). Moreover, expanded notions of security are little more than an instrument for legitimizing geopolitical, militaristic and interventionary tendencies among the world's major powers.

Globalization and the transformation of warfare

Just as industrialization engendered a new mode of warfare, so too the information revolution has been associated with a revolution in military affairs (RMA). Within the West, strategic thinking has moved on from twentieth-century notions of total and limited war to fourth generation or network-centric warfare, emphasizing mobility, speed, accuracy, flexibility and lethality in the projection of force (Freedman 2006). Although the friction of distance remains an important constraint on the projection of force, 'it has been significantly undermined by revolutions in communications, transport and military delivery systems' (Ferguson and Mansbach 2004: 252). In the information age, strategic globality has acquired a new meaning articulated in a new Western mode of warfare. Martin Shaw, inspired by Kaldor's earlier analyses of modes of warfare – the social relations and institutions which underpin the material production, organization, and deployment of military force – refers to it as 'global surveillance warfare' (Shaw 2005: 62). Whereas industrialized total war in the twentieth century demanded or threatened the complete mobilization or destruction of societies, global surveillance war is conducted by largely demilitarized societies with limited objectives and precision force on the perimeters of the West (Shaw 2005). It is a mode of warfare which, as evidenced in the campaigns in Kosovo and Afghanistan, relies on global infrastructures of command, control, communication, logistics, and military organization. It is a mode of warfare which has much in common with new globalized modes of post-Fordist production in terms of outsourcing, flexibility, just-in-time methods, and decentralization. In many respects, it represents a response not simply to military-technological change but also to transformations in the nature of strategic threats in a globalized world.

Paradoxically the same global infrastructures that make it possible to organize production on a worldwide basis can also be exploited to lethal effect. Modern societies are extremely vulnerable to disruption of those complex systems which enable them to function effectively, from transport to banking. Although this has always been the case, it is perhaps compounded today because of greater reliance on vital foreign primary products (from food to oil), the transnationalization of production, and the critical role of communications and transport infrastructures. Whereas total war implied the 'destruction' of the enemy, and in the Cold War depended on maintaining a strategic deterrent, in contemporary circumstances modern societies are seriously vulnerable to those who, with minimal coercive capability, threaten or seek to disrupt, rather than destroy, them. Using the 'weapons of the weak', from box-cutters to home-made explosives, the potential for non-state groups to leverage their coercive power through the disruption, criminalization or terrorizing of societies presents a significant threat to civil and international order. Furthermore, the potential of this 'asymmetric warfare' is magnified for two reasons. First, borders are no longer barriers, so that disruption of critical infrastructures by cyber-attacks, or alternatively the perpetration of terrorist attacks, can be organized effectively across distant regions of the globe (Lukasik, Goodman and Longhurst 2003). Often the sources of collective violence are no longer rooted in the locales where the violence is directly experienced, whether in the form of acts of terrorism in London or gang warfare on the streets of Chicago. In Keohane's view, the 'barrier conception of geographical space, already anachronistic with respect to thermonuclear war . . . was finally shown to be thoroughly obsolete on September 11th' (2002: 276). Second, the proliferation of highly lethal weapons systems, not to mention technologies of mass destruction, radically alters the scale of potential threats. Asymmetric warfare, under conditions of globalization, transforms the potential threat environment confronting states such that distinctions between vital strategic regions and non-strategic regions no longer holds, while orthodox notions of territorial security are made problematic. For if potential threats can be organized, resourced or directed from multiple sites across the globe, countering them requires more than simply domestic security measures and must include a global surveillance infrastructure. National security increasingly begins abroad, not at the border, since borders are as much carriers of as barriers to transnational organized violence. Security, in different contexts, is being decoupled from a statist territoriality. This has become increasingly evident in relation to what Kaldor (1998) calls the 'new wars' – complex irregular warfare in the global South.

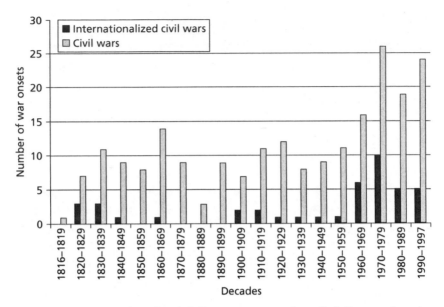

Figure 4.3 Internationalized civil wars compared to all civil wars, decades from 1810 to 1997

Source: Sarkees, Wayman and Singer 2003.

Organized violence remains a defining feature of the contemporary global condition. However, by comparison with previous epochs, particularly that of the early twentieth century, it has acquired a substantially different form and scale (Ferguson and Mansbach 2004). Interstate war has been almost entirely supplanted by intrastate and trans-state conflict located in the global South, or on the perimeters of the West. These so-called 'new wars' (or internationalized civil wars) are primarily located in failing states and rooted in identity politics, local conflicts and rivalries (Kaldor 1998; and see figure 4.3). They involve complex irregular warfare between military, paramilitary, criminal and private forces which rages through, but often around and across, state borders with little discrimination between civilians and combatants (Duffield 2001; Kaldor 1998). The UN estimates, for instance, that thirty-five people die every hour across the globe as a consequence of irregular armed conflict (Keane 2004: 8).This is a form of warfare which would be more readily recognizable to medieval warlords or Shoguns than it is to a military schooled in total war.

Yet these 'new wars', whether in Bosnia, Darfur or Venezuela, are curiously modern since they are sustained largely by the capacity of combatants to exploit global networks to provide finance, arms, émigré support, or aid, as well as to facilitate profiteering, racketeering and shadow economies, such as the diamond trade, which pay for arms and influence (Duffield 2001; Tilly 2003; Kaldor 1998).

Despite their apparently localized quality, 'new wars' are in fact a manifestation of the contemporary globalization of organized violence. They represent a mode of warfare which, according to Duffield, 'stands comparison with the manner in which Northern political and economic actors have similarly adapted to the pressures and opportunities of [economic] globalization' (2001: 14). The dynamics of such conflicts often generate complex humanitarian emergencies, which rapidly draw in international and external agencies, fuelling demands for humanitarian intervention, as in Kosovo and Somalia in the 1990s. Significantly, as Duffield argues, 'the increasing interconnectedness of the global system has magnified the threat of the internationalization of instability in the South' (2001: 37). Several consequences flow from this interconnectedness: a convergence between global security and development objectives (as aid is tied to security, and security to development); and the emergence of global security complexes, spanning the North–South divide, in which the West seeks, through selective incorporation, the pacification of its turbulent frontiers. In effect, 'as disorder in one part of the world has combined with IT and the speed of travel to feed insecurity in another, security has become increasingly diffuse and borders more complicated to defend' (Avant 2005: 33).

Global security complexes bind together the security of societies across the North–South divide. So too do the illicit global trade in arms, the operations of private security companies, organized crime, and transnational terrorist networks. Over the last five decades there has been a remarkable expansion in parallel transnational networks which operate alongside, through or beyond the formal military networks between states – the world military order. From the illicit trade in small arms or weapons technologies, such as the Khan network which supplied nuclear technology to Libya and Iran, to the operations of private security companies, such as Executive Outcomes, which was employed by the central government in Sierra Leone in the 1990s to impose civil order, these parallel transnational networks represent the emergence of a burgeoning global market for force and the means of violence. Frederick the Great, as the commander of an army half of whom were foreigners, would probably not find this a terribly novel situation. Historically such a market has always existed. However, as Singer and Avant among others emphasize, the end of the Cold War, the opportunities opened up by intensifying globalization, the privatization and commercialization of military production and services in the North, and the endemic disorder in several regions of the world have combined to produce a huge expansion in the global market for force (Singer 2003; Avant 2005). In much the same way as production has been outsourced and globalized, so too have many aspects of organized violence. As Singer remarks, 'A new global industry has emerged. It is outsourcing and privatizing of a twenty-first century variety, and it changes many of the old rules of international politics and warfare' – and, one might also add, of the maintenance of peace (Singer 2003: 9).

Globalization, commercialization and criminalization combined, it can be argued, highlight a major disjuncture between the distribution of formal military power and the actual distribution of effective coercive power. Al-Qaeda, the Triads, narco-terrorism, and the illicit arms trade are very much part of what Keohane refers to as agencies of informal organized violence, or what Ferguson and Mansbach call post-international violence (non-state, privatized, outsourced, globalized violence) (Keohane 2002; Ferguson and Mansbach 2004). Transnational terrorist and criminal organizations, alongside those transnational social forces operating in the shadow global economy, have been able to exploit the infrastructures of globalization for their own illicit and destructive purposes. So much so that some conclude that 'the transnational expansion of these dangerous trades has come to form part of the essential machinery of globalization' (Bhattcharya 2005: 32). Domestic policing increasingly has a transnational dimension. Deadly violence on the streets of the world's major cities can often be traced to the distant actions of trans-state organized criminal and gang networks. Among realists and liberals schooled in Weber's classic understanding of the state as 'a human community that claims the monopoly of the legitimate use of violence within a given territory', this is profoundly unsettling (Ferguson and Mansbach 2004: 232). Keohane poses the issue starkly: 'States no longer have a monopoly on the means of mass destruction: more people died in the attacks on the World Trade Center and the Pentagon than in the Japanese attack on Pearl Harbor in 1941' (2002: 284).

In her historical study of the modern state and organized violence, Janice Thompson (1994) describes how, by the early twentieth century, states had purposively acquired a monopoly of force, and how this became an international norm. Although this was a generalized historical process, it was never entirely universal: significant exceptions remained, while even the most advanced states relied on the private sector for the production of the means of violence. Indeed, as Victoria Hui has recently written, the modern Western state historically has lacked the kind of centralized control of organized violence which defined the ancient Chinese state (Hui 2005). Caution is therefore required in interpreting contemporary developments as necessarily denoting the generalized erosion or demise of the state monopoly of organized violence (Singer 2003).

That there are in the order of 30,000 noncitizens in the US military, that private military companies have trained the military in forty-two countries, that in 2004 there were 20,000 private security personnel from sixty different international firms operating in Iraq all are hugely significant facts. Yet, as Avant argues, the commercialization and globalization of organized violence compromise rather than erode the state's monopoly of organized violence, while the actual consequences vary among strong and weak states (Avant 2005). Although in some contexts control over organized violence may be redistributed, in other contexts states are able to enhance the provision of security with no substantial diminution of control. Deudney makes a helpful distinction here in arguing that 'states have a monopoly on the ability to legitimize violence, but they do not have the ability to monopolize violence' (quoted in Clark 1999: 119). However, it is also clear that the state's capacity to legitimize violence is partly conditional: witness the contestation of the 2003 US-led decision to intervene in Iraq, given international legal constraints and the pressure by non-governmental organizations (NGOs) and transnational social movements (Leander

2002). Rather than the state's effective monopoly of force being automatically eroded, it is perhaps more accurate to conclude that a global market for force is both complicating the business of control and also normalizing the practice of private ownership of the means of destruction – that organized violence is not (or should no longer be) a public monopoly (Leander 2002; Avant 2004). One paradox is that this tends to blur the distinction between legitimate and illegitimate organized violence which is essential to the identity of the modern state, and articulated every day in the global war on terror.

If the modern state's legitimate monopoly of organized violence is in question, its autonomous capacity to produce the means of destruction, with the exception of a few cases, has become somewhat compromised in recent decades. Just as manufacturing production has become globalized, so too has production of the means of violence, although in a more controlled and restrained manner because of the primacy of national security considerations. Sustaining or nurturing an autonomous industrial base for national defence remains central to the very existence of the modern state, yet in truth it is perhaps more the exception than the norm. Since the 1960s, technologies of military production have become increasingly diffused around the globe, such that many more countries beyond the US and Europe have developed the capability to produce missiles, advanced fighters, and chemical and biological weapons systems. Moreover, with rapid industrialization has come the increased capacity of many states to manufacture an array of lethal weapons. The proliferation of technologies of weapons of mass destruction (nuclear, chemical or biological), whether to states or non-state organizations, also remains a critical global security problem because of the accelerated diffusion of knowledge to and operation of illicit global networks. However, since the 1990s, intensified rationalization and concentration within the defence industrial sector in response to the end of the Cold War has been accompanied by its significant transnationalization, so that, apart from the first-tier arms producers (US, UK, France, Germany, Russia, China), few other states can claim to sustain a completely autonomous defence industrial base (Sköns and Wulf 1994). As Bitzinger observes, 'The industry has undergone an unprecedented restructuring, both on a national and a global scale.' A recent

Swedish defence review acknowledged publicly that the country 'can no longer afford to sustain a national defense industry to the extent that this was possible in the past', while even Japan has recognized that *kokusanka* (autonomy) is unrealistic (Bitzinger 2003: 53). For many countries beyond the first tier of high-tech arms production the national defence industrial base has become integrated into a broader global division of labour in arms production (Bitzinger 2003). To a more limited extent this is also true of the first-tier producers, although they retain a singular capacity for military-defence innovation. Even so, as Bitzinger concludes, 'the bulk of arms production has become more of a global, integrated and hierarchical affair' (2003: 81).

If the state's monopoly of the production of the means of destruction has been eroded, this is also the case for the organization and deployment of military forces. Increasingly states operate within the context of institutionalized alliances, such as NATO, or cooperative security arrangements with major powers or regional security organizations. In the process, multilateral and transgovernmental politics is constitutive of national decisions about the organization, deployment and use of military power. Furthermore, the huge expansion in multilateral peacekeeping activities by the UN, NATO and other regional bodies, such as the African Union, reinforces the notion that national security is no longer simply a national affair. This is particularly the case in relation to the threatened or actual use or deployment of military force, the legitimacy of which can no longer be justified by a simple appeal to raison d'état. In certain respects, the state's normative monopoly on decisions concerning the legitimate use of force, to varying degrees and in different contexts, is circumscribed (Leander 2002, 2004a; and see chapter 2).

One of the more significant qualifications to the primacy of orthodox notions of the state and international security is expressed in the institutionalization of the human security discourse – protecting and advancing the material and developmental welfare of individuals and communities (Thomas 2000; E. Newman 2001). Human security, as a regulative principle of world order, circumscribes the legitimacy of the state's monopoly on security since it privileges individuals and societies, in some contexts in opposition to national security. Underlying the normative shift to human security, which has found institutional expression in the UN Commission on Human Security and in the global development-security complex, is a cosmopolitan philosophy which, as with the universal human rights regime, is in tension with the Westphalian statist principles which historically have informed the rules of world order. Cosmopolitanism privileges individuals and the conditions necessary for human flourishing (see chapter 3). It emphasizes that, in a densely interconnected world, ethical duties and responsibilities are not territorially bounded but, on the contrary, given a shared fate, they necessarily transcend borders. Innocuous as this may appear, it raises the profoundly difficult and controversial question as to whether such duties may require or can justify military intervention on humanitarian grounds: whether, in other words, globalization implies there is a moral duty to save strangers (Wheeler 2000).

Humanitarian intervention sits uneasily with a Westphalian world order which privileges state sovereignty and territorial integrity. However, if in an interconnected world the problems of domestic insecurity, underdevelopment and violent conflict spill across borders and regions, the international community is necessarily confronted, as it was in Kosovo, Somalia and many other places, with the practical issue of whether or not to intervene. Similarly, globalization presents the international community with stark moral choices where governments may be engaged in crimes against humanity or significant abuses of their citizens. Although the ethical issue of duties beyond borders predates contemporary globalization, it has become increasingly salient and pressing: complex emergencies are not only given immediacy by a globalized media, but in addition the international capacity to intervene or ameliorate injustice is generally not in doubt. Globalization is not an ethical justification for saving strangers, since such duties can be said to exist irrespective of the intensity of worldwide interconnectedness, but it has undoubtedly made more urgent and politically salient the ethical debate concerning duties beyond borders, whether in relation to humanitarian intervention or to global distributive justice (making poverty history) (Caney 2005).

Beyond the matter of saving strangers, the globalization of organized violence has destabilized other norms and regimes with respect to the regulation of force. In particular, the character of complex irregular warfare, such as that pursued by al-Qaeda, has generated ethical and legal uncertainty concerning the rationale and justification for preventive and pre-emptive war. Globalized informal violence also raises more fundamental questions concerning the normative and legal claims of states to a monopoly of legitimate violence, whether such claims are conditional or qualified, and whether or in what circumstances informal or non-state violence might be legitimate. Moreover, the commercialization and privatization of organized violence raises serious questions about what norms and legal rules should apply to these forces and how they are to be governed (Singer 2004; Avant 2005). Already, in the absence of formal (national or international) public regulation, the governance of commercial forces is developing independently within mixed (public–private) global regimes (Avant 2005; Tripathi 2005). One such regime is the Voluntary Principles on Security and Human Rights, which has established and implemented a normative framework for the regulation of public and private security activities within the global extractive industry (IWG 2005). The globalization and commercialization of organized violence, combined with the rise of complex irregular warfare, not to mention transnational organized crime, are creating, some would argue, a radical decentralization of control over the use of force, and with it the erosion of legal and normative restraints on collective violence (Leander 2002, 2004a, 2004b; Ferguson and Mansbach 2004: 245). Significantly the indiscriminate use of violence which is eroding the effective distinction between combatants and non-combatants is but one major consequence of these developments. As Ferguson and Mansbach conclude, 'post-international violence today commonly involves non-sovereign participants fighting for anything but reasons of state' and thus often effectively beyond normative and legal restraints on the use of force (Ferguson and Mansbach 2004: 272). In these respects the globalization of organized violence invites serious ethical deliberation about the substantive norms and legal principles which should inform the global regulation of collective violence and military force.

Two popular metaphors for describing the current global condition are the 'new medievalism', or 'dark ages', and the 'liberal (democratic) peace'. Drawn principally from Hedley Bull's classic analysis of the future of world order, the 'new medievalism' describes for some the coming dystopia: a world unified in a struggle between opposing ways of life, in which political authority is highly fragmented, control over organized violence is highly decentralized, and endemic conflict on the periphery is encroaching on the pacific core (Bull 1977). This is the world of a globalizing modernity and resistance to it, in which control over the means of violence is becoming increasingly diffused, a world of permanent war for permanent peace, and one in which states share political authority with public and private agencies astride, below and beside them. As a description, rather than explanation, of our times it captures elements of the current condition. But in several respects it exaggerates 'the coming anarchy' and overlooks the ways in which the zones of stability in the world are collectively managed and regulated without resort to violence or warfare. The utopian metaphor is that of the 'liberal or democratic peace'. Where democracy, economic interdependence and multilateralism reinforce each other, as in the Western community of states, a distinctively liberal zone of peace can be identified in which, according to this account, war has become obsolete (Mueller 1989; Russett 1993; Russett and Oneal 2001). For some, therefore, globalization is almost entirely associated with peace rather than war. Given a liberal faith in the possibilities of progress, the logical extrapolation of this argument is that a more peaceful world can be engineered by expanding the zone of peace. Russett, for instance, concludes:

> A different kind of world can be nurtured, one in which most conflicts of interests are not managed primarily by the threat of violence . . . The benefits of liberalism need not be confined, therefore, to the powerful. Nor should the powerful seek to impose liberalism on others . . . Extending the Kantian system will require cooperation. Multilateralism will be crucial . . . If multilateralism is to be effective, international organizations will have to play an important role. (Russett and Oneal 2001: 303–4)

Other globalists, however, argue that this position is simply a veiled justification for liberal imperialism, or to paraphrase Appiah, 'liberalism on safari' (Appiah 2005). For these critical thinkers the transformations in warfare noted above are primarily driven by the dynamics of the new global capitalism and the consequent need to pacify the hinterlands lest conflicts spread. Organized violence is very much constitutive of contemporary globalization, since its economic, political and cultural impacts are significant factors in the endemic disorder, conflict and violence which plague many regions of the world. It appears somewhat curious to argue, as do many liberals, that economic globalization generates the conditions for a democratic peace among the affluent – since the causal logic is the reverse – and to ignore the ways in which, either directly or indirectly, it contributes to collective violence in global capitalism's borderlands. There is considerable evidence to suggest that economic globalization in particular has contributed significantly to the social, ethnic and political strains in many developing states and regions which have resulted in collective violence and 'new wars' (Duffield 2001; Black 2004; Kaldor 1998). As Black concludes of collective violence on the periphery, 'Globalism . . . is one of the major causes, as it accentuates the possibility of conflict' (2004: 4). Equally global infrastructures have undoubtedly sustained many such conflicts, from Zaire to Colombia, well beyond what purely indigenous resources might permit. Moreover, resistance to cultural globalization and Westernization has spawned considerable violence within and across states and societies in the North and South. To the extent that North and South are increasingly connected by flows of people, goods, images, weapons, microbes and illicit activities, etc., the contingency and vulnerability of the democratic peace are robustly exposed. This is precisely why in recent years, even before the second Iraq war, the question of humanitarian and military intervention acquired such salience on the global political agenda (Wheeler 2000).

Writing before 9/11, Scholte presciently observed that 'equations of globalization and peace might prove to be dangerously complacent' (2000b: 211). As Kaldor, Duffield, and Barnett, among others, argue, the long-term sustainability of the liberal peace depends on recognizing the shared nature of security across the shifting borders of the North–South divide – the global political, economic and security complexes which bind together different human communities of fate (Duffield 2001; Barnett 2004; Kaldor 1998). To date this has encouraged a securitization of development, especially in the wake of 9/11, as societies or social formations are selectively included in or excluded from the formal infrastructures of globalization. The problem is that, even if they are excluded from these formal networks, it is almost impossible to exclude social forces from the parallel globalizations of informal and illicit networks. As Duffield observes, 'The networks that support war cannot be easily separated out and criminalized in relation to the networks that characterize peace; they are both part of a complex process' of globalization (Duffield 2001: 190). In key respects, precisely because of globalization, the zones of perpetual peace and perpetual war may be geographically discontinuous but materially, socially and existentially radically conjoined. This leads to a 'recognition of the integral relations between developments in the (liberal democratic) core and elsewhere and so prompts an analysis of the [global] system not as divided into zones of [liberal] peace and war but as a structured whole'; a structured totality in which organized violence is deployed, by state and non-state forces, for 'the purposes of extending or defending liberal spaces both at home and abroad', or alternatively, by those resisting and contesting such purposes, for advancing other ways of life (Barkawi and Laffey 1999: 412, 422). The globalization of organized violence and the inherent violence of globalization are organically related, whether described as 'humanitarian interventionism', liberal imperialism or 'empire-lite'.

There is one point of agreement between sceptics and globalists: namely that some of the new emerging threats to security are likely to prove a potential source of increased conflict. In this respect, Hirst (2001) argues that these new insecurities, most significantly climate change, are likely to become a significant source of conflict between states. This is evident already in the manner in which the issue of climate change has become imbued with a geopolitical logic – as an instrument in the struggle between the US and China for economic primacy. Even Gray predicts that 'the political context for future war is going to be impacted massively, perhaps dominated, by the . . . negative consequences of climate change'(C. Gray 2005).

Global insecurity and environmental change

For most of human history, the main way in which environmental impacts spread around the world was through the unintentional transport of flora, fauna and microbes. The great plagues, such as the Black Death of the mid-fourteenth century, showed how dev-astating the effects could be. The European colonization of the New World within a generation killed a substantial proportion of the indigenous populations of the Caribbean, Mexico and other parts of Latin America. Over the following centuries these societies saw their ecosystems, landscapes and agricultural systems trans-formed. Early colonialism also damaged the environment in new ways. The Sumatran and Indian forests were plundered to meet consumer demand in Europe and America; seals were overhunted in many places, to dangerously low levels, and some species of whale became extinct.

But most forms of environmental impact were largely localized until the middle of this century. Since then, the impact and scale of environmental change have intensified. Sixty years of resource-intensive and high-pollution growth in the OECD and the even dirtier industrialization of Russia, Eastern Europe and the ex-Soviet states have taken their toll on the environment. Now China, along with some other countries in the developing world, are industrializing at breakneck speed, putting further pressure on non-renewable resources and our ecosystems.

The globalization of environmental threats and risks has, it is important to stress, taken a number of forms, including the encounters between previously separated ecological systems from different parts of the planet; the pollution and degradation of the global commons (such as the oceans and the atmosphere); the ter-ritorial overspill of the effects of environmental pressures (envir-onmental refugees); transborder pollution and risks (nuclear power, acid rain); and the transportation and diffusion of wastes and polluting products across the globe (the toxic waste trade). As a result, humankind faces an unprecedented array of environmen-tal threats which have the potential to disrupt not just established ways of life but also the very existence of some societies. The section below discusses perhaps the most critical of these: global warming or climate change. It reviews the debate about climate change as a new global security threat (which may be even more significant than military threats such as terrorism). In discussing this issue, the evidence supporting the globalist arguments about climate change as a threat to national and international security will be presented first, followed by the sceptical position.

Environmental risk and insecurity: the globalist case

There is a consensus that global temperatures are increasing (see figure 4.4). Consider the following facts:

- Over the last century the average temperature has climbed about 1 degree Fahrenheit (0.6 of a degree Celsius) around the world.
- The Intergovernmental Panel on Climate Change (IPCC) of the United Nations projects that global temperatures will rise an additional 3 to 10 degrees Fahrenheit (1.6 to 5.5 degrees Celsius) by century's end.
- The spring ice thaw in the northern hemisphere occurs nine days earlier than it did 150 years ago, and the autumn freeze now typically starts ten days later.
- The 1990s was the warmest decade since the mid-1800s, when record-keeping started. The hottest years recorded were 2006, 1998, 2002, 2003, 2001 and 1997.
- Rising temperatures have a dramatic impact on Arctic ice, which serves as a kind of 'air conditioner' at the top of the world. Since 1978 the Arctic sea ice area has shrunk by some 9 per cent per decade, and thinned as well. (See Handwerk 2004.)

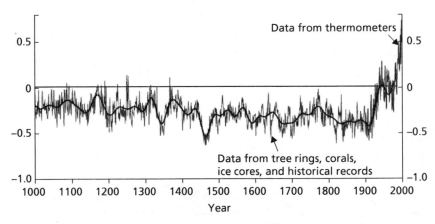

Figure 4.4 Temperature rise since the early 1900s (departure in temperature (°C) from the 1961–90 average, Northern Hemisphere)

Source: World Bank 2006; Intergovernmental Panel on Climate Change.

While these facts are regarded as irrefutable, the causal forces at work are contested. For example, over the last million years the earth has fluctuated between colder and warmer periods. The shifts have occurred at intervals of roughly 100,000 years and are thought to be regulated by sunlight. The earth's sunlight quota depends, then, on its orbit and celestial orientation. But to what extent? And to what extent have human factors intervened? The main issue of contention is whether human beings, through industrialization and fossil fuel consumption, are causing global warming now.

The overwhelming body of scientific opinion supports the position articulated by the Intergovernmental Panel on Climate Change.* In its assessment, the earth's climate is being affected by human activities: 'Human activities . . . are modifying the concentration of atmospheric constituents . . . that absorb or scatter radiant energy . . . [M]ost of the observed warming over the last 50 years is likely to have been due to the increase in greenhouse gas concentrations' (McCarthy 2001: 21). This position is supported by every major scientific body in the United States which specializes in the study of climate change: the American Meteorological Society, the American Geophysical Union, and the American Association for the Advancement of Science have all issued statements supporting the evidence for anthropogenic climate change. Moreover, *Science*, the most respected scientific journal in the world, conducted a study to measure how much consensus there was on anthropogenic climate change. This survey of 928 peer-reviewed studies of climate change conducted between 1993 and 2003 found that they all either supported the human-caused global warming thesis or did not dissent from it. The article concluded that 'politicians, economist, journalists, and others may have the impression of confusion, disagreements, or discord among climate scientists, but that impression is incorrect' (Oreskes 2004).

---

* Created in 1988 by the World Meteorological Organization and the United Nations Environmental Programme, the IPCC's purpose is to evaluate the state of climate science as a basis for informed policy action, primarily on the basis of peer-reviewed and published scientific literature. See www.ipcc.ch. The IPCC's latest (4th) Assessment Report became available in early 2007 and upheld scientific opinion about the scale of global warming and its human causes. See also IPCC 2007.

Scientific opinion on the human causes of climate change		
1 Strongly agree	50 (9.4% of valid responses)	Above-median positions total 55.8%
2	134 (25.3% of valid responses)	
3	112 (21.1% of valid responses)	
4	75 (14.2% of valid responses)	
5	45 (8.5% of valid responses)	Below-median positions total 29%
6	60 (10.8% of valid responses)	
7 Strongly disagree	54 (9.7% of valid responses)	
Source: Bray 2005.		

Yet the consensus is not quite complete. An international survey of scientists from 2005 shows there is no absolute agreement that climate change has been the result of human action. Only 9.4 per cent of the respondents 'strongly agreed' that climate change was the result of anthropogenic causes (measured on a 1–7 scale where 1 is 'strongly agree') (Bray 2005: 25). Nonetheless, the distribution of the responses to the thesis clearly demonstrates that, weighing positions on either side of the median position, those on the agreeing side are in a substantial majority (see the box).

The chief British scientist, Sir David King, warned in 2004 that 'climate change is the most serious problem we are facing today, more serious than the threat of terrorism' (King 2004). Irrespective of whether or not one agrees with this statement, global warming, in the view of the broad opinion of the scientific community, has the capacity to wreak havoc on the world's diverse species, biosystems and socioeconomic fabric. Violent storms will become more frequent, water access will become a battleground, rising sea levels will displace millions, the mass movement of desperate people will become more common, and deaths from serious diseases in the world's poorest countries will rise rapidly (largely because bacteria will spread more quickly, causing greater contamination of food and water). Moreover, global warming constitutes a serious threat not just in the long term, but the here and now. The failure to cut emissions could lead to a downturn in the global economy of a kind not seen since the Great Depression and the two world wars (Stern 2006).

Humankind is increasingly aware that it faces an unprecedented array of global environmental threats which no national community or single generation can tackle alone. The Kyoto Protocol, signed in 1997, was a step forward in trying to regulate greenhouse gases, yet the United States, the biggest single contributor to greenhouse gas emissions, refused to sign (see Held et al. 1999: 389–99). Shifts in international political discourse have been significant, and the capacity of environmental NGOs to mobilize domestic support for international environmental problems has increased considerably. But so far there has simply not been the political commitment, domestic support or international authority on a scale to do any more than limit the very worst excesses of these global environmental threats. Whether this will change, under the pressure of mounting public concern, remains to be seen.

So *much hot air: the sceptical response*

While there is a consensus that global temperatures are increasing, there is controversy about whether human beings are causing global warming and, thus, whether or not it represents a real or imaginary global security threat. The most sceptical public campaigns in the US on anthropogenic climate change accept the scientific consensus that global ground-level temperatures are rising (Murray 2006: 1). Such accounts argue, however, that there is no need for public concern, because either it is questionable that global warming is anthropogenic, or it is the case that global warming will not have the harmful effects predicted, and may even be beneficial. One line of scepticism runs as follows. While global surface temperatures have risen over the last few decades, mid-tropospheric temperatures have not warmed as much – which suggests an inconsistency with the climate change models often employed. Some hold that atmospheric temperatures have not altered since 1979. Based on what is known about how the greenhouse effect works, atmospheric temperatures would be expected to be more than surface temperatures, and thus such phenomena call into question the climate change account as it is conventionally presented.

Sceptics like to contend that many of the well-known indicators of global warming are misleading or inaccurate. For example:

- the Arctic was as warm or warmer in 1940 than it is today;
- the Greenland ice sheet may be growing on average, and hence pushing ice off its coastal perimeter, generating images that suggest it is melting and breaking off;

- Alpine glaciers have been in retreat since the early nineteenth century. Since 1970 many of the glaciers have stopped retreating and some are now advancing again (and it is not known why this is happening). (Lindzen 2006)

More recently, the Centre for the Study of Carbon Dioxide and Global Change and the Competitive Enterprise Institute have argued that:

> Warming has been shown to positively impact human health, while atmospheric CO_2 enrichment has been shown to enhance the health-promoting properties of the food we eat, as well as stimulate the production of more of it. . . . In addition, elevated levels of atmospheric CO_2 have been shown to increase the amounts and effectiveness of disease-fighting substances found in plants that protect against various forms of cancer, cardiovascular and respiratory diseases . . . it is abundantly clear that we have nothing to fear from increasing concentrations of atmospheric CO_2 and global warming.' (Idso, Idso and Idso 2003)

In short, the sceptical contention is that global warming is not extensive, that most models exaggerate the future of the warming, and that benefits may outweigh costs (Murray 2006).*

Bjørn Lomborg has added two additional arguments to the literature. First, he has sought to show that the costs of taking action against climate change are extremely high, and this is especially the case because one has to consider the difference between taking action in the present and taking action in the future when society is richer and has better information about global problems (Lomborg 2004a: 311–12, 322–3). Further, there are striking opportunity costs. Taking action on a specific problem and spending scarce resources on it (for instance, on climate change) means not spending resources elsewhere (for instance, on global public health). Lomborg compares the trade-off between, for example, estimates by UNICEF, the UN Children's Fund, of what it would cost for all developing country inhabitants to have access to basic health, education, water, sanitation, etc., and addressing

---

* The Royal Society has prepared a document seeking to dispel some of the myths on anthropogenic climate change, at www.ipcc.ch/pub/wg2SPMfinal.pdf.

climate change, and ultimately opts for the former. As he succinctly puts it:

> We should not spend vast amounts of money to cut a tiny slice of the
> global temperature increase when this constitutes a poor use of
> resources and when we could probably use these funds far more
> effectively in the developing world. . . . global warming is not any-
> where near the most important problem facing the world. What
> matters is making the developing countries rich and giving the citi-
> zens of developed countries even greater opportunities. [. . .] the
> same resources could do much more good, saving many more people
> from dying from involuntary risks. [. . .] To use a harsh – albeit
> fitting – metaphor, we could say that when we ignore the cost of our
> environmental decisions on the lesser regulations in other areas, we
> are in reality committing statistical murder. (Lomborg 2004a:
> 322–3, 342)

Following this line of reasoning, Lomborg has sought to establish
a 'Copenhagen Consensus', which, he hopes, will become a powerful source of agenda-setting and research (Lomborg 2004b). In
its most recent ranking of global priorities, out of a list of forty,
addressing climate change in the form of the Kyoto Protocol
appears only twenty-seventh, behind other global social priorities
such as improving health services, an expansion of education and
improving infant and child nutrition.*

Yet, clearly, these positions can be disputed. First, the sceptical
position on anthropogenic climate change is clearly controversial,
as noted previously. A large majority of scientific opinion is against
it. Second, in considering spending trade-offs, Lomborg's analysis,
and the Copenhagen Consensus project more generally, focuses
specifically on the redeployment of economic surplus within the
category of beneficial activities and explicitly avoids analysis of the
potential of redirecting areas of vast expenditure, such as military
spending. This weakens the analysis and creates striking biases.
Third, if humankind takes the advice of the sceptical position on
human-based climate change, it will lose pressing opportunities to
act according to the precautionary principle; that is, the principle
of acting to avoid harm (or further harm) now in order to mitigate

---

* For the 2006 list, see www.copenhagenconsensus.com/Default.aspx?ID=728.

risks that may well build up for the future. To the extent that there is uncertainty in the debate, it might be a costly mistake, to say the very least, to ignore the potential threat by failing to act in the present.

5

A New World Economic Order?
Global Markets and State Power

Some two decades ago Robert Gilpin published *The Political Economy of International Relations* (now a classic text), which confirmed the coming of age of international political economy as a separate field of academic enquiry (Gilpin 1987). At the beginning of the new century, Gilpin issued a second edition but retitled it *Global Political Economy*, reflecting, as noted in the book's preface, the fundamental changes which had taken place in the intervening period in the nature of the international economic order. In particular, the most significant change he observes is 'the globalization of the world economy' (Gilpin 2001: 3). Economic globalization, however, remains a deeply contested subject in the academy and beyond. Within the academy, the very concept of economic globalization remains controversial because of its questionable validity both as a description and an explanation of the contemporary world economic order. Engaging with these controversies, this chapter examines the key points of contention which revolve around principal issues:

- economic globalization as a social ideology as opposed to a really existing condition;
- the extent to which the world economy is becoming more integrated or more segregated;
- the relationship between global markets and state power;
- the (apparent) mobility of capital and its implications for national welfare regimes and national models of capitalism;
- the limits to, and possibilities for, effective national and multilateral regulation of global markets; and

73

- whether the concepts of geopolitics, imperialism or empire, as opposed to globalization, provide more convincing accounts of the dominant tendencies in the contemporary world economic order.

In examining these questions the chapter will begin with a discussion of world economic trends, followed by the sceptical and globalist interpretations of these trends. The chapter is ordered in this way because much of the debate between sceptics and globalists concerns what these trends disclose.

Recent trends in the world economy: globalization, regionalization or triadization?

It is the confluence of secular trends and patterns of world trade, capital flows, production and migration which is central to any evaluation as to whether the principal tendency in the world economy is one of globalization, regionalization (segmentation into regional blocs), or triadization (segmentation into three metropolitan cores: the Americas, Asia and Europe).

For most of the postwar period, world trade has grown much faster than world output, and significantly so since the 1990s (see figure 5.1) (Irwin 2002; WTO 2006b). World exports, measured as a proportion of world output, were three times greater in 1998 than in 1950; the WTO estimates this ratio stood at 29 per cent in 2001 and was around 27 per cent in 2005, by comparison with 17 per cent in 1990 and 12.5 per cent in 1970 (WTO 2001; WTO 2006b). Despite the 11 September attacks and the subsequent downturn in the world economy, world trade measured as a proportion of world output remains at levels well in excess of the high points of 1990s globalization (WTO 2003, 2006a; A.T. Kearney/Foreign Policy 2003). World merchandise trade exceeded $10 trillion in 2005 ($10,159 billion), almost sixty-five times the value of world trade in 1963 ($157 billion), and services trade stood at $2,415 billion, compared to $365 billion in 1980, an almost sevenfold increase (WTO 2006b).

Trade now involves a larger number of countries and sectors than at any time in the recent past, while developing economies today account for a growing share of world export markets

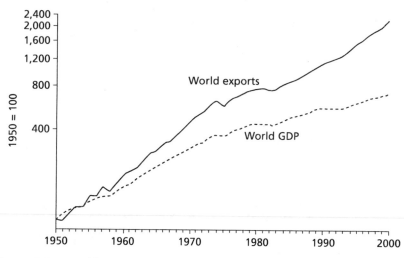

Figure 5.1 World trade and world GDP, 1950–2000

Source: Irwin 2002, based on World Trade Organization data.

(increasing from 19.2 per cent in 1970 to 32.1 per cent in 2005), particularly but not exclusively in manufactures (Held et al. 1999; WTO 2002, 2006b; UNCTAD 2005: 11). Over the postwar period the ratio of exports to GDP for all countries increased from 5.5 per cent in 1950 to 17.2 per cent in 1998 (see table 5.1), and for many of the major OECD and developing states it more than doubled (Kaplinsky 2006). Trade now reaches deeper into more sectors of many national economies as an expanded array of goods and services have become tradeable (see figure 5.2).

Table 5.1 Merchandise exports as a percentage of GDP in 1990 prices, world and major regions, 1870–1998

	1870	1913	1950	1973	1998
Western Europe	8.8	14.1	8.7	18.7	35.8
Western offshoots	3.3	4.7	3.8	6.3	12.7
Eastern Europe and former USSR	1.6	2.5	2.1	6.2	13.2
Latin America	9.7	9.0	6.0	4.7	9.7
Asia	1.7	3.4	4.2	9.6	12.6
Africa	5.8	20.0	15.1	18.4	14.8
World	4.6	7.9	5.5	10.5	17.2

Source: Maddison 2001: 127.

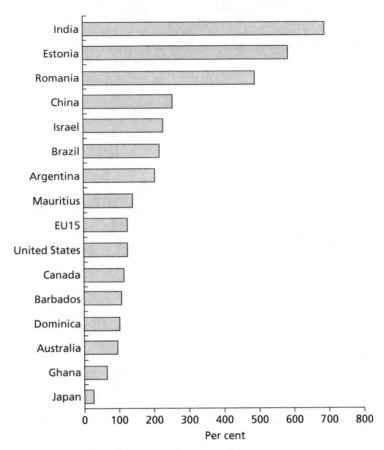

Figure 5.2 The cumulative growth of services exports for a range of countries, 1994–2003 (percentages)

Source: World Bank 2006, based on data from International Monetary Fund, *Balance of Payments Statistics.*

Of course, world trade remains highly concentrated: in geographical terms, OECD countries account for the largest proportion of world merchandise trade (some 65 per cent), and a small number of East Asian countries for the bulk of developing country trade; in sectoral terms, in 2005 manufacturing constituted 58 per cent of total world trade (in value terms), fuels 13.9 per cent, services 20 per cent, and agriculture only 6.7 per cent (Held et al. 1999; UNCTAD 2005: 133; WTO 2006b). This concentration is hardly surprising given that OECD countries account for the

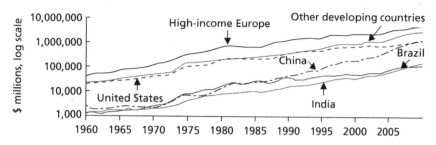

Figure 5.3 The rise in China's exports: recently exceeding those of the United States

Source: World Bank 2006.

largest share of world economic output and are by far the largest economic units. Yet, since the 1990s, this dominance has been diluted (the developed economies' market share of world merchandise exports fell back from 75 per cent in 1970 to 64.8 per cent in 2003) as new trading powers have emerged (such as Brazil, Russia, India and China – BRIC) (see figure 5.3), consequent on structural changes in the world economy associated with a new global division of labour (changes in countries' trade specialization in the world economy) and the intensification of worldwide competition through trade (UNCTAD 2005: 133).

Patterns of trade have altered significantly over the last four decades and particularly so in the last few years. A new geography of trade (or global division of labour) is emerging which reflects the changing location of manufacturing production as East Asia and other newly industrializing economies (NIEs) take on a new role as the world's factories. At the same time, most OECD economies have experienced a significant rise in their trade in services, which now account for almost a quarter of their exports (WTO 2006b). Falling costs of transportation, the communications revolution, liberalization and the growth of transnational corporations have all contributed to a new global division of labour. This restructuring is evident in the current pattern of developing country exports, in which fuels account for 18 per cent (by value), commodities 12.7 per cent, and manufactures 68.1 per cent, compared to 38.8 per cent, 26 per cent, and 31.4 per cent respectively in 1980 (UNCTAD 2005: 91). In just over a quarter century their share of manufactured exports has more than doubled. This shift has also been accompanied in recent

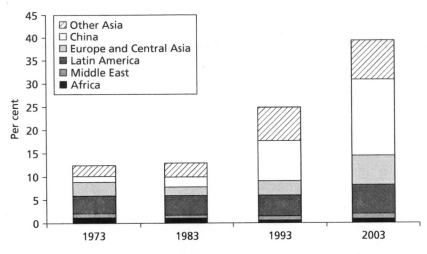

Excludes trade among EU15 countries.

Figure 5.4 Shares of the manufactures imported by high-income countries which originated in developing countries, 1973–2003

Source: World Bank 2005, based on data from World Bank Integrated Trade Solution (WITS) and staff calculations.

years by a significant expansion in trade between developing economies (South–South trade), which has also almost doubled from 22.9 per cent to 40.9 per cent of their total exports (UNCTAD 2005). However this South–South trade is highly concentrated among East Asian economies, which accounted for some 66 per cent of it in 2003 (UNCTAD 2005). Even so, the NIEs are becoming increasingly important engines of global trade, such that some have argued 'the South is gradually moving from the periphery of global trade to the centre', while a recent World Bank report observes that 'growth in the global economy will be powered increasingly by developing countries' (UNCTAD 2004b; World Bank 2006: xii).

These structural shifts are also associated with an intensification of economic competition. In 2003, 40 per cent of manufactured imports into the OECD economies were produced in developing economies compared with 12 per cent in 1973 (World Bank 2006: xix; and see figure 5.4). In both the manufacturing and, increasingly, the services sectors the expansion of trade increases competitive pressures on domestic businesses both North and South. Lower-cost imports impose greater price competition, while the dominance of intra-industry trade (trade in similar products or services) between OECD economies brings domestic business and labour into direct competition with their foreign counterparts. This has significant distributional consequences for employment and wage levels within countries, although separating out the effects is a complicated matter and the implications for labour remain hotly contested (Lawrence 1996). Seeking competitive advantage is articulated either through more efficient domestic production methods or the fragmentation of production, that is, 'slicing up the value chain' or outsourcing production so that firms draw on worldwide networks of suppliers producing in places where the greatest economies of scale or efficiency gains can be realized. One recent study suggests that intra-industry and interfirm trade accounts for at least 30 per cent of the growth of world trade in the period 1970–90 (Hummels 2001). It is not just that OECD economies confront cheaper imports from the world's new manufacturing zones, in East Asia or Latin America, or lower-cost services from India and South Africa, but that competition among and between the OECD economies and developing economies has also intensified as production and markets have become globalized. This new geography of trade has major distributional consequences, both in relation to world economic and productive power, and for patterns of global and national inequality. In just over three decades, China has evolved from a negligible force in global trade to the world's third largest exporter in 2005, and the second in 2007 (World Bank 2006; WTO 2006a).

Global markets in goods and services exist in so far as dense trade flows occur between the major regions of the world economy – Asia-Pacific, the North American Free Trade Agreement (NAFTA) area, and European Union core. The most obvious examples of such markets are those in key primary commodities, such as oil or wheat, which set benchmark world prices. But global markets are far from the textbook notion of the perfectly integrated market. Despite the dramatic trade liberalization of the last forty years, in which formal tariffs have become negligible (average world tariff rates almost halved from 15 per cent to 8 per cent between the 1970s and 1990s), significant non-tariff barriers to trade remain (such as particular health and safety standards), while distance, history and culture still continue to influence patterns of world trade (Bourguignon et al.

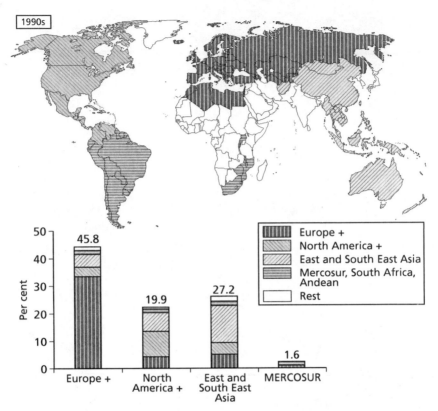

Figure 5.5 The regionalization of world trade: degrees to which regions trade within their own region and with others outside it

Source: World Bank 2005.

2002). Such factors make the scale and continuing annual growth of trade – some 13 per cent in 2005 and averaging 10 per cent 2000–5 – all that more remarkable (WTO 2006b: 3). However, much trade is conducted regionally, leading to the suggestion that the dominant tendency is one of regionalization rather than globalization (Chortoreas and Pelagidis 2004: 20; and see figure 5.5). This is particularly evident in the significant growth of regional trade agreements and clubs over recent decades. Yet, as Baldwin concludes in an exhaustive study of contemporary regional trading arrangements, there are good theoretical and empirical reasons to believe that 'multilateral and regional liberalization proceeded in tandem since 1947' (Baldwin 2006: 24). Moreover, the increasing fragmentation of production creates significant pressures for competitive liberalization and makes it difficult to sustain any effective trade bloc 'when part of your wall encompasses the enemy camp' (Baldwin 2006: 29).

There is also evidence of a tendency for price differentials for traded goods to narrow, as might be expected in a global marketplace (IMF 2002: 122). Studies suggest that distance is no longer as crucial a determinant of patterns of world trade as in the past (Coe et al. 2002). Nor does regionalism appear to be producing a segmentation of the world economy into separate regional markets. Although patterns of regional trade present a complex picture, *intraregional* trade as a proportion of world merchandise trade, at an estimated 36 per cent, was lower in 2001 than throughout the 1990s (WTO 2001: 6). As figure 5.6 shows, the evidence does not demonstrate a secular trend towards the regional segmentation of the world economy. On the contrary the evidence is rather inconclusive, since in the cases of both the European Union and Japan *inter*regional trade rose between 1990 and 2000, but remained constant for NAFTA, while simultaneously the growth of *intra*regional trade outpaced the growth of interregional trade in several regions during the same period. Since 2000 the pattern is similarly inconclusive except in the case of NAFTA (UNCTAD 2004a; WTO 2006b). However, what is interesting is that 'with the exception of MERCOSUR, all regions that have experienced an increasing share of intra-regional trade in total trade have also seen the ratio of extra-regional trade in GDP increase' (World Bank 2005a: 59; see also figure 5.7).

Through its very existence and functioning, the WTO defines a global regulatory framework which effectively constitutes the normative and legal foundations of global markets and their operation. In this respect, global markets are not just spontaneous constructions but partly the product of the regulatory activities of multilateral bodies, not to mention the expanding role of transnational private merchant law (the new *lex mercatoria*) (Gill 1995; Cutler 2003). This institutionalization of global rule-making and adjudication in trade matters marks a seminal development in the political construction of a truly global trade system. To this extent, trade globalization is not simply about trends in world trade but also the critical importance of global and transnational trade authorities in the *constitution* of global markets.

81

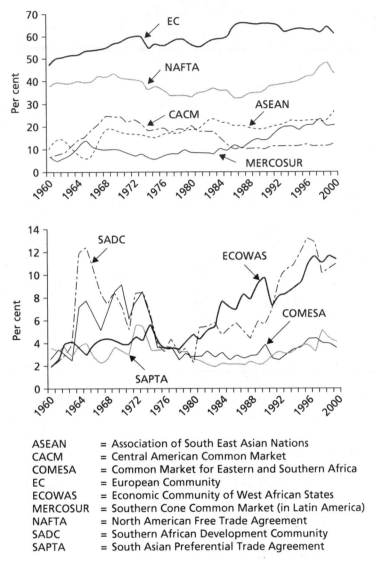

ASEAN	= Association of South East Asian Nations
CACM	= Central American Common Market
COMESA	= Common Market for Eastern and Southern Africa
EC	= European Community
ECOWAS	= Economic Community of West African States
MERCOSUR	= Southern Cone Common Market (in Latin America)
NAFTA	= North American Free Trade Agreement
SADC	= Southern African Development Community
SAPTA	= South Asian Preferential Trade Agreement

Figure 5.6 Evolution of the share of intraregional imports in total imports, 1960–2000

Source: World Bank 2005.

Until comparatively recently, international finance was considered principally an adjunct to trade, a necessary mechanism for enabling the international exchange of goods and services (Eichengreen 1996; Germain 1997). This direct association between finance and trade

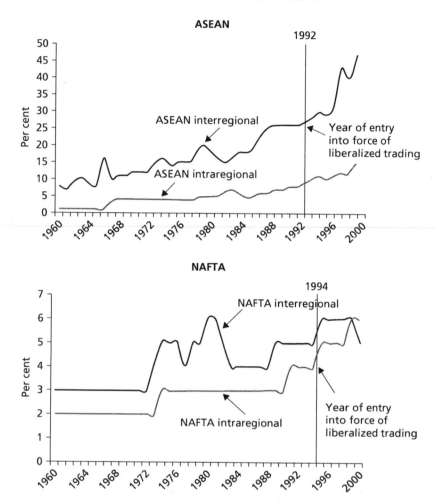

Figure 5.7 The ratio of interregional and intraregional trade to GDP, 1960–2000

Source: World Bank 2005.

began to dissolve in the nineteenth century. By the twenty-first century it had become irrelevant, or marginal at best. Daily turnover on foreign exchange markets rose from $590 billion in 1989 to an astonishing $1,880 billion in 2004 (compared to daily world exports of approximately $33 billion in 2005) (BIS 2001, 2005a: 5; Grieco and Ikenberry 2002: 214; see table 5.2). On a similar scale, daily cross-border trading in derivatives (derivatives being financial

Table 5.2   Average daily foreign exchange turnover, 1989–2004 ($US billions)

1989	1992	1995	1998	2001	2004
590	820	1,190	1,490	1,210	1,880

Decline in 2001 largely due to introduction of the euro according to the *Quarterly Review* of the Bank for International Settlements.
Source: Bank for International Settlements, *Quarterly Review*, various issues.

instruments which hedge financial risks) almost tripled from $880 billion in 1995 to $2,410 billion in 2004 (BIS 2005a: 16). This activity, facilitated by instantaneous global communications, is conducted around the clock between the world's major financial centres on each continent. A worldwide foreign exchange market exists that determines the value of traded currencies, influencing the level of key financial variables such as national interest rates, and enabling the rapid movement of capital around the globe.

By comparison with trade, which exhibited a compound growth rate of almost 10 per cent over the period 1964–2001, transborder financial flows grew at a compound rate of almost 19 per cent (Bryant 2003: 141). To put this in context, Bryant calculates for the period 1964–2001 that if the growth of international bonds – a form of securitized international lending/borrowing measured here in terms of stocks not flows – had been at an equivalent level to the growth rate of all OECD economies, stocks of international bonds would be valued today at some $776 billion, only 11 per cent of the actual $7.2 trillion (Bryant 2003: 142). Similar patterns are evident for all other types of transborder capital flows, from international issues of shares (which expanded from $8 billion in the 1980s to a peak of $300 billion in 2000, subsequently surpassed in 2005 ($307.5 billion)), to cross-border trading in derivatives (which grew, measured in gross value, from $618.3 billion in 1986 to $4,224 billion in 2001, and more than doubled to $10,605 billion in 2005 (the value of world merchandise trade)), and transborder bank lending (which increased tenfold from $2,095 billion in 1983 to $27,272 billion in 2005) (Held et al. 1999: ch. 4; Bryant 2003: 140; BIS 2003, 2005a; 2005b, 2006).

As with trade, the bulk of capital flows (some 66 per cent) is accounted for by the major OECD economies. While these

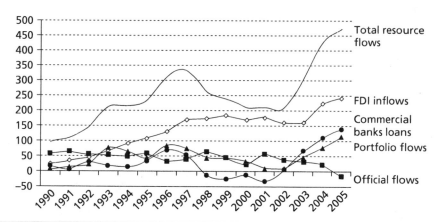

The World Bank's classification of developing countries is used here. It includes new EU member states from Central and Eastern Europe and excludes high-income countries such as the Republic of Korea and Singapore.

Figure 5.8 Total net resource flows to developing countries by type of flow, 1990–2005 ($billion)

Source: UNCTAD 2006b, based on World Bank data.

interregional flows have intensified – 64 per cent of transborder investments in stock markets are intercontinental – this is not replicated everywhere (IMF 2003). Transborder financial flows are highly uneven, so that while most emerging market economies have increasingly acquired access to world financial markets, many of the poorest economies remain subject to, rather than active participants in, their operation (BIS 2005b). Capital flows to developing states have fluctuated considerably over the last three decades, peaking in the mid-1990s before the East Asian crash and subsequently falling back, although by 2006 they had rebounded to the level of the previous peak in 1997 (IMF 2003; World Bank 2006: 15; and see figure 5.8). The distribution of these flows is significantly concentrated among the principal emerging market economies of Latin America, East Asia and the European transition economies. Geography and history still exert influence on capital flows, although there is much less evidence of regionalization (G. Thompson 2006). However, few economies can insulate themselves against the consequences of financial contagion in a real-time global financial system (Desai 2003).

Despite the unevenness of transborder capital flows, the evidence suggests that since the 1980s there has been a significant

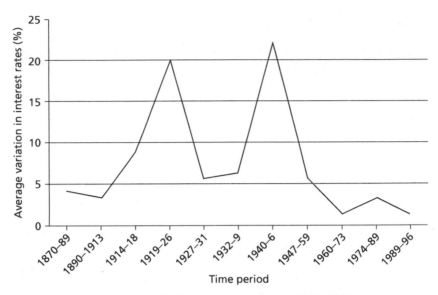

Figure 5.9 Worldwide variation in interest rates, 1870–1996

Source: Grieco and Ikenberry 2003, based on Obstfeld and Taylor 1998: 366, table 11.3.

integration of financial markets (A. Taylor 1996; Lane and Milesi-Ferretti 2003; Obstfeld and Taylor 2004). Financial integration is a matter of degree, or a tendency, expressed in relative measurements of either greater or lesser intensity. It is assessed by a variety of measures (including stocks and flows of capital, asset and interest rate price convergence, synchronization of stock markets and national business cycles). Obstfeld and Taylor's econometric studies, among others, identify a narrowing of interest rate differentials between all the major OECD economies after 1960 (they returned to their pre-1914 levels), as might be expected under conditions of high capital mobility and openness (see figure 5.9; also Fujii and Chinn 2001; Goldberg, Lothian and Kunev 2003; Obstfeld and Taylor 1998, 2003, 2004). Although short of complete convergence, international differentials remain comparable to those within most national economies (for a given financial asset), while they persist for much shorter periods than in the past, which might be expected in the context of 24-hour global financial trading (Goldberg, Lothian, and Kunev 2003; Fujii and Chinn 2001; Obstfeld and Taylor 2004).

By contrast, Feldstein and Horoika's classic study (1980) concludes that levels of national savings and investment appear to be highly correlated, as most domestic savings are invested at home, indicating significant barriers to international financial integration. This finding has also been confirmed by other studies and in much of the orthodox literature it is regarded as a 'stylized but very robust fact' (Obstfeld and Taylor 2004: 62). For orthodox economists this robust fact presents somewhat of a puzzle in so far as the relative ease of global capital mobility today theoretically should imply low, rather than the observed high, correlations between domestic savings and investment. Accordingly this F-H puzzle has attracted much attention as a measure of global financial mobility and integration. A broad range of recent studies have 'solved' the puzzle in that they provide significant empirical evidence that the savings–investment correlation appears to have weakened since the 1990s – a period of intense transborder capital flows (Coakley, Kulasi and Smith 1998; Abbott and De Vita 2003; Banerjee and Zanghieri 2003; Coakley, Fuertes and Spagnolo 2004; Giannone and Lenza 2004). Other studies have questioned the methodological and theoretical robustness of the F-H puzzle, rather than the empirical findings, as a measure of capital mobility and integration (Baxter and Crucisi 1993; Hoffmann 1998; A. Taylor 1996). These suggest that the observed correlations – more likely a product of the theoretical assumptions and econometric modeling – are not inconsistent with high capital mobility and so an imperfect measure of global financial integration.

Other measures, such as the stock of foreign assets as a proportion of world GDP, indicate a much less ambiguous conclusion in so far as this has increased from 6 per cent in 1960, to 25 per cent in 1980 and 92 per cent in 2000 (Obstfeld and Taylor 2004: 55). Similarly flows of capital as share of GDP have grown since the 1960s, although they have not necessarily returned to the levels of the belle époque (Obstfeld and Taylor 2004: 60). Furthermore, there is considerable evidence that capital controls – legal restrictions on capital flows – have declined significantly since the 1970s for OECD states and since the 1980s for most developing economies (and associated with the shift to a floating exchange rate regime) (Obstfeld and Taylor 2004: 165). Bryant accordingly concludes in his recent study of global finance that 'the analogy of nearly autonomous national savings [and investment] reservoirs is no longer appropriate' (Bryant 2003: 152). Capital is by no means perfectly mobile in so far as global financial markets are imperfect. Even so, the dominant tendency has been in the direction of greater (uneven) financial integration.

Tendencies towards financial integration have also been accompanied by processes of financial deepening (measured in terms of contagion effects or the synchronization of financial markets and national business cycles) (Obstfeld and Taylor 2004). Finance pervades the operation and management of all modern economies, representing for many, to borrow Hilferding's vocabulary, a new epoch of finance capitalism. To the extent that national financial systems are increasingly integrated (in real time) with global capital markets, the consequences of financial developments or volatility abroad are magnified and diffused rapidly at home. For instance, on 27 August 1998 the stock markets on every continent fell significantly in reaction to the spread of currency crises from Asia to Russia and Latin America (Desai 2003: 198). Irrespective of contagion effects at times of crisis, the evidence suggests that major stock markets and stock market returns have become increasingly synchronized in the last three decades (Longin and Solnik 1995; Bekaert and Hodrick 2005). This synchrony in financial market movements across the globe is not uniform, since local conditions do make a difference, while it is more evident at times of crisis. Nevertheless it denotes the heightened significance of global financial conditions for domestic financial stability and vice versa (Eichengreen 2002).

Indeed Bordo, in a study of business cycles over the last 120 years, points to evidence of a 'secular trend towards increased synchronization' (Bordo and Helbling 2003: 42). Evidence of this is to be found during the 1990s, for instance, in increased foreign holdings of national public debt – in the euro zone an increase from 16 to 30 per cent and in the United States from 19 per cent to in excess of 35 per cent today – not to mention increased foreign holdings of shares, private financial assets, and the almost doubling of the ratio of foreign assets to national GDP for most OECD economies (Held et al. 1999; IMF 2002; Mosley 2003). In 2005 foreigners owned some 50 per cent of the total stock of US Treasury Bonds, enabling the US both to maintain lower interest rates than would otherwise be the case and to fund its historic twin deficits (fiscal and balance of payments) (Warnock and Warnock 2006: 1–4). Furthermore, although many studies have pointed to the 'home bias' effect, which refers to investors' proclivity for domestic assets, such that the international diversification of investment portfolios appears relatively low (in the US foreign equities constitute around 12 per cent of total holdings), recent studies have qualified these findings (G. Thompson 2006). Cai and Warnock, for instance, demonstrate that this is in part a product of how home bias is measured, which does not distinguish the kinds of domestic assets purchased. In doing so, they 'nearly eliminate the home bias puzzle' (Cai and Warnock 2006: 3).

Associated with this financial deepening is a process of institutionalization, as the organization and infrastructures of transborder finance become regularized and systematized through the activities of (public and private) global agencies and networks. This institutionalization is evident in the enormous expansion of multinational banking – for example, HSBC, 'the world's local bank' – as well as the surveillance and global standard-setting activities of the IMF, the Bank for International Settlements (BIS) and the multiplicity of official and private transborder networks, from the Financial Action Task Force (FATF) to the International Accounting Standards Board (IASB). It is through the operation of these institutions that the essential infrastructure of global financial markets is developed and extended, from the SWIFT global financial interbank payments system, to mechanisms for managing sovereign (national) 'bankruptcy'. In the process, the global or interregional integration of financial markets is reinforced.

Although data on transborder capital flows include foreign direct investment (FDI), political economists single out FDI since effectively it denotes the transnationalization of production. Outsourcing production around the world is now widespread in the most dynamic industrial sectors. Indeed, both investment in overseas production facilities (FDI) and its fragmentation (as in the outsourcing of production to foreign independent third parties integrated within transnational production chains or networks) have increased dramatically over the last three decades (UNCTAD 2002, 2006b). Driving and dominating this process is the transnational corporation (TNC). By comparison with the recent past (say,

1990), transnational production rather than trade has become the principal means of servicing foreign markets. Transnational corporations account currently for more than 25 per cent of world production, 80 per cent of world industrial output, approximately 40 per cent of world merchandise trade, and 10 per cent of world GDP (compared to 7 per cent in 1990) (Gilpin 2001: 289; UNCTAD 2001, 2003, 2006b). They have become important determinants of the location and organization of production and services in the world economy, especially in the most advanced and dynamic economic sectors, integrating and reordering business activity between and within the world's three principal economic regions and their associated hinterlands. These developments are characterized by, among other factors, an increased scale and scope; processes of transnational economic restructuring; and the consolidation of a new global division of labour.

Over the last three decades, flows of FDI have not only become geographically more diffuse but also much more intense (Dunning 2000; UNCTAD 2001). At the turn of the new century total world (inward) FDI reached a new peak of $1,409.6 billion, almost four times the level of 1995 and over six times that of a decade earlier (see figure 5.10; and UNCTAD 2001: 3, 2006b). After 2001, FDI flows declined dramatically, with the slowdown in the world economy, but have subsequently increased to just over $916 billion in 2005 compared to an average of $548 billion in 1994–9 (UNCTAD 2003: 2, 2006b: 2). FDI today is well over ten times that of 1982 and has grown at rates well in excess of those of two decades earlier, outstripping world GDP growth, exports and capital investment (UNCTAD 2006b: 7). With this has come a cross-border mergers and acquisition boom, as the pressure for global corporate consolidation intensifies – previous historic highs in 2000 have been exceeded, with deals to the total value of a record $3,900 billion (*Financial Times*, 21 Dec. 2006, p. 1). Furthermore significant flows (more than $10 billion) reach more than fifty countries (including twenty-four developing economies), compared to seventeen (and seven LDCs) respectively in 1985 (UNCTAD 2001: 4). As UNCTAD notes, the 'trend towards integration on ever larger geographical scales is relatively new. Supply chains have extended to new areas of the globe and integrated formerly distinct regional production activities' (2002: 13). This

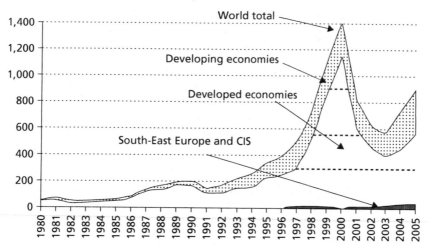

Figure 5.10 Inflows of foreign direct investment, global and by groups of economies, 1980–2005 ($billion)

Source: UNCTAD 2006b.

reflects a variety of factors, including proximity to new markets and technological shifts in the capacity to organize and manage production at a distance (Dicken 2003). But it is no longer simply manufacturing production which is on the move, but increasingly – with the digitization of information and advances in communications – the provision of services, such as call centres, information processing, and legal and banking services (Held et al. 1999: ch. 5; UNCTAD 2001: 6).

Widely diffused as FDI is, both flows and stocks nevertheless remain concentrated among and within the major OECD economies. Moreover, official FDI flows significantly understate actual levels of foreign investment, since some estimates indicate that FDI finances only 25 per cent of the total of such productive investment abroad (Held et al. 1999: 237). Some FDI reaches every continent, and though it remains highly uneven in its dispersion, this is changing. In 2000, OECD economies were the destination for some 80 per cent of FDI (inflows), the source of 88 per cent of FDI (outflows), and accounted for 86 per cent of the world stock of (outward or exported) FDI, and 67 per cent of the world stock of (inward) FDI (UNCTAD 2006b: 7). However, as Obstfled and Taylor observe, 'this trend may have turned, with FDI to poorer countries increasing in magnitude, and, importantly, reaching a more widely dispersed group of recipient countries' (2004: 83; see figure 5.10 above). Recent years have witnessed a significant change in the pattern of inward and outward FDI flows – with an almost doubling of the share accounted for by developing economies (inward from 17.5 per cent in 1990 to 36 per cent in 2005 and outward 6.9 per cent and 12.3 per cent respectively) – and also in FDI stocks (inward from 20.7 per cent in 1990 to 27.2 per cent in 2005 and outward 8.3 per cent to 11.9 per cent respectively) (UNCTAD 2006b: 2, 7). This exceeds quite significantly the average shares of FDI invested in or by developing countries throughout the 1990s. Developing economies, most especially in East Asia, are increasingly significant both as a destination for, and as a source of, FDI.

These trends disclose a concentration of investment within and between the European Union, United States and Japan, as the largest economies, and between these economies and the NIEs of Asia, Latin America (to a lesser extent) and the East European transition economies. This concentration has been variously conceived as triadization or regionalization but this misrepresents the complex matrix of intraregional and interregional flows of FDI and networks of production (Dicken 2003; Dunning 2000). It is the very clustering of FDI around the three major economic regions, combined with the intensity of interregional flows, that reinforces the dynamic of global economic integration.

In linking the dynamics of economies, FDI is also associated with processes of economic restructuring. Although the notion of 'footloose capital' is very much a cliché, the consequences of the mobility of capital are evident in structural changes across many OECD economies and in the rise of NIEs in Asia and Latin America (Rowthorn and Wells 1987; Castells 1996; Dicken 2003; Kapstein 2000; Hoogvelt 2001). There is much debate both about the significance of the deindustrialization of OECD economies in recent decades and its causes (Piore and Sabel 1984; Krugman 1994; Wood 1994; Lawrence 1996; Rodrik 1997; Burtless et al. 1998; Schwartz 2001). Although the impact of globalization, as opposed to technological change, on the decline of manufacturing employment in many OECD economies is disputed, there is general agreement that capital mobility and increasing outsourcing nevertheless plays a significant role in their continuing economic transformation. Deindustrialization in these economies is linked directly with the industrialization of many developing economies as production is shifted to lower-cost locations both through expanded FDI and increasingly through outsourcing arrangements (which require no capital input) (Rowthorn and Wells 1987; Wood 1994; Lawrence 1996; Rodrik 1997; Dicken 2003; Munck 2002; UNCTAD 2002, 2006a). This is not to argue that the mobility of productive capital is unconstrained, since it is not. Proximity to local markets, institutional factors, and productivity calculations limit the potential for industrial capital to relocate abroad, either rapidly or at all. Nevertheless, over time the cumulative impact of such mobility, along with the expansion of trade, has contributed to major structural changes in the world economy.

As noted, a significant shift has occurred in the location of manufacturing production from OECD economies outwards to NIEs in East Asia, Latin America and other parts of the developing world (Gilpin 2001: 140). Some estimates suggest that between 1977 and 1999 alone some 3 million US manufacturing jobs were lost as production relocated abroad. This contraction in domestic employment was almost four times greater than the actual number of jobs created in developing countries (Harrison and McMillan 2006: 40–1). This suggests outsourcing may lead to a net loss of jobs overall as production efficiency gains are maximized. To a more limited extent, a similar trend is evident in the services sector, most notably in back office functions, customer services, data and information processing, etc. (WTO 2001, 2006b). As a result of these shifts, the geography of world economic activity has been transformed in recent years, with important consequences for the distribution of productive power and wealth, and ultimately for the politics of global economic relations (Gilpin 2001; Crafts and Venables 2003). This is patently evident with the rise of China, India and Brazil as key players in the global political economy.

A second, and related, structural change has been the intensification of transnational and interregional competition for market share, technological advantage and rapid product innovation. Such competition is no longer necessarily best conceived as occurring simply between self-contained national economic units, but rather increasingly between firms and businesses in different regions of the globe, in so far as the new geography of world economic activity links distant markets through the operations of giant multinational corporations and interregional production networks (Gilpin 2001: 180–2). Economic and corporate competition becomes globalized since it transcends regions, biting deeper into national economies and magnifying the consequences of local conditions and differences (Held et al. 1999: ch. 5). Domestic competition between supermarket chains for agricultural produce, for instance, turns farmers at home and abroad into direct competitors. Given the existence of instantaneous communications, it is not only the scope but also the rapidity with which global competition evolves which contributes significantly to its intensity (Harvey 1989; Castells 1996).

A third significant change is in the nature of production processes, most especially in manufacturing but also in services, which is not effectively captured by flows or stocks of FDI. Outsourcing, or the cross-border fragmentation of production, is increasingly a key means by which production in many sectors is located and relocated abroad to realize efficiency and competitive gains (although it tends to be concentrated in the low value added segments of the production cycle or service provision) (Dicken 2003; Kaplinsky 2006). Since it requires minimal capital investment or ownership but rather involves collaborative or contractual relationships between producers and a range of suppliers, it is increasingly open to a much wider range of economic agents, from small publishing houses to major transnational corporations. Outsourcing relies on complex transborder production chains, within and between regions of the world economy, such that paradoxically it involves the global integration of productive processes through their increasing geographical fragmentation or dispersion (Gereffi and Korzeniewicz 1994). The significant reliance on production chains presents a challenge to orthodox conceptions of the world economy as constituted by discrete national economic spaces since it suggests that a better depiction (a messier but perhaps more accurate one) is of a networked global economy – what in the context of trade Baldwin refers to as the spaghetti or noodle bowl metaphor (Castells 2000; Brenner 2004; Baldwin 2006; Sassen 2006).

By comparison with capital and goods, labour is relatively much more immobile. That said, labour flows (especially unskilled) are

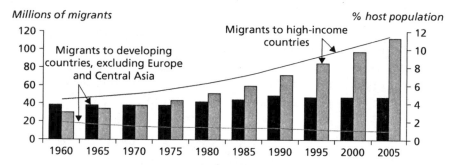

Bars are measured on the left axis; lines are measured on the right axis.

Figure 5.11 Migration to high-income countries, 1960–2005 (absolute numbers and as share of host population)

Source: World Bank 2006.

geographically extensive and, in terms of direction, reflect an almost mirror image of capital flows in so far as they have become primarily South *to* North (Held et al. 1999; Castles and Miller 2002; Chiswick and Hatton 2003; see figure 5.11). As the 2005 report of the World Migration Organization noted, 'no country remained untouched by international migration' (WMO 2006: 381). Outward flows of people are a phenomenon predominantly associated with developing countries and, despite greater restrictions, they are, surprisingly, on the scale of the mass migrations of the early twentieth century (Chiswick and Hatton 2003: 74). Though complex in origin and destination, interregional, as opposed to intraregional, migration has expanded enormously over the period 1950–2000 (Chiswick and Hatton 2003). In 2005, migrants totalled around 190 million of the world's population, more than twice the 1970 level at 82.5 million, making up some 3 per cent of the global workforce but 9 per cent of that in the developed world (Freeman 2006: 2). Inward migration is somewhat concentrated, in that 75 per cent of migrants were domiciled in just twenty-three countries in 1970 and some twenty-eight countries by 2000 (WMO 2006: 382). Furthermore, migration tends to be an increasingly urban and gendered phenomenon in so far as migrants concentrate in major urban areas (23 per cent of Parisians, 28 per cent of Londoners and 30 per cent of Abidjanis (Nigeria) were born abroad), where there are more employment opportunities, while now 50 per cent are female

(Freeman 2006: 4–5). Migration of skilled labour from South to North is also on the increase, linked to skills gaps and demographic trends in the North. Significantly, too, the huge expansion of temporary workers moving between world regions, facilitated by low cost transport infrastructures, is additional to these official figures and is of growing importance to certain sectors (for instance, construction and agriculture) within many developed economies (including the US, UK and even South Africa, which annually hosts 100,000 guest workers) (Freeman 2006: 8).

These developments reflect tendencies towards the integration of distant labour markets (Silver 2003). Such tendencies might be expected to produce some convergence in wage rates (both North and South), most especially for the skilled, but overall there is a growing divergence between rates for skilled and unskilled workers, given the preponderance of the latter among migrants and within the South. There is some evidence to confirm these trends although the causal weight of migration – as opposed to other factors such as trade, technology or capital mobility – is debated (Galbraith 2002; Firebaugh 2003; Lindert and Williamson 2003). One incontrovertible trend, however, is the growing scale and importance of remittances by migrants, which quadrupled between 1990 and 2004 and which for many labour-exporting countries in the South has become 'an increasingly important source of foreign exchange' (UNCTAD 2006b: 100). According to UNCTAD estimates, the level of migrants' remittances in1990 was about 50 per cent of total official aid flows or on a similar scale to FDI flows, from North to South, but today it far exceeds the former and for many countries the latter too (remittances to India in 2005 totalled $20.5 billion compared to inward FDI of $11.9 billion) (UNCTAD 2006b: 100). Migration is of growing significance to the transnationalization of labour markets, and economic activity more generally.

The persistence of national economies and geopolitics

Remarking on a previous epoch of global economic transformation, the economist John Maynard Keynes wrote of 'an extraordinary episode in the economic progress of man' in which 'the internationalization of . . . economic and social life . . . was nearly complete' (quoted in Grieco and Ikenberry 2002: 6). Many of his liberal contemporaries, such as Norman Angell, associated (what later became known as) this belle époque (1880–1914) with the emergence of a new world order in which war was becoming increasingly unthinkable (McGrew 2002). The guns of August 1914 brutally suppressed such liberal idealism. This first age of liberal, or more accurately imperial, global economic integration has acquired totemic status in the current debates about globalization. For those of a sceptical persuasion it is the 'gold standard' against which the many empirical claims concerning contemporary economic integration can be debunked (Hirst and Thompson 1999). This has given rise to a voluminous literature of comparative economic history, dissecting and contrasting the two great ages of globalization in the search for conclusive – or rather elusive – evidence as to which can lay claim to being the more 'globalized' (see table 5.3). The real significance of this enterprise, however, is more political than historical. For the critical issue is not the comparative scale of globalization so much as what the comparison discloses about the limits to, or scope for, national politics under conditions of global economic integration. Or, as Bordo et al. put it, 'why globalization a century ago did not create the same dilemmas as now' (Bordo, Eichengreen and Irwin 1999).

For Gilpin, 'although globalization had become the defining feature of the international economy at the beginning of the twenty-first century' the current world economy, by comparison with the belle époque, remains considerably less globalized and integrated (Gilpin 2001: 3). This is a view shared with other economic historians (for instance, O'Rourke and Williamson 1999). The implication is that, far from being unprecedented, economic globalization today is essentially a return to the developmental trajectory of the world economy inaugurated by the birth of the industrial age. In their study of global finance Obstfeld and Taylor (2004) identify a more differentiated picture in which, on some measures (gross capital flows and stocks of foreign capital), globalization is considerably greater today; on others, it has converged on pre-1914 levels (interest rate differentials, national savings and investment correlations); and on others still, it is below that of the pre-1914 era (flows of capital to the South and net capital flows). By contrast, for Gilpin and for O'Rourke and Williamson, among

Table 5.3 Epochal shifts in globalization since 1820

Epoch	Intercontinental commodity market integration		Migration and world labor markets		Integration of world capital markets
	Change in price gaps between continents	Why they changed	How the migrant shares changed in the receiving countries	Why they changed	What happened to integration (Feldstein Horioka Slope Coefficient)
1820–1914	Price gaps cut by 81%	72% due to cheaper transport, 28% due to pre-1870 tariff cuts	Migrant shares rise	Passenger transport cost slashed, push and pull (Immigration policies remain neutral)	60% progress from complete segmentation toward market integration
1914–1950	Gaps double in width, back to 1870 level	Due to new trade barriers only	Migrant shares fall	Restrictive immigration policies	Revert to complete market segmentation
1950–2000, especially since 1970	Price gaps cut by 76% now lower than in 1914	74% due to policies freeing trade, 26% due to cheaper transport	Migrant shares rise	Transport costs drop, push and pull again (No net change in immigration policies)	Again 60% progress from complete segmentation toward market integration
Overall 1820–2000	Price gaps cut by 92%	18% due to policies, 82% due to cheaper transport	No clear change in US migrant shares, but rises elsewhere	Policy restrictions, offsetting transport improvements	60% progress from complete segmentation toward market integration

Source: Lindert and Williamson 2003.

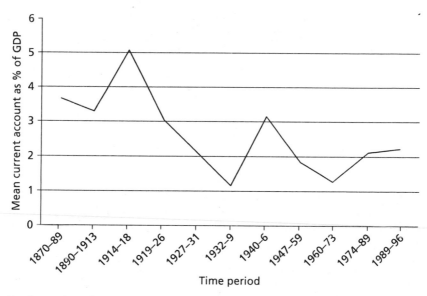

Absolute value of current account balance is used to calculate percentages.

Figure 5.12   Estimated extent of international capital flows, 1870–1996

Source: Grieco and Ikenberry 2003, based on Obstfeld and Taylor 1998: 359, table 11.1.

others, the world economy still has some way to go in order to achieve the comprehensive levels of global capital, trade, commodity and labour market integration of the pre-1914 era (Gilpin 2002b; O'Rourke and Williamson 1999; and see figure 5.12). As O'Rourke and Williamson emphasize

> By 1914, there was hardly a village or town anywhere on the globe whose prices were not influenced by distant foreign markets, whose infrastructure was not financed by foreign capital, whose engineering, manufacturing, and even business skills were not imported from abroad, or whose labour markets were not influenced by the absence of those who had emigrated or by the presence of strangers who had immigrated. (1999: 2)

They go on to conclude that this 'involved the most extensive wage and living standard convergence the Atlantic economy has ever seen' (1999: 14). Indeed Hoogvelt (2001) describes the current era as one of the implosion of global economic activity, as it has become increasingly concentrated in the OECD and a handful of

Table 5.4 Geography matters: predicted percentage reductions in types of economic exchange as distance increases

	Trade	Foreign direct investment	Equity flows	Technology (R&D stocks)
1,000 km	0	0	0	0
2,000 km	58	25	45	35
4,000 km	82	44	69	72
8,000 km	97	58	83	95

Source: Based on Thompson 2006.

NIEs by comparison with the age of empire. The implication is that the significance of today's 'second age' of economic globalization is considerably exaggerated and thus its consequences significantly overstated, most especially in respect of national politics and the continuing centrality of state power to the proper functioning of the world economy (Hirst and Thompson 1999).

In a globalized economy, market forces (theoretically) might be expected (as discussed above) to produce a convergence in the real value of key economic variables (production, prices, wages and interest rates). Just as local economies are integrated through national markets, so, suggests the strong sceptical position, the valid test of economic globalization is that of global economic integration, that is, the existence of economic convergence (Hirst and Thompson 1999; O'Rourke and Williamson 1999; Grieco and Ikenberry 2002). Studies of the significant impacts of history, geography, borders, culture and politics on worldwide economic integration suggest that the present phase of economic globalization has not overcome the fundamental barriers of distance, national borders and market segmentation (Feldstein and Horioka 1980; Gordon 1988; Boyer and Drache 1996; Burtless et al. 1998; Garrett 1998; Weiss 1998; Rieger and Liebfried 2003). Gravity models of international trade, which take account of geographic distance, demonstrate an almost exponential decline in trade activity the greater the distance between the trading partners (Carrere and Schiff 2003; G. Thompson 2006; see table 5.4). Moreover, border and home bias effects (which measure economic divergence between countries and the tendency of investors or consumers to buy domestic assets/goods respectively) do not appear to be diminishing. For instance, there appears to be very little evidence of a significant trend towards international financial diversification (Cavaglia, Brightman and Aked 2000; G. Thompson 2006). The implication is that if globalization is the dominant tendency today, much higher levels of trade and financial flows should be expected, as well as much greater economic convergence, than presently exist (G. Thompson 2006). To take Joseph Stiglitz (2005) at his word, 'globalization is oversold'.

Furthermore, a more critical interrogation of actual international economic trends over the last three decades attests to the increasing segmentation rather than integration of the world economy (G. Thompson 2006; Hirst and Thompson 1999, 2003; Hay 2000, 2005; Rugman 2001, 2005; Grieco and Ikenberry 2002; Dowrick and DeLong 2003). Hay (2005), Thompson (2006) and Rugman (2005) argue that notwithstanding the evidence of a huge expansion of cross-border economic activity (discussed above), the geographical patterns of trade, capital and production flows confirm that the dominant tendencies in the world economy over recent years have been increasing regionalization and triadization, but not globalization. In every region intraregional trade now outstrips extraregional trade. Moreover, this is being steadily reinforced by the recent huge expansion in the numbers of preferential trade agreements (agreements between groups of states giving each preferential access to the others' markets) covering an increasing proportion of world trade (Crawford and Fiorentino 2005; figure 5.13). This segmentation of the world economy along regional lines and the continuing dominance of OECD economies account for the absence of the substantive global economic convergence to be expected under conditions of globalization. It might therefore be convincingly concluded that regionalization or segmentation, rather than globalization, of the world economy is the dominant tendency today, or, as Thompson concludes, in the most generous interpretation the system is 'one poised between "globalization" and supranational "regionalization"' (Hay 2000; G. Thompson 2006).

Rather than a global economy, the sceptics interpret current trends as evidence of a significant, but not historically unprecedented, internationalization of economic activity, that is, an intensification of linkages between discrete national economies. Internationalization complements rather than displaces the

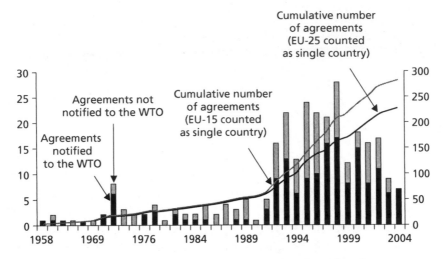

Bars are measured on the left axis; lines are measured on the right axis.

Figure 5.13   The soaring numbers of regional trade agreements in the 1990s

Source: World Bank 2005, based on World Trade Organization (WTO) data.

predominantly national organization and regulation of economic and financial activity, since virtually all such activity remains principally national or local. Even the trend towards internationalization repays careful scrutiny, for it betrays a concentration of trade, capital and technological flows between the major OECD states to the exclusion of much of the rest of the world. The structure of world economic activity is dominated (and increasingly so) by the OECD economies and the growing links between them (Jones 1995). By far the largest proportion of humanity remains excluded from the so-called global market; there is a growing gap between the North and most of the South. Drawing on a range of statistical evidence, Hoogvelt argues that by historical standards the world economy is imploding rather than expanding its reach. Measured in terms of trade, capital, and people flows, the core of the world economy is now less integrated with the periphery than before the industrial revolution (Hoogvelt 2001; Obstfeld and Taylor 2004; Kiely 2006). Far from the present being an era of economic globalization, it is, especially by comparison with the belle époque, one defined by the growing fragmentation of the world economy into a multiplicity of regional economic zones dominated by powerful mercantilist forces of national economic competition and economic rivalry (Hart 1992; Sandholtz et al. 1992; Rugman 2001).

Such a conclusion undermines the orthodoxy that a new pattern of interdependence is emerging between North and South. Popular belief that the deindustrialization of OECD economies is primarily a consequence of outsourcing manufacturing business and jobs to NIEs and LDCs, where wage rates are lower and regulatory requirements much less stringent, is a drastic oversimplification (Lawrence 1996; Burtless et al. 1998). The new geography of the world economy does not bear out such a dramatic shift, and the argument overgeneralizes from the East Asian experience (Callinicos et al. 1994; Hirst and Thompson 1999). The bulk of the world's poorest economies remain reliant on the export of primary products, while the OECD economies continue to dominate trade in manufactured goods (Hirst and Thompson 1999). Deindustrialization cannot be traced to the effects of foreign trade, especially cheap exports from the developing world, but rather is a consequence of technological change and changes in labour market conditions throughout the OECD economies (Rowthorn and Wells 1987; Krugman 1994, 1995). In exaggerating the significance of changes in the international division of labour, globalists run a serious risk of overlooking the deeper continuities in the world economy. Despite internationalization and regionalization, the role and position of most developing countries in the world economy have changed remarkably little over the entire course of the last century (Gordon 1988). The present international division of labour is one Marx would instantly recognize.

If the sceptical argument is dismissive of the notion of a new global economy, it is equally critical of the concept of global capitalism. While not denying that capitalism, following the collapse of state socialism, is the 'only economic game in town', or that capital itself has become significantly more internationally mobile, such developments, it is argued, should not be read as evidence of a new 'turbo' capitalism, transcending and subsuming national capitalisms (Callinicos et al. 1994; Ruigrok and Tulder 1995; Boyer and Drache 1996; Hirst and Thompson 1999; Kiely 2006). On the contrary, distinct national capitalist social formations continue to flourish on the models of the European social democratic mixed economy, American liberal capitalism and the developmental states of East Asia (Hay 2000, 2002). Despite the aspirations of its most powerful protagonists, the neoliberal tide of the 1990s has not produced a genuine or substantive convergence between these distinct regimes (Scharpf 1991; Hart 1992). The idea of global capitalism, personified by the business empires of figures such as George Soros and Bill Gates, may have great popular appeal but it is, ultimately, misleading since it ignores the diversity of existing capitalist social formations and the rootedness of all capital in bounded national economies.

Although images of dealing rooms in New York or London reinforce the idea that capital is essentially 'footloose', the reality is that all economic and financial activity, from production, research and development to trading and consumption, occurs in geographical not virtual space. To talk of the 'end of geography' is a gross exaggeration when place and space remain such vital determinants of the global distribution of wealth and economic power. Granted that, in a world of almost real-time communication, corporate capital and even small businesses may have the option of greater mobility, the fate of firms, large or small, is still primarily determined by local and national competitive advantages and economic conditions (Porter 1990; Ruigrok and Tulder 1995; G. Thompson 1998b). Even among the largest multinationals, competitive advantages are principally a product of their respective national systems of innovation, while production and sales tend to be strongly regionally concentrated (Ruigrok and Tulder 1995; G. Thompson and Allen 1997; Rugman 2005). In effect, multinationals are little more than 'national corporations with international operations', since their home base is such a vital foundation for their continued success and identity (Hu 1992). Furthermore, as UNCTAD's figures confirm, the majority of MNCs are headquartered outside the US, UK, Germany or Japan. Indeed, the 'myth' of global capitalism appears as a convenient cover for the internationalization of American or Western business above all else (Callinicos 2003; Callinicos et al. 1994; Burbach, Nunez and Kagarlitsky 1997). Governments, or at least the most powerful governments, thus retain considerable bargaining power with MNCs, because the latter require access to vital national economic resources and markets. Corporations do not rule the world. Simple economic comparisons of MNCs and states (measured by the size of sales and

A New World Economic Order?

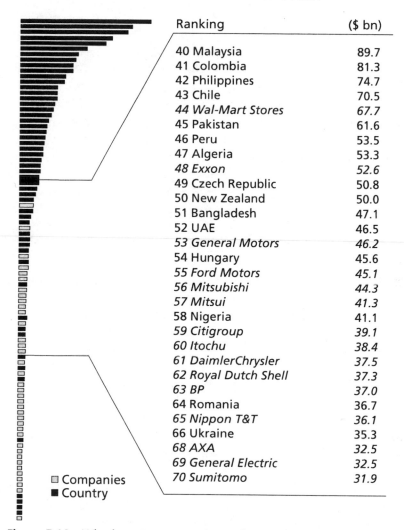

Ranking	($ bn)
40 Malaysia	89.7
41 Colombia	81.3
42 Philippines	74.7
43 Chile	70.5
44 Wal-Mart Stores	*67.7*
45 Pakistan	61.6
46 Peru	53.5
47 Algeria	53.3
48 Exxon	*52.6*
49 Czech Republic	50.8
50 New Zealand	50.0
51 Bangladesh	47.1
52 UAE	46.5
53 General Motors	*46.2*
54 Hungary	45.6
55 Ford Motors	*45.1*
56 Mitsubishi	*44.3*
57 Mitsui	*41.3*
58 Nigeria	41.1
59 Citigroup	*39.1*
60 Itochu	*38.4*
61 DaimlerChrysler	*37.5*
62 Royal Dutch Shell	*37.3*
63 BP	*37.0*
64 Romania	36.7
65 Nippon T&T	*36.1*
66 Ukraine	35.3
68 AXA	*32.5*
69 General Electric	*32.5*
70 Sumitomo	*31.9*

□ Companies
■ Country

Figure 5.14 Who is on top: countries and companies ranked according to value added or GDP

Source: Wolf 2002: 7, adapted from World Bank and *Fortune* magazine data.

gross domestic product (GDP) respectively) are therefore hugely misleading. True measures of the economic power of MNCs (by value added compared with GDP) show that none get into the list of the top forty largest economies in the world (and see figure 5.14). States, for the most part, remain the dominant economic players in the world economy.

Although the post-1945 era witnessed significant institutional innovations in international economic governance, especially with the creation of a multilateral system of economic surveillance and regulation – the Bretton Woods regime – the position of the US, as the world's largest single economic power, remains critical to the smooth functioning of the world economy. In effect, the governance of the world economy still remains reliant, especially in times of crisis, on the willingness of the US, as the hegemonic power, to police the system – as the East Asian crash of 1997–8 demonstrated so dramatically (Gilpin 2001). However, even in normal times, it is the preferences and interests of the most economically powerful states, in practice the G7 governments, that take precedence. Economic multilateralism has not rewritten the basic principles of international economic governance, for it remains a realm in which might trumps right: one where the clash of competing national interests is resolved ultimately through the exercise of national power and bargaining between governments (Gilpin 1987; Sandholtz et al. 1992; Kapstein 1994). In this respect, multilateral institutions have to be conceived as instruments of states – and the most powerful states at that. This suggests that the global governance complex is effectively a new instrument of Western, but particularly US, domination, as opposed to a genuine system of global coordination and regulation (Harvey 2003; Kiely 2006). The discourse of global governance, as with the discourse of globalization, conceals the most important developments in the global political economy, namely the reassertion of geopolitics and the new imperialism (Harvey 2003; Callinicos 2007).

Whereas much liberal scholarship tends to presume that markets and empire are ultimately incompatible forms of political and economic organization, Marxist and realist scholars have recognized their long, albeit contradictory, historical association (Colas 2006). Thus Gilpin argues that both globalization and global economic governance are expressions of US hegemonic power – a process of Americanization (Gilpin 2001, 2002a). Alternatively both are conceived as products of a new Western imperialism which seeks to extend the liberal core while at the same time deploying military power, whether unilaterally or multilaterally, to protect the West's vital interests (Harvey 2003; Kiely 2006).

States, or at least the most powerful states, remain central to the governance of the world economy, since they alone have the legal and political authority to regulate economic activity. Rather than conceiving national governments as simply the 'victims' of global economic forces, the sceptical position acknowledges their strategic role (especially that of the most powerful) in creating the necessary conditions for global markets to flourish. In this respect, states are the architects of the world economy. Indeed the belle époque, the first age of globalization, was precisely the era during which nation-states and national economies were being forged (Gilpin 1981; Krasner 1993). Thus there is little reason to suppose that contemporary conditions pose a real threat to national sovereignty or autonomy. Far from economic interdependence necessarily eroding national economic autonomy or sovereignty, it can be argued that it has enhanced the national capabilities of many states. Openness to global markets, many economists argue, provides greater opportunities for sustained national economic growth. As the experience of the East Asian 'tigers' highlights, global markets are entirely compatible with strong states (Weiss 1998, 2003). Even where state sovereignty is compromised by international agreements, as in the case of the European Union, national governments effectively pool sovereignty in order to enhance, through collective action, national control over international developments. Although the limits to and the constraints on national economic autonomy and sovereignty have become more visible, especially in democratic states, historically they are no greater than in previous epochs, when, as noted previously, international interdependence was much more intense.

While international financial markets and international competition may well impose similar kinds of economic disciplines on all governments, this does not prefigure a convergence in national economic strategies or policies. Such pressures, as noted earlier, are mediated by domestic structures and institutional arrangements which produce enormous variations in outcomes (Garrett and Lange 1996; Weiss 1998; Swank 2002a). States can and do make a difference, as the continuing diversity of national capitalist formations confirms. This is especially the case in relation to macroeconomic and industrial policy, where significant national differences continue to exist even within the same regions of the world (Dore 1995; Boyer and Drache 1996; Garrett 1998). Nor is there really convincing evidence to suggest that international financial disciplines by themselves either preclude governments from pursuing progressive redistributive fiscal strategies or, alternatively, provoke the demise of the welfare state or robust policies of social protection (Garrett 1996, 1998; Rieger and Liebfried 1998; Hirst and Thompson 1999; Swank 2002a). On the contrary, welfare spending has grown most rapidly in the most open economies, while actual levels of national welfare spending (or social transfers) and social protection continue to diverge, even within the EU, suggesting that social democracy and internationalization are entirely compatible (Rodrik 1997; Hay 2001; Garrett and Nickerson 2003; Hay 2005; see figure 5.15). In explaining this apparent contradiction, Rieger and Liebfried (2003), among others, argue that strong welfare regimes make globalization possible precisely because they provide compensation to its losers, making such openness politically sustainable. This is crucial, for as the next chapter makes clear, there is fairly general agreement that the openness of economies to international markets creates significant losers as well as winners.

A planetary economy

As Garrett remarks, 'No matter how many different numbers are presented . . . the growth of international activity in the past thirty years remains staggering' (Garrett 2000). A planetary economy is in the making, constituted by, and through, the infrastructures and dynamics of economic globalization. Globalization is the dominant, but not the sole, tendency in the world economy, while regionalization (or segmentation) is a complementary rather than competing tendency. Economic globalization today unfolds on a historically unprecedented scale (O'Brien 1992; Altvater and Mahnkopf 1997; Greider 1997; Rodrik 1997; Dicken 1998; Baldwin and Martin 1999). Daily turnover on the world's foreign exchange markets (currently $1.88 trillion a day; see table 5.2 above), for instance, is more than sixty times the level of annual world merchandise exports. National economies, with some exceptions, are presently much more deeply enmeshed in global systems

108

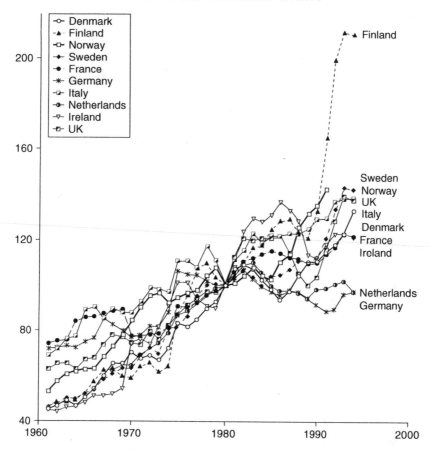

Figure 5.15 Social transfers of EU member states as a percentage of GDP (1980 = 100)

Source: Hay 2006: 9, fig. 2.

of production and exchange than in previous historical eras, while few states, following the collapse of state socialism, are immune from the volatility of global financial markets. Patterns of contemporary economic globalization have woven strong and enduring webs across the world's major regions with the result that their economic fates are intimately connected.

Given the scale and density of cross-border economic flows, national economies no longer function, if they ever did, as autonomous systems of wealth creation, for national borders are no longer significant barriers to the conduct and organization of economic activity. Accordingly, contemporary economic globalization, the globalists suggest, is distinguished from past phases by the existence of a single global economy transcending and integrating the world's major economic regions (Geyer and Bright 1995; Dickson 1997; Scholte 1997; Dicken 1998; Frank 1998). By comparison with the belle époque, an era distinguished by relatively high levels of trade protectionism and imperial economic zones, the present global economy is much more open and its operations have an impact on all countries, even those nominally 'pariah' states such as Cuba or North Korea (Nierop 1994). Although the contemporary global economy is structured around three major centres of economic power – unlike the belle époque or the early postwar decades of US dominance – it is best described as a post-hegemonic order in so far as no single centre, not even the US, can dictate the rules of global trade and commerce (Gill 1992; Geyer and Bright 1995; Amin 1996). Of course, it remains highly stratified in that by far the largest share of global economic flows – such as trade and finance – is concentrated among the major OECD economies. But this dominance of OECD economies is being diluted as economic globalization significantly alters the geography of world economic activity and power.

What distinguishes the present global capitalist economy from that of prior epochs, argue the globalists, is its particular historical form (see table 5.3 above, p. 98). Just as the twentieth century witnessed the global diffusion of industrial capitalism, so at the century's end postindustrial capitalism is taking its place. This is not to argue, as some do, that this new global economy has transcended the 'boom and bust' logic of capitalism, or entered the era of the 'weightless economy' in which information has replaced manufactured goods. Nevertheless, capitalism has experienced a dramatic alteration in its configuration and organization. In seeking to capture the qualitative shift occurring in the spatial organization and dynamics of this new global capitalist formation, globalists refer variously to 'global informational capitalism', 'manic capitalism', 'turbocapitalism', or 'supraterritorial capitalism' (Castells 1996; Greider 1997; Scholte 1997; Luttwak 1999). In the age of the internet, to simplify the argument, capital – both productive and financial – has been liberated from national and territorial constraints, while markets have become globalized to the extent that the domestic economy constantly has to adapt to global competitive conditions. In a wired world, software engineers in Hyderabad can do the jobs of software engineers in London for a fraction of the cost. Inscribed in the dynamics of this new global capitalism is a powerful imperative towards the denationalization of strategic economic activities.

Central to the organization of this new global capitalist order is the transnational corporation. In 2005 there were 77,000 TNCs worldwide with 770,000 foreign subsidiaries selling $22.17 trillion of goods and services within every continent, equivalent to some 50 per cent of world GDP, and employing 62 million workers (UNCTAD 2006a). They span every sector of the global economy – from raw materials, to finance, to manufacturing – integrating and reordering economic activity within and across the world's major economic regions. In the financial sector, multinational banks are by far the major actors in global financial markets, playing a critical role in the management and organization of money and credit in the global economy (Walters 1993; Germain 1997). It is global corporate capital, rather than states, contend many globalists, that exercises decisive influence over the organization, location and distribution of economic power and resources in the contemporary global economy (Gill 1995, 2003; Castells 1996; Amin 1997; Cutler 2003). Contemporary patterns of economic globalization have been accompanied by an increasingly unified world for elites, national, regional and global, but increasing division within nations as the global workforce is segmented, in rich and poor countries alike, into winners and losers. This is associated with new patterns of global and local stratification or inequalities (see chapter 6) which transcend both postindustrial and industrializing economies (Reich 1991; Amin 1997; Hoogvelt 2001; Rodrik 1997; Castells 1998; Dicken 1998). Sandwiched between the constraints of global financial markets and the exit options of mobile productive capital, national governments across the globe confront a common set of policy dilemmas: in particular, whether or how rapidly to adopt broadly market-friendly (neoliberal) economic strategies which require liberalization, deregulation and financial prudence (Gill 1995; Strange 1996; Amin 1997; Greider 1997; Hoogvelt 1997; Scholte 1997; Yergin and Stanislaw 1998; Luttwak 1999). In Eatwell's view, 'Faced with an overwhelming scale of potential capital flows, governments must today as never before attempt to maintain market "credibility" ' (Eatwell and Taylor 2000: 52). Whether globalization imposes a 'golden straitjacket' on states, producing a convergence among national models of capitalism – in the direction of the competition state as opposed to the welfare state – remains the subject of some considerable controversy (Campbell 2004).

Many studies have argued that the disciplines of intensifying financial globalization, capital mobility, and trade competition undermine social democracy and erode the solidarity which is its social glue (Gourevitch 1986; Julius 1990; Frieden 1991; Garrett and Lange 1991; Scharpf 1991; O'Brien 1992; Moses 1994; Wood 1994). These disciplines or tendencies alter the strategic context for social democratic governments in several important ways: through markets imposing financial penalties on governments with (perceived) unsustainable levels of deficit-financed public expenditure, thus heightening the need for macroeconomic stability and fiscal prudence; through the greater structural opportunities for capital to relocate production and employment, generating significant downward pressure on corporate tax rates and encouraging the cultivation of business interests and the promotion of market-enhancing fiscal and welfare policies; and through the significant redistributive consequences of trade liberalization and global competition which, in the context of multilateral trade managment, are more politically difficult and costly to address by resort to unilateral protectionist measures (Scharpf 1991; Garrett 1998; Held et al. 1999; Jessop 2002; Schmidt 2002; Swank 2002b; Devereux, Lockwood and Redoano 2003; Mosley 2003).

Empirical evidence for a crisis of social democracy or secular convergence towards the competition state, however, is limited. One reason is that, as many studies have demonstrated, national vulnerabilities to economic globalization vary considerably, according to the scale and the configuration of national enmeshment in the world economy and the mediating role of domestic institutional and political structures (Garrett 1998; Mosley 2000, 2003; Swank 2002a). Swank concludes that globalization has differential consequences depending on the type of welfare regime: it is associated with retrenchment in liberal welfare regimes but not in comprehensive welfare regimes (Swank 2003). Garrett's studies, too, confirm such differential impacts, with more open economies having higher welfare spending than less open economies (Garrett 2001; Garrett and Nickerson 2003). It is within the South that the correlation between globalization and the decline of the welfare state is strongest (Rudra 2002). Rather than a secular trend towards convergence, a more complex pattern emerges of the differential consequences of economic globalization. As Mosley concludes, this suggests that politics still matters very much: 'There is a good deal left – for the left, center, or right – in domestic politics' in so far as governments 'that conform to capital market pressures in select macroeconomic areas, such as overall government budget deficits and rates of inflation, are relatively unconstrained in supply side and microeconomic policy areas' (Mosley 2003: 69, 3; also Garrett 1998). However, this is also an acknowledgement that the autonomy of states, although historically never absolute, is constrained by the forces of economic globalization.

To paraphrase a former British Chancellor of the Exchequer, Norman Lamont, under conditions of globalization 'politicians and governments too often give the appearance of being in office without being in power'. Governing the economy has become a more complex and uncertain process under conditions of intensifying globalization. Realizing macroeconomic goals, delivering core policy programmes and resolving domestic crises increasingly involve the state in a negotiated order between diverse agencies, both public and private, within and increasingly beyond the state. In a more interconnected world, simply to achieve domestic objectives national governments must engage in extensive multilateral collaboration and cooperation. This, however, creates its own dilemmas in so far as a trade-off exists between the effectiveness of national policy and national autonomy (that is, self-governance). No government can transcend the 'holy trinity' of open economy macroeconomic management: the inescapable theoretical and practical trade-off between exchange rate policy, domestic monetary policy, and capital mobility (Obstfeld, Sambaugh and Taylor 2003; Obstfeld and Taylor 2004). Governments can control any two but it is theoretically impossible to control all three simultaneously (Obstfeld, Sambaugh and Taylor 2003). As Obstfeld and Taylor elaborate: 'An open capital market . . . deprives . . . government of the ability simultaneously to target its exchange rate and to use

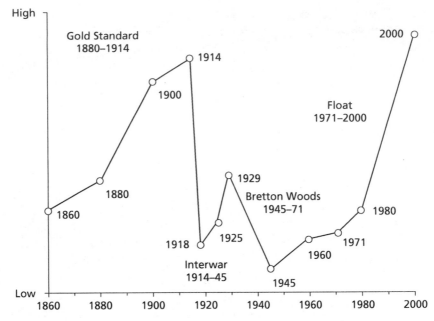

Figure 5.16   A stylized view of capital mobility in modern history

Source: Obstfeld and Taylor 2004.

monetary policy in pursuit of other economic objectives' (2004: 29). Given that globalization necessarily implies capital mobility, the economic policy autonomy of states is necessarily circumscribed. This in turn explains, in part, why there has been an almost universal shift to floating exchange rates, which, given capital mobility (see figure 5.16), are a precondition for greater domestic (or in the case of the eurozone, regional) monetary policy autonomy.

   Under these conditions, argue the more critical globalists, states effectively make an accommodation with global capital (Amin 1996; Cox 1997). Furthermore, the existing multilateral institutions of global economic governance, especially the IMF, World Bank and WTO, in so far as they promote and pursue policies which simply extend and deepen the hold of global market forces on national economic life, become the principal agents of global capital and the G7 states (Gill 1995; Korten 1995; Cox 1996). For the most part, the governance structures of the global economy operate to nurture, reproduce and discipline what is a nascent 'global market civilization' (Gill 1995; Korten 1995; Burbach,

Nunez and Kagarlitsky 1997; Hoogvelt 1997; Scholte 1997). In this view, global politics is dominated by the activities of powerful transnational social forces – elite, political, corporate, and bureaucratic networks – centred on the US (but not controlled by it), whose wealth, power and position are bound up with the reproduction and expansion of global corporate capitalism. In effect, political empires have been replaced by what Hardt and Negri (2000) refer to as the empire of global capitalism. National governments and the institutions of global governance are principally transmission belts for securing and managing this global capitalist order in accordance with the disciplines of global market forces and the imperatives of accumulation. Suturing this empire together is an emerging transnational class formation – the cosmocracy. This cosmocracy blends the interests and aspirations of key national business and state elites across the globe with those of transnational corporate capital and international bureaucrats into an unofficial global directorate, staffing and managing the citadels of world power in accord with the precepts of an evolving global capitalist order.

Acknowledging the power of capital, liberal globalists nevertheless argue that global governance structures have considerable autonomy from the dictates of corporate capital and/or the dominant G7 states (Rosenau 1990; Shaw 1994; Shell 1995; Cortell and Davies 1996; Castells 1997; Hasenclever, Mayer and Rittberger 1997; Milner 1997; Herod, Tuathail and Roberts 1998). Indeed, multilateral institutions have become increasingly important sites through which economic globalization is contested, both by weaker states and by the agencies of transnational civil society. Even the G7 states and global capital can find themselves in contravention of their rules, requiring adjustments in policy (as with the scrapping of US steel quotas following WTO rulings) or accommodation to their regulatory arrangements. Moreover, the political dynamics of these multilateral institutions tend to mediate great power control, for instance through consensual modes of decision-making, such that they are never solely tools of dominant states and social forces (Keohane 1984, 1998; Ruggie 1993a; Hasenclever, Mayer and Rittberger 1997; Roberts 1998). Alongside these global institutions there is also a parallel set of regional bodies, from MERCOSUR to the EU, which constitute a further layer in an emerging system of multilayered global economic governance (Rosenau 1990, 1997; Ruggie 1993b). Within the interstices of this system operate the social forces of transnational civil society, from the International Chamber of Commerce to the Global Justice movement, seeking to promote, contest, resist and bring to account the institutions of global economic governance and thereby the forces of economic globalization (Scholte 2005; Rosenau 1997; Higgott 2000; O'Brien, Goetz and Scholte 2000; Castells 2005). In this respect, the politics of global economic governance is far more pluralistic than many critical globalists or sceptics admit in so far as global and regional institutions exercise considerable independent authority. Economic globalization, in this respect, destabilizes the modern historical correspondence between political authority, legal sovereignty, territory and nationhood (Sassen 2006). A power shift is underway as political authority and power are diffused above, below and alongside the state. The classic ideal of the command and control state is being displaced by a philosophy of economic governance which privileges the strategic coordination role of national governments in the context of a multilayered system (see chapters 2 and 7).

6

The Great Divergence? Global Inequality and Development

Average world income per head stood at around $8,833 in 2004 (UNDP 2006). However, the income of the vast proportion of the world's population was considerably below this level: $4,775 for all developing countries and $1,350 for the poorest, while the average for the 900 million people in the world's affluent regions was over $27,500 (Davies et al. 2006; UNDP 2006). A comparable pattern is evident in the distribution of world wealth: world per capita net worth was $26,421 in 2000, while the OECD per capita average was $113,675 compared to $5,485 for 40 per cent of the world's inhabitants (Davies et al. 2006). In the world's poorest states average life expectancy is forty-two, compared to seventy-eight in the richest states (UNDP 2006). For the majority of the world's citizens, life is short, brutish and nasty, as Hobbes once put it. Global inequality and poverty, in all its dimensions, undoubtedly ranks as 'by far the greatest source of human misery today' (Pogge 2001: 8).

For many, the principal source of this misery is globalization, and in particular its dominant neoliberal form – the Washington Consensus in its various guises (Thomas 2000; Harvey 2006). In determining the location and distribution of productive power and wealth in the world economy, economic globalization is a primary force in shaping patterns of global inequality and exclusion (see chapter 5). These patterns have dramatic consequences for the life chances and material prospects of households, communities and nations across the globe. They also impact, as chapter 4 has discussed, on the prospects for global stability and order. However, while there may be a general consensus on the scale of the human

Table 6.1 Comparison of the three concepts of inequality

	Concept 1: Unweighted international inequality	Concept 2: Weighted international inequality	Concept 3: 'true' world inequality
Main source of data	National accounts	National accounts	Household surveys
Unit of observation	Country	Country (weighted by its population)	Individual
Welfare concept	GDP or GNP per capita	GDP or GNP per capita	Mean per capita disposable income or expenditures
National currency conversion	Marked exchange rate or PPP exchange rate		
Within-country distribution (inequality)	Ignored	Ignored	Included

Source: Milanovic 2005.

suffering involved, there exists considerable disagreement on four fundamental matters:

1 how global poverty and inequality are to be determined and what is a valid measure (see table 6.1);
2 what the empirical evidence discloses about the real trends in global poverty and inequality;
3 the causal links, if any, between globalization and these trends;
4 the most effective development strategies for reducing global poverty and inequality.

On these questions there is perhaps more disagreement within the respective globalist and sceptic camps than there is between them. This is because there is little consensus within each camp on how to characterize trends in global inequality, their underlying causes and appropriate remedies. Even so, what does generally distinguish the two positions is that whereas the globalists acknowledge that globalization has some causal connection with global inequality, the sceptics overwhelmingly reject this, arguing that there are more fundamental causal forces at work, such as imperialism or national development strategies. Furthermore, both start from similar working assumptions. Three in particular are important. The first is that it is necessary to distinguish absolute inequality or poverty – measured against some financial baseline such as the World Bank's $1 a day – from that of relative inequality – the distribution of income or life chances. The second is that income inequality is only one measure of relative deprivation and that health, morbidity and other statistics provide measures that are just as important: for instance, in subsistence economies measures of income inequality may not capture the true pattern of relative deprivation. The third is that there are important distinctions to be made between three accepted kinds of income inequality measured by the GINI coefficient:* international (that between countries); intranational or national (that within countries); and global (that between individuals or households irrespective of their country location). Different conclusions may therefore sometimes be drawn as a result of what measures and assumptions are used in the analysis.

The persistence of world inequality

Sceptics are doubtful about either the novelty or significance of contemporary globalization. This scepticism extends to questions of global inequality and poverty, which are conceived, within a longer historical perspective, as enduring features of world order or the capitalist world-economy (Krasner 1985; see table 6.2 and figure 6.1). That both have tended to worsen in recent times is generally acknowledged, although some analyses give greater emphasis to the relative improvement in both over the longer term (Fieldhouse 1999). In accounting for the worsening trends in international inequality and poverty, some sceptical arguments emphasize the growing 'involution' of the world economy as opposed to its globalization (Callinicos et al. 1994; Gordon 1988; Hirst and Thompson 1999). Much of the less developed world has been steadily marginalized, as trade, investment and technological flows

---

* The GINI coefficient is a measure of income dispersion such that 0 would be absolute equality. The closer to 1.0, or 100%, the greater the level of inequality.

Table 6.2 Summary of globalization's effects on world inequality

Epoch	Global inequality trend	Inequality between nations		Inequality within nations	
		Trend	Effects of globalization	Trend	Effects of globalization
1500–1820	Rising inequality	Rising inequality	No clear net effect	Rising inequality (Western Europe)	No clear net effect
1820–1914	Rising inequality	Rising inequality	Participants gain on non-participating countries. Among participants, migration reduced inequality more than capital flows raised it. Freer trade may have reduced inequality, with exceptions	No clear trend	Globalization raised inequality in the New World, reduced it in participating Old World nations
1914–1950	No clear inequality trend	Rising inequality	Retreat from globalization widened the gaps between nations	Falling inequality (in OECD)	No clear net effect
1950–2000, esp. since 1970	Slightly rising inequality	Slightly rising inequality	Globalized trade and migration narrowed the gaps among participants. Non-participants fell further behind	Slightly rising inequality (in OECD)	Globalization raised inequality within OECD countries. In other countries, non-participating regions fell behind
Overall 1820–2000	Rising inequality	Rising inequality	Globalized trade and migration narrowed the gaps among participants. Non-participants fell further behind	No clear trend	No clear net effect

Source: Lindert and Williamson 2003.

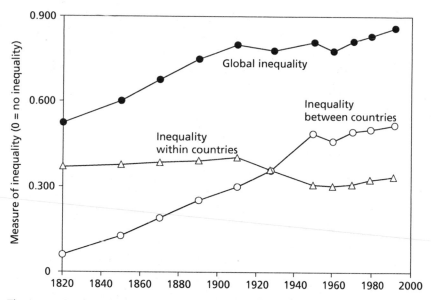

The 'countries' here consist of 15 single countries with abundant data and large populations, plus 18 other country groups. The 18 groups were aggregates of geographical neighbours having similar levels of GDP per capita.

Figure 6.1 Global inequality of individual incomes, 1820–1992

Source: Bourguignon and Morrisson 2002; figure reproduced in Lindert and Williamson 2003.

become increasingly concentrated in the OECD core of the world economy (Hirst and Thompson 1999; Petras and Veltmeyer 2001). The division of the world into core and periphery, North and South, remains very much a structural feature of the contemporary global system.

This structural division, according to many Marxist accounts, is a consequence not so much of globalization as of the process of uneven capitalist development which is inherent in the very logic of accumulation (Rosenberg 2005; Callinicos 2007). That the worldwide expansion of capitalist relations historically has produced differential incorporation and thus uneven development within and even between countries is hardly new (Brewer 1980; Wallerstein 1983; Wood 2003). As economic activity becomes increasingly concentrated in the regional cores of the OECD, the result is to limit or block the development prospects of many less developed states. Policed by the institutions of liberal global governance, such as the IMF and the WTO, this pattern of international economic activity reinforces historic structures of dominance and dependence, inequality and poverty (Cammack 2002; Pieper and Taylor 1998). As a result, the benefits from trade and foreign investment flow disproportionately to the major capitalist economies, while the gap between rich and poor states accelerates (Burbach, Nunez and Kagarlitsley 1997). It is this system, driven by the exploitative dynamics of metropolitan capitalism, which is responsible for global poverty and inequality, rather than 'globalization'. As Petras and Veltmeyer note, globalization is 'not a particularly useful term . . . it can be counterposed with a term that has considerably greater descriptive value and explanatory power: imperialism' (2001: 12). So long as capitalism exists, imperialism will remain and global poverty and inequality will continue to endure. Genuine development therefore has to be rooted in a transformation or delinking from the world economy: more anti-capitalism than anti-globalization (Callinicos 2003).

In contrast, although accepting that global inequality is one of the most intractable problems on the global agenda, realist sceptics take issue with the notion of imperialism (Gilpin 2001; Krasner 1985). While there is a general acceptance that the structure of global economic power shapes the context of development, the fact that many states in East Asia and Latin America grew rapidly throughout the 1980s and 1990s highlights the vital role of national development strategies and effective economic governance. Indeed, the growing divergence in the economic fortunes of developing states (see figure 6.2), from the deepening impoverishment of sub-Saharan Africa to the rising affluence of Singapore, suggests that patterns of global inequality and poverty are not dictated solely or even principally by the 'exploitative' structure of the global economy (Landes 1989). In short, states still matter. Moreover, national or local factors, from resource endowments to state capacity, are perhaps of increasing significance in lifting nations and communities out of poverty (Gilpin 2001; Hirst 1997; Weiss 1998). As a leading realist sceptic observes, not only is the significance and impact of globalization considerably exaggerated, but it blinds scholars to the ways in which 'states continue to use their power to implement policies to channel economic forces in ways favourable to their own national interests and . . . a

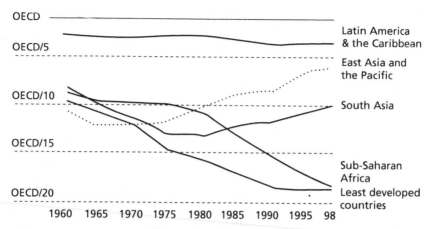

High-income OECD excludes OECD members classified as developing countries and those in Eastern Europe and the former Soviet Union.

Figure 6.2 Comparing incomes between the developing regions and high-income OECD, 1960–1998 (regional average GDP per capita (1985 US$ purchasing power parity) as a ratio of that of high-income OECD countries)

Source: UNDP 2001: 16, based on World Bank Data.

favourable share of the gains from international economic activities' (Gilpin 2001: 21; see also Krasner 1985). Increased global inequality and poverty is, by implication, more the product of national political choices or state failure than of the structural features of the global economic order. Accordingly, the eradication of global inequality requires much more than simply repeating the tired rhetoric of anti-imperialism, anti-capitalism or, even worse, 'making globalization work for the poor'.

Assuming, however, that the reform of global institutions will necessarily produce benign consequences in contributing to 'making poverty history' is simply naive. For in a world in which power politics is the dominant reality, the endemic struggle for national relative advantage ensures that international inequality can never be eradicated (Woods 1999; Hurrell 2001). As Gilpin states, 'One must begin with the fact that every international system throughout history has been hierarchical and composed of dominant and subordinate states; there has never been, and in the future there is not likely to be, an egalitarian and democratic international system' (Gilpin 2002a). This is because states will always seek to maintain a relative advantage over their nearest competitors (Gilpin 2001). Moreover, since global institutions are the instruments of the most powerful states, they are unlikely to acquire the necessary authority to ensure that affluent states (not natural altruists) comply with redistributive global policies – few at the moment contribute the Millennium target goal of 0.7 per cent of GDP to official aid flows (Hurrell 2001; Krasner 1985). On the contrary, as is evident with multilateral aid flows, the disbursement of funds is increasingly linked to the political and security objectives of the major Western powers, while these funds come with significant conditionalities. Increasingly multilateral agencies and major donor governments coordinate their aid and development funding, targeting them on strategic zones of conflict and instability in the South (Duffield 2001). This has been especially the case, following 9/11, in respect of official foreign aid disbursements; as Woods (2005) observes, these appear to signal the replacement of a development-led approach by a security-led approach. These sobering realities affirm that it is only through and within the national state – as a moral and political community – that effective and legitimate solutions to the problem of global social injustice can be realized (Hirst and Thompson 1999).

Although some global reforms may moderate some of the worst excesses of world markets, it is only through the apparatus of national welfare regimes and the determined pursuit of national wealth and economic power that global poverty and inequalities can be successfully addressed in the long term. This demands, however, a coherent national development strategy, which, for some, is to be found in the developmental state model associated with 'the economic miracle' of East Asian industrialization. The developmental state model represents a distinctive brand of capitalism, which differs in significant ways from its European and American counterparts. It simultaneously combines strong state direction of the economy with managed liberalization to produce high rates of economic growth but crucially without increased inequality, thereby maintaining social cohesion (Haggard 2000; Chang 2003; Kiely 2006). Rooted in institutional economics, which emphasizes the importance of state intervention to correct for the failure of markets, and strategic trade theory, which emphasizes the role of government investment in national comparative trade advantage, state-led development has considerable appeal, primarily because 'it appears to be the appropriate means for combining economic development with political independence' (Gilpin 2001). It is therefore an attractive political alternative to liberal orthodoxy, which transfers considerable control over the economy to foreign capital and international markets. National governments, contend many sceptics, are the only politically viable structures for ameliorating and combating the scourge of world inequality and uneven development – that is, for realizing international justice (Gilpin 2001; Hirst and Thompson 1999).

One world, divided?

Among globalists, there is considerable disagreement on these issues. Broadly, a distinction can be made between the orthodox and the critical accounts of globalization. These differences, both in assumptions and underlying theoretical commitments, produce significantly divergent analyses of the current global condition. These differences relate to the evidence and interpretation of actual trends in world inequality, its sources, consequences and remedies.

Although there is perhaps no disputing that the absolute gap between the world's richest and poorest states is now at historic levels and accelerating – the income gap between richest and poorest has doubled since 1960 – economic orthodoxy suggests this tells us little about underlying trends in global inequality (UNDP 1999). Since the absolute gap is a product of two centuries of industrialization, a far more relevant measure of trends, it is argued, is the relative income gap.* Studies by the World Bank and UNDP demonstrate that the relative income gap between OECD countries and the rest is narrowing – the gap declined from a high of around 88 per cent of world average income in 1970 to 78 per cent in 1995 (World Bank 2001a; UNDP 2001; Wade and Wolf 2002). Of course, there are vast differences between regions, with East and South Asia rapidly closing the gap, while for sub-Saharan

---

* The relative income gap measures the difference between the income of the typical individual and world average income, calculated as a percentage of the latter.

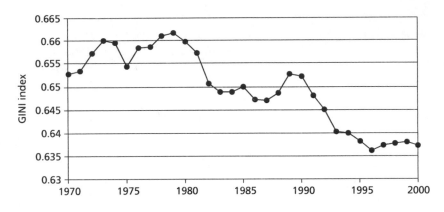

Figure 6.3   Declining world income inequality, 1970–2000

Source: Xavier Sala-i-Martin 2005: fig. 8.

Africa the gap is still widening (UNDP 2001). Furthermore, Dollar (2005) notes that international equality (measured by the GINI index of inequality between economies) reduced from 0.67 to 0.64 between 1980 and 2000. Although modest, 'it represents an important reversal of a long historical pattern of rising inequality' (Dollar 2005). Other studies have confirmed this decline or agree that the trend towards rising international inequality has been halted (see figure 6.3; also Bourguignon and Morrisson 2002; O'Rourke 2001; Sala-i-Martin 2002; Lindert and Williamson 2003). Furthermore, over the last century the distribution of world income does not show a 'twin peaks' effect (that is, income polarization evident in peaks at both ends of the distribution as the rich get richer and the poor poorer) but rather greater income dispersion (Bourguignon and Morrisson 2002; and see figure 6.4).

If world inequality is narrowing, perhaps more significant is the fact that absolute poverty is rapidly declining. By comparison with 1980, 200 million fewer people live in absolute poverty – defined as subsisting on less than $1 per day – while the proportion of the really poor has fallen from 31 per cent of the world's population to 20 per cent today (Wolf 2002). This decline represents, according to Dollar (2005), 'an important historical shift' (see figure 6.5). Of course, these trends conceal significant regional variations in that much of the decline is accounted for by Asian growth, particularly by India and China, the two most populous countries in the

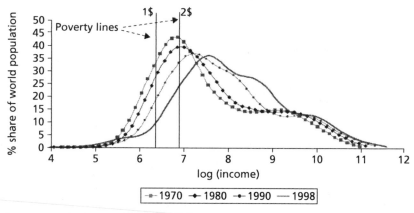

Figure 6.4 Estimated world income distributions (various years)

Source: Xavier Sala-i-Martin 2002: fig. 4.

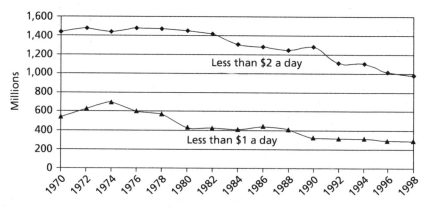

Figure 6.5 Declining poverty, 1970–1998 (in millions of people)

Source: Xavier Sala-i-Martin 2002: fig. 6.

world. Regional disparities exist, with an increase in poverty in Africa and a growing relative income gap between many of the poorest countries and other developing countries (Dollar 2005).

Nevertheless the orthodox economic account concludes that the key trends are that 'the last two decades saw a decline not just in absolute poverty but also in world-wide inequality among households' (Wolf 2002). This has been complemented by rising life expectancy and a general improvement in most measures of human development for much of the world's population (UNDP 2006; see

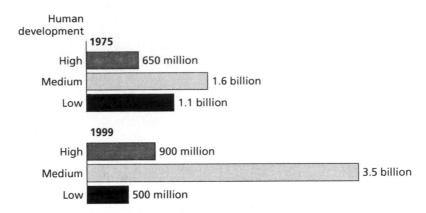

Data are in terms of numbers of people and refer only to countries for which data are available for both 1975 and 1999.

Figure 6.6 How the structure of human development in the world has shifted

Source: UNDP 2001: 11.

figure 6.6). If global economic well-being is improving, this is strongly associated with economic globalization. As Lindert and Williamson's study concludes, 'we find clear signs of income convergence among countries that integrate more fully into the world economy but divergence between these active participants and those who elect to remain insulated from global markets' (Lindert and Williamson 2003; see also table 6.3). Along with Dollar and Kraay (2002) they argue that globalization is largely responsible for the reductions in world poverty and inequality, since it stimulates economic growth and rising incomes, and thereby a decline in relative and absolute poverty. Thus Dollar and Kraay observe: 'Growth spurred by open trade . . . benefits the poor as much as it does the typical household'. In the same study they even go so far as to suggest 'the lack of any evidence of a significant negative impact of openness to international trade on the incomes of the poor' (Dollar and Kraay 2001).

Rather than stunting development and heightening inequality, globalization enhances the development prospects of states in the South by stimulating higher economic growth rates, contributing significantly to making the world a less unequal place (Bhagwati 2004; Wolf 2004). The new global division of labour greatly assists this growth (see chapter 5). In the last quarter-century of intensive

Table 6.3 Trade policy orientation and growth rates in the Third World, 1963–1992

Orientation	Average annual growth rates of GDP per capita (%)		
	1963–73	*1973–85*	*1980–92*
Strongly open to trade	6.9	5.9	6.4
Moderately open	4.9	1.6	2.3
Moderately anti-trade	4.0	1.7	−0.2
Strongly anti-trade	1.6	−0.1	−0.1

In all periods the three strongly open economies were Hong Kong, South Korea and Singapore. The identities of the strongly anti-trade countries changed over time. In 1963–73, they consisted of Argentina, Bangladesh, Burundi, Chile, the Dominican Republic, Ethiopia, Ghana, India, Pakistan, Peru, Sri Lanka, Sudan, Tanzania, Turkey, Uruguay and Zambia. For the two overlapping later periods the strongly anti-trade group consisted of the previous sixteen plus Bolivia, Madagascar and Nigeria, but minus Chile, Pakistan, Sri Lanka, Turkey and Uruguay. For the identities of the moderate-policy groups, see World Bank (1987: 78–94).
Source: Lindert and Williamson 2003, based on World Bank data.

globalization, significant progress in advancing human development has been achieved (see figure 6.5 above; UNDP 2001: 11). Thus the orthodox account suggests that economic globalization is the only effective path to global poverty reduction and economic development. By contrast, the causes of enduring inequality are to be located principally in the failure of countries to integrate fast enough or deep enough into the world economy. More, rather than less, globalization is the orthodox prescription for eradicating global poverty.

By contrast, many globalists critical of this liberal orthodoxy argue that it provides a very distorted interpretation of the actual trends in world poverty and inequality. With regard to poverty levels, the claimed decline in numbers living on incomes below the World Bank's thresholds of $1 and $2 a day, according to recent studies by Reddy and Pogge (2003) and by Robert Wade (2004), is primarily the result of methodological and statistical changes in the way the figures are actually calculated. Rather than decreases in world poverty, Wade, among others, suggests there have been increases (Wade 2004; Reddy and Pogge 2003; Kaplinsky 2006; and see table 6.4). Furthermore, Milanovic's studies covering the period 1950 to 2000 show that international inequality (between countries) and global inequality (between individuals) increased as

Table 6.4 Contrasting estimates of global poverty

	1987	*1990*	*1993*	*1998*
World Bank				
Number living below $1 per day (million)	1,197	1,293	1,321	1,214
% of global population	29.7	29.3	28.5	24.3
Sala-i-Martin				
Number living below $1 per day (million)	390	400	371	353
% of global population	8.8	8.6	7.6	6.7
Pogge and Reddy				
Number living below $1 per day (million)				1,640
% of global population				32.2

Source: Kaplinsky 2006; comparisons based on www.worldbank.org/research/ povmonitor/; Sala-i-Martin 2002; calculations from Pogge and Reddy (see Reddy and Pogge 2003).

the economic fortunes of both countries and individuals diverged (Milanovic 2002a, 2002b, 2005). International inequality (measured by the GINI coefficient) rose from 0.44 in 1950 to 0.55, while global inequality rose from 0.62 in 1988 to 0.64 in 1998. If this were converted into actual dollars then the ratio of the top 10 per cent of incomes to the bottom 10 per cent would be approximately 320:1, 'probably among the highest, or perhaps the highest, inequality level ever recorded' (Milanovic 2005). And certainly higher than any individual country measure.

This pattern is reproduced in relation to industrial pay inequalities within countries, which have widened significantly since 1982 according to Galbraith (2002). Further evidence indicates that on every other single measure, from income gaps to health gaps, the gulf between the richest and poorest states has been accelerating (Bradshaw and Wallace 1996). In 1960, the income of the richest 20 per cent of the world's people stood at about thirty times that of the poorest 20 per cent; by 1997 the corresponding figure was seventy-four (UNDP 1997). Wade's illustrative 'champagne glass' figure (see figure 6.7) maps in stark form the contours of this gulf between the richest and poorest in the global economy (see also figure 6.2 above). Global wealth or assets are even more unequally distributed. Estimates indicate that the richest 10 per cent of the world's population own 85 per cent of the world's wealth – a GINI of 0.89 – compared to most countries, where the richest 10 per cent in most economies own 50 per cent of total wealth – a GINI of 0.7,

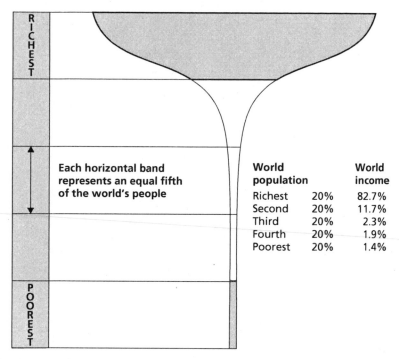

Figure 6.7 The 'champagne glass' pattern of inequality between the world's rich and poor

Source: Wade 2001a.

with only a few above 0.8 (Davies et al. 2006). Some 17.5 million people have assets of more than $1 million, and 499 more than $1 billion (Davies et al. 2006; and see table 6.5). The actual trends therefore denote a real increase in both global inequality and world poverty.

Economic globalization, in this account, is identified as the principal cause of growing international and world inequality as mobile capital relocates jobs and production in the world economy, trade intensifies international competitive pressures, and global finance constrains the welfare and redistributive capacities of states (Rodrik 1997; Tanzi 2001; Thomas 1997; Castells 1998; Wade 2004; Kaplinsky 2006). This produces four mutually reinforcing dynamics: the increasing segmentation of the global workforce into winners and losers from productive and financial integration; the growing marginalization, exclusion and impoverishment of the

Table 6.5 The distribution of net worth by World Bank country group, 2000

World Bank country group	Percentage share of world population	Net worth per capita	Net worth per adult	Percentage of world net worth per capita	Real GDP per capita	Percentage of world GDP
High income OECD (24)	14.81					
Purchasing power parity		113,675	151,308	63.73	27,367	53.55
Market exchange rates		115,565	153,824	83.29	27,430	76.92
GINI		0.240	0.242			
High income non-OECD (43)	0.93					
Purchasing power parity		91,748	147,524	3.23	21,475	2.35
Market exchange rates		81,233	123,485	3.67	17,708	3.08
Upper middle income (39)	11.37					
Purchasing power parity		21,442	33,968	9.23	9,342	13.91
Market exchange rates		9,626	15,249	5.33	4,058	8.74
Lower middle income (59)	33.01					
Purchasing power parity		12,436	19,445	15.54	4,446	18.90
Market exchange rates		3,573	5,590	5.74	1,285	8.02
Low income (64)	39.87					
Purchasing power parity		5,485	10,520	8.28	2,241	11.29
Market exchange rates		1,017	1,950	1.97	0.372	3.24
World totals (229)						
Purchasing power parity		26,421	43,628		9,186	
GINI		0.581	0.534			
Market exchange rates		20,551	33,893		6,205	
GINI		0.747	0.712			

All figures are in year 2000 US$; figures are weighted by country population.
Purchasing power parity (PPP) and market exchange rates are alternative ways of making comparisons between countries with different currencies.
Source: Davies et al. 2006.

losers both across and within states; the erosion of social solidarity as welfare regimes are unable, or politicians unwilling, to bear the costs of protecting the most vulnerable; and the intensification of economic polarization and exclusion within, between and across states (Birdsall 1998; Castells 1998; Dickson 1997; J. Gray 1998; Lawrence 1996; Sklair 2001; Thomas 1997). This segmentation and exclusion does not just occur between rich and poor states but within them. The new global division of labour simply reorganizes, rather than ameliorates, patterns of global inequality and exclusion. The world is no longer divided as it once was on geographic lines, that is, between North and South, but rather exhibits a new social architecture (Castells 1998; Hoogvelt 2001). This architecture – which divides humanity into elites, the bourgeoisie, the marginalized, and the impoverished – cuts across territorial boundaries, rearranging the world into the winners and losers of globalization, with a growing gap between the two (Hoogvelt 2001). Indeed the evidence, suggests Wade (2004), is that orthodox arguments concerning the 'benign effects of globalization on growth, poverty, and income distribution [do] not survive scrutiny'.

In challenging the prevailing liberal orthodoxy concerning globalization and development, critical globalist studies suggest a much more complex relationship between liberalization and patterns of economic development (Wade 2004; Ugarteche 2000; Garrett 2001). For instance, China and South Korea have witnessed rapid economic growth but in relatively closed economies, while many Latin American states liberalized rapidly in the 1990s but witnessed low growth rates. As Ugarteche (2000), among many others, suggests, liberal orthodoxy presents a false dilemma, since countries can gain from engaging with the global economy without fully liberalizing. Thus an alternative strategy for developing countries is that of selective or managed liberalization and integration with the global economy (Rodrik 2006). This alternative to orthodox development aims 'to make markets work for people, not people for markets' (UNDP 1997: 91). It starts from the assumption that 'all economics is local', and seeks above all the empowerment of peoples, human security and environmental sustainability through selective local engagement with, rather than systematic delinking from, the world economy (Bello 2002).

By itself this is likely to be insufficient to facilitate balanced development without vital changes in the global economic structures and policies. For in the case of some states, among them the world's poorest, globalization has been associated with patterns of distorted development, if not underdevelopment, as a consequence of selective inclusion in, or structural exclusion from, the global economy (Hoogvelt 1997; Amin 2004). Addressing these problems requires a reformed and more robust system of global economic governance that can regulate global markets and redistribute opportunities and wealth (UNDP 1999; Milanovic 2005).

One strategy for realizing this is emerging, it is argued, in the form of the 'new regionalism' among developing states and emerging economies (Hettne 2007). This recognizes that, in a more interconnected and less stable world order, effective development policies are 'possible only in concert with others, such as regional trading groups . . . By forming such groups, poor countries combine increased competition with economies of scale and a better division of labour – while retaining some protection from competition from more advanced countries' (UNDP 1997: 91). New regionalism also potentially enhances the bargaining power of subordinate states within the institutions of global economic governance. It also supports a form of international solidarity, which can take account of the enormous diversity among developing states, in terms of levels of industrialization, geopolitical situation and forms of governance. Amin (1997) refers to this new regionalism as 'polycentric regionalism', since it is a strategy for further eroding the old North–South hierarchy and building a more pluralistic world order. Furthermore, rather than being constructed in opposition to globalization, it is, on the contrary, buttressed by a growing enmeshment in the global political economy. For the new regionalism constitutes a form of 'open regionalism', with the object of deepening global engagement while at the same time creating an institutional and political capacity to 'modify the conditions of globalization' (Gamble and Payne 1991; Amin 1997: 75). This is evident in the growing intensity of interregional diplomacy, such as that between MERCOSUR and the EU, as regional groups seek to establish open trading and investment areas embracing all their member states. However, the limits to this new regionalism are all too evident in the potential it has to intensify interregional competition and conflict and to erode global solidarity. As a political strategy for developing countries faced with a globalizing world, regionalism is thus by no means purely benign in development terms.

New regionalism, however, is simply a necessary building block, as Amin (1997) notes, towards global institutional reform. Collectively and individually, developing states have sought to exploit the rules of the global governance system in order to advance development goals. This has been combined with collective initiatives – as with the attempts of the G20 to ensure that the WTO Doha Trade Round gave priority to development – to demand reforms to both the institutions and the rules of global economic governance. Governments in the emerging economies of Asia and Latin America are increasingly resorting to the WTO trade dispute settlement mechanisms in their conflicts with the EU and the US, since, in a rule-based system, might has less chance of trumping right. Of course, the WTO is also used by the more powerful to annul some of the traditional protection that the poorest states have received and to advance the trade liberalization agenda. Besides 'working through the system', there is growing collective political pressure from governments of developing countries in the G77 for reforms to both the rules and the institutions of global economic governance. Following the East Asian crash in 1997, with financial stability acquiring priority, reforms to the rules and architecture of global finance have dominated the international financial agenda. Alongside reforming the rules of the global economy, there is also an ongoing debate about the reform of the institutions of global economic governance in order to give emerging and developing states greater representation in key decision-making bodies. In the case of the IMF there have been moves to widen consultation and participation in rule-making beyond the G7 to embrace the more representative G22 – a formal grouping which includes the major emerging economies from each world region. The non-aligned movement has also formed the G15 of leading developing states which seeks to establish a role as a kind of 'poor man's G7' (Sindharan 1998).

These developments reflect one of the most fundamental challenges of globalization to existing modes of global economic governance: how to ensure that priority is given to human security and development over the requirements of global markets – making globalization work for the poor. Just as the Bretton Woods conference in 1944 created the framework of an open world economic order conducive to social democracy within states, so it should not be beyond the contemporary political imagination, argue many globalists, to construct a global New Deal in order to govern the global economy in ways which will promote a more equal, just, humane and secure world (global social democracy). This reformist prescription is explored more substantively in a subsequent chapter (see chapter 11).

7

(Mis)Managing the World?

For the protesters at G8 summits, from Genoa to Gleneagles, or WTO meetings, from Cancún to Hong Kong, globalization is a political project promoted, sometimes coercively, by a global directorate of Western powers and a transnational elite class dominated by the corporate sector – the cosmocracy – to the principal advantage of a minority of humankind. It is this cosmocracy, they argue, centred on the United States, which advocates and organizes globalization, principally through both formal institutions and informal elite networks of global economic governance, with the most important institutions being the IMF, World Bank, WTO, G8 (the G7 plus Russia) and the EU. Dominated by powerful vested interests, the structures of global economic management constitute the core of a wider system of liberal global governance subordinating the world and its peoples to the dictates of a liberal ideology and global corporate capitalism. By contrast, others contest this radical interpretation, arguing that it both exaggerates the power of global capital and overlooks the complex multilateral politics of global economic governance, not to mention the relative autonomy of global institutions and the countervailing influence of transnational civil society forces. In this respect, the globalization debate projects into a new context the cardinal questions of political life concerning power and rule: who rules, in whose interests, by what means, and for what ends?

As the earlier discussion of political globalization showed (see chapter 2), the last five decades have witnessed a significant institutionalization of global politics. A thickening web of multilateral agreements, global and regional institutions and regimes, and transgovernmental policy networks and summits has evolved, and these regulate and intervene in virtually all aspects of transnational activity or world affairs, from global finance to the other WTO, the World Toilet Organization ('improving toilets and public sanitation globally'). This evolving global governance complex is far from being a world government, with ultimate legal authority and coercive powers, but it is far more than a disarticulated system of limited intergovernmental cooperation. It comprises a vast array of formal suprastate bodies and regional organizations, with the UN at its institutional (but not political) core (see figure 7.1), as well as regimes and transnational policy networks embracing government officials, technocrats, corporate representatives, pressure groups, and non-governmental organizations. Limited political direction is given to this complex through the activities of the G8, operating as a kind of global directorate, and through the UN's setting of global priorities, such as the Millennium Development Goals. Nevertheless, in general, the global governance complex lacks the kind of centralized, coordinated political programme that is associated with national government, or at least the ideal of strong national government. This is evident in its failings in the provision of many essential global public goods (those which markets fail to provide effectively), from health to environmental security (Kaul et al. 2003). Few, however, would dismiss it outright as irrelevant. Indeed the expanding jurisdiction or scope of global policy-making, most especially its growing intrusion into the domestic affairs of states, large and small – witness, for example, the rulings of the WTO's trade dispute panels – makes it increasingly visible and controversial. As Murphy (2000) notes, whatever its limits and faults, the current system of global governance is a principal arena 'in which struggles over wealth, power and knowledge are taking place'. The following sections examine the debate about global governance by examining, first, in the sceptical camp, the arguments of realists, among others; and second, in the globalist camp, the positions of radicals and institutionalists.

International governance: an instrument of domination

Whether they stress the realities of power politics or a globalized monopoly capitalism, sceptics do not dispute that there has been a significant expansion of international regulation in recent years, or that it involves a complex politics between states, civil society and international organizations. On the contrary, as Robert Gilpin attests, 'the rapid globalization of the world economy has elevated the governance issue to the top of the international economic agenda . . . the battleground has become the entire globe, and the types as well as the number of participants have greatly expanded to include states, international organizations, and nongovernmental organizations' (2001: 378, 402). What the sceptics do vigorously contest, however, is the belief that this constitutes a system of effective global governance which transcends geopolitics or in which global institutions, alongside the agencies of transnational civil society, acquire effective power or resources to shape the important rules of world order.

For these thinkers, geopolitical realities, and especially US super-hegemony, remain the principal force determining the dynamics of, and limits to, what they refer to as international, rather than global, governance. Subtle though the distinction is, it is substantive not semantic. It represents a crucial difference of interpretation in so far as governance beyond the state is conceived primarily as an intergovernmental affair – dominated by power politics and the historic struggle for relative national advantage (including the competition between national monopoly capitalisms) (Krasner 1985). In this view, far from multilateralism taming power politics or establishing the international rule of law, it is simply another mechanism through which the struggle for power and national advantage is expressed (Gilpin 2002a).

International governance is a contingent rather than an institutionalized feature of world order: it exists, and continues to exist, only to the extent to which the most powerful states conceive it as being in their national interests. International institutions, therefore, are principally devoid of autonomous power, and function largely as instruments for the advancement of the interests of the most dominant states or coalitions of states. This is evident in those limits to their power that exist not only formally, as in weighted voting systems and institutionalized vetos embedded in the operations of many IGOs (see table 7.1), but also more informally in so far as it is widely understood that the most powerful states may sometimes, or even often, act unilaterally in transgression of global

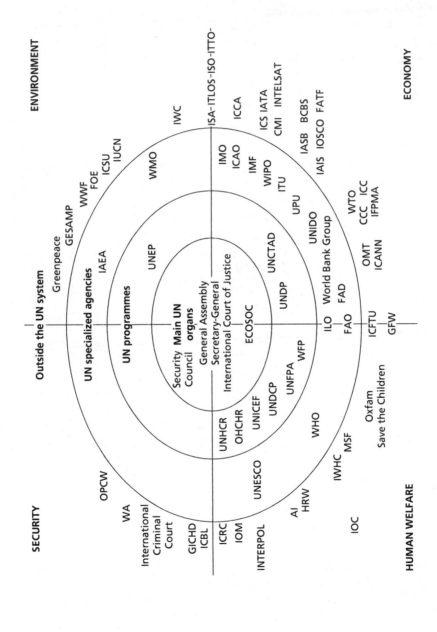

SECURITY

ENVIRONMENT

Outside the UN system

UN specialized agencies

UN programmes

Main UN organs

Security Council
General Assembly
Secretary-General
International Court of Justice
ECOSOC

Greenpeace
GESAMP
WWF
FOE
ICSU
IUCN
IWC
ISA-ITLOS-ISO-ITTO-

OPCW
WA
International Criminal Court
GICHD
ICBL
ICRC
IOM
INTERPOL
UNESCO
AI
HRW
IWHC
MSF
IOC

IAEA
UNEP
WMO

IMO
ICAO
ICCA
IMF
WIPO
ITU
UPU
ICS IATA
CMI INTELSAT
IASB BCBS
IAIS IOSCO FATF

UNHCR
OHCHR
UNICEF
UNDCP
UNFPA
WFP
WHO

UNCTAD
UNDP
UNIDO
World Bank Group
ILO
FAD
FAO
ICFTU
GFW
Oxfam
Save the Children
OMT
ICANN
WTO
CCC ICC
IFPMA

ECONOMY

HUMAN WELFARE

Key to abbreviations

AI	Amnesty International
BCBS	Basel Committee on Banking Supervision
CCC	Customs Cooperation Council
CMI	Comité Maritime International
ECOSOC	UN Economic and Social Council
FAO	Food and Agriculture Organization
FATF	Financial Action Task Force
FOE	Friends of the Earth
GESAMP	Joint Group of Experts on the Scientific Aspects of Marine Environmental Protection
GFW	Global Fund for Women
GICHD	Geneva International Centre for Humanitarian Demining
HRW	Human Rights Watch
IAEA	International Atomic Energy Agency
IAIS	International Association of Insurance Supervisors
IASB	International Accounting Standards Board
IATA	International Association of Transport Airlines
ICANN	Internet Corporation for Assigned Names and Numbers
ICAO	International Civil Aviation Organization
ICBL	International Campaign to Ban Landmines
ICC	International Chamber of Commerce
ICCA	International Council of Chemical Associations
ICFTU	International Confederation of Free Trade Unions
ICRC	International Committee of the Red Cross
ICS	International Chamber of Shipping
ICSU	International Council for Science
IFAD	International Fund for Agricultural Development
IFPMA	International Federation of Pharmaceutical Manufacturers Associations
ILO	International Labour Organization
IMF	International Monetary Fund
IMO	International Maritime Organization
INTELSAT	International Telecommunications Satellites Organization
INTERPOL	International Criminal Police Organization
IOC	International Olympic Committee
IOM	International Organization for Migration
IOSCO	International Organization of Securities Commissions
ISA	International Seabed Authority
ISO	International Organization for Standardization
ITLOS	International Tribunal for the Law of the Sea
ITTO	International Tropical Timber Organization
ITU	International Telecommunication Union
IUCN	World Conservation Union
IWC	International Whaling Commission
IWHC	International Women's Health Coalition
MSF	Médecins Sans Frontières
OHCHR	Office of the High Commissioner for Human Rights
OMT	World Tourism Organization
OPCW	Organization for the Prohibition of Chemical Weapons
UNCTAD	UN Conference on Trade and Development
UNDCP	UN Drug Control Programme
UNDP	UN Development Programme
UNEP	UN Environment Programme
UNESCO	UN Educational Scientific and Cultural Organization
UNFPA	UN Population Fund
UNHCR	UN High Commissioner for Refugees
UNICEF	UN Children's Fund
UNIDO	UN Industrial Development Organization
UPU	Universal Postal Union
WA	Wassenaar Arrangement on Export Controls for Conventional Arms and Dual-Use Goods and Technologies
WFP	Word Food Programme
WHO	World Health Organization
WIPO	World Intellectual Property Organization
WMO	World Meteorological Organization
WTO	World Trade Organization
WWF	Worldwide Fund for Nature

Figure 7.1 The organizational infrastructure of global governance: a UN-centric view

Source: Koenig-Archibugi 2002.

Table 7.1 Current voting power in the International Monetary Fund (in votes and in percentages)

Group of countries	Votes quota	Basic votes	Total votes	% total votes quota	% total basic votes	% total votes
G7 countries	983,720	1,750	985,470	46.17	3.80	45.29
Other industrial countries	332,624	4,750	337,374	15.61	10.33	15.50
Total industrialized countries	1,316,344	6,500	1,322,844	61.78	14.13	60.79
Africa	110,734	12,750	123,484	5.20	27.72	5.67
Asia	219,957	7,750	227,707	10.32	16.85	10.46
Middle East	163,007	4,000	167,007	7.65	8.70	7.67
Latin America and the Caribbean	159,339	8,000	167,339	7.48	17.39	7.69
Transition economies	161,156	7,000	168,156	7.56	15.22	7.73
Total developing countries	814,193	39,500	853,693	38.22	85.87	39.23
Total	2,130,537	46,000	2,176,537	100.00	100.00	100.00

Basic votes are according to population; votes quotas are according to share of financing of the IMF.
Source: International Monetary Fund, 'Quotas: a fact sheet'.

rules, norms or agreements. Since global institutions have no authority or powers to ensure compliance, the global interest is often trumped by powerful national interests. On a diverse range of global issues, from the eradication of poverty to humanitarian intervention and global warming, the formal and informal 'veto' power of dominant states constructs the effective limits to concerted global action. International governance, in key respects, is the contemporary equivalent of old-style imperialism in so far as it represents a distinctive political mechanism which entrenches a system of global domination of the weak by the strong (Callinicos et al. 1994; Gowan 2001).

This dominance is articulated in the way in which the hierarchy of global power moulds not only the institutional architecture but also the substantive purposes and priorities of international governance. The present liberal world order – of free trade and unhindered capital flows – is primarily a product of US global hegemony, although it relies on the consent of other G7 powers. The structural power of the US is reinforced and extended by the very existence of global institutions and the liberal constitution of world order. International governance, as with globalization, is thus little more than a process of the Americanization of world order. As one arch-sceptic observed many decades ago, 'Power is an indispensable instrument of government. To internationalise government in any real sense is to internationalise power; and international govern-ment is, in effect, government by that state which supplies the power necessary for the purpose of governing' (Carr 1981: 107). Of course, this is not to argue that this system is simply a trans-mission belt for US policy, or Western interests, since these same institutions are also arenas through which their dominance is resis-ted. Nevertheless, for sceptics, 'hard power' – that is, economic and military might – not 'soft power' retains a disproportionate role in shaping the structures, patterns and outcomes of international gov-ernance. It is for this reason that most sceptics doubt that, without a profound change in US policy or a fundamental challenge to US hegemony, international governance will ever be in a position to tame globalization or to advance global social justice.

Sceptics are highly critical of the unreflective nature of much of the existing debate about global governance. This scepticism arises from three principal conclusions: that globalist accounts tend to exaggerate the autonomous power and efficacy of global institutions and civil society; that US hegemony, not international governance, is the principal source of the maintenance and management of the liberal world order; and, finally, that in failing to penetrate beyond the appearances of global governance to the underlying structures of power, much of the globalist 'babble' presents a fundamentally flawed analysis of the present condition of, and the future possibil-ities for, the international governance of globalization. (See table 7.2 for a summary of the sceptics' and globalists' views.)

Among the most damning criticisms of global governance is its continuing failure to effectively address, let alone moderate, increasing global poverty and global warming (see table 7.3). In what sense is the discourse of global governance meaningful given the obvious incapacity to act on two of the most urgent issues con-fronting the global community today? For this reason alone, most sceptics tend to conclude that global governance is an idea whose time has not yet come.

Table 7.2 Contrasting interpretations of global governance

	Sceptics	Globalists
Who governs?	US, G7 states *versus* National monopoly capital through dominant capitalist states	US, G7 global directorate, transnational capitalist class (informal empire) *versus* Multiplicity of agencies: national/suprastate, governmental, non-governmental and corporate, varying from issue to issue
In whose interests?	US, Western, national interests *versus* National capital	Global corporate capitalism, US and G7 states *versus* Diverse global and particular interests varying from issue to issue within a framework of distorted global governance
To what ends?	Maintain US/Western dominance, sustain Western security community, defend and promote an open liberal world order	Promote and reproduce global liberal capitalist order *versus* Plurality of purposes, regulating and promoting globalization, advancing global public policies
By what means?	International institutions, hegemonic power and hard power – coercion, geopolitics	Liberal global governance, hegemony and consent *versus* Multilayered global governance: suprastate agencies, regimes, NGOs, global networks
Key source of change?	Dependent on challenge to US hegemony	Dependent on structural limits to global capitalism and its contestation by diverse anti-capitalist forces *versus* Transformations produced by complex global interdependence, agencies of transnational civil society, and globalization of political activity/governance

Table 7.3 Degree of progress in providing many global public goods

Good	Role of developing countries	Progress of international efforts
Global commons		
Climate change	Limited current contributors, but major future source, of carbon emissions; potentially disastrous impact on many countries	Current mitigation efforts insufficient to stabilize global temperature
Biodiversity and ecosystems	Main reservoir of many species	Rate of species extinction rising; tropical forest cover declining
Water resources	Over 600 million people face acute fresh water shortage	Little international effort beyond increasing awareness; 2–3 billion people may face severe fresh water shortage by 2020
Fisheries	Many countries dependent on ocean fisheries for exports and domestic consumption	75 per cent of commercial fish stocks exploited at or above sustainable levels
Human issues		
Infectious diseases	Developing countries could suffer severe losses in a global flu pandemic; already suffer millions of deaths from tropical diseases	Flu pandemic avoided (for now); limited progress in containing malaria, measles, AIDS in developing countries
Peace keeping	Millions killed in civil wars and intercountry conflicts	Some interventions successful (Kosovo in the Republic of Serbia); others less so (Sierra Leone)
Poverty	1 billion people living on less than $1 a day	Asia expected to see continuing decline in people living in extreme poverty; Africa likely to see rise
Regulatory framework		
Trade	Developing countries account for 27 per cent of global merchandise exports; goods and services	Trade rules effective, but limited progress on removing trade barriers critical to developing countries

(*continued*)

Table 7.3   *(continued)*

Good	Role of developing countries	Progress of international efforts
	exports represent 33 per cent of developing countries' gross domestic product	
Financial architecture	Total fiscal costs of systemic crises in developing countries since 1975 exceeds $1 trillion	Crisis interventions have mixed success; little change in global rules that would dampen volatility

Source: World Bank, 2006.

Governing globalization: the ambiguities of global governance

Globalists, in general, would accept Murphy's characterization of global governance as having become a key arena for the promotion and contestation of globalization. However, divergent accounts exist of how this global governance complex operates, in whose interests, and to what ends, producing different assessments of its effective capacity to manage globalization for the benefit of humankind as opposed to vested interests and dominant powers. (See figure 7.2 for the constellation of organizations in this complex.)

Radical and neo-Marxist accounts consider global governance little more than a convenient political shell for the exercise of US global dominance and, thereby, as a key instrument for sustaining and expanding the global reach of corporate capitalism (Gowan 2001). In a post-imperial world, the institutional infrastructure of global governance legitimizes a new form of global domination, but one that crucially gives the appearance of an inclusive and progressive system privileging global concerns over the interests of the most powerful states and social forces. In effect, global governance is essentially *liberal* global governance since it promotes and advances the project of a liberal world order in which global markets, the international rule of law, liberal democracy and human rights are taken as the universal standards of civilization

146

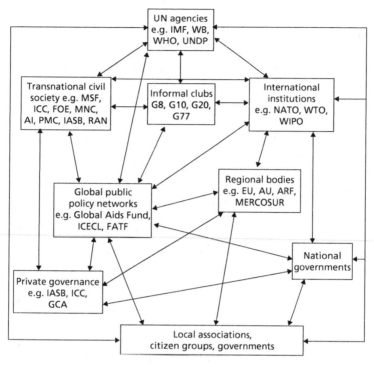

Figure 7.2 The global governance complex

Source: McGrew 2005.

KEY:

IMF	International Monetary Fund	IASB	International Accounting Standards Board
WB	World Bank		
WHO	World Health Organization	ICECL	International Convention on the Elimination of Child Labour
UNDP	UN Development Programme		
G8	Group of 8 (US, Italy, UK, France, Germany, Russia, Canada, Japan, EU)	FATF	Financial Action Task Force (on money laundering)
G77	Group of 77 developing countries	GCA	Global Credit Agencies, e.g. Moodies, Standard & Poor
MSF	Médecins sans Frontières		
ICC	International Chamber of Commerce	ARF	ASEAN Regional Forum
FOE	Friends of the Earth	EU	European Union
AI	Amnesty International	MERCOSUR	Southern American Common Market
PMC	Private military companies, e.g. Sandline	AU	African Union
		NATO	North Atlantic Treaty Organization
MNC	Multinational corporations, e.g. Shell	WTO	World Trade Organization
		WIPO	World Intellectual Property Rights Organization
RAN	Rainforest Action Network		

(Duffield 2001). Of course, these values are not promoted in a balanced way, as is evident by the priority that is attached to the expansion and reproduction of global markets – to be seen in the activities of the WTO – almost to the exclusion of other values, such as equality or human rights. Moreover, where values clash, as they often do, liberal economics normally wins out against other liberal values. This is principally because the project of liberal global governance is informed by an unwritten constitution that structurally privileges the interests and agenda of Western globalizing capital, more often than not at the expense of the welfare of the majority of nations, communities and the environment (Braithwaite and Drahos 1999: 515).

As productive and finance capital have become globalized, the policy priorities of liberal global governance have become increasingly dominated by the need to extend, promote and secure the effective conditions for continued economic globalization. This is evident not only in the vigour with which structural adjustment policies have been pursued by the IMF and World Bank, and the pace and intensity of trade liberalization promoted by the WTO, but also in the merging of the development and security agendas, especially in the wake of 11 September. The growing emphasis on good governance, democracy and where necessary humanitarian intervention – what some have referred to as global 'riot control' – represents attempts to stabilize world order around the liberal-capitalist model. By comparison, effective global action to combat the accelerating gap between rich and poor through redistributive mechanisms, from official aid to technical assistance, remains negligible in relation to the scale of global poverty.

Liberal global governance sutures together the divergent interests of corporate, national, technocratic and cosmopolitan elites, crystallizing in the process a nascent transnational capitalist class whose principal objective is the widening and deepening of the global capitalist project (Sklair 2001). While some hold that corporations rule the world and/or that liberal global governance is simply the instrument of a transnational capitalist class, others emphasize its ambiguity, since it is also a crucial arena within which corporate globalization is contested. In this regard, it is a site of struggle that harbours the political potential for mitigating, if not transforming, relations of domination in the existing world order.

Recent years have witnessed the emergence and growing mobilization of what has been termed the global anti-capitalist and global justice movements (Callinicos 2003; Tormey 2004; Desai and Said 2001). Embracing a diversity of social movements and non-governmental organizations, from anarchists to social democrats, the anti-capitalist and global justice movements have evolved as a powerful reaction against corporate-driven and state-promoted globalization (Callinicos 2003; Tormey 2004). Mobilizing both local and global action, the movement has made use of direct action, transnational campaigns and the politics of protest to bring to the world's attention the subordination of human and ecological security to the interests of global capital or US hegemony (Tarow 2005). In the last few years the annual summits of all the major global and regional institutions have confronted mass street protests, including the meetings of the World Bank, the IMF and the world's bankers, and the G8, the EU and APEC.

Beyond mass protest, single-issue campaigns, including Jubilee 2000 seeking debt cancellation, Make Poverty History, mobilization against the Multilateral Agreement on Investment proposing a global charter of rights for MNCs, and the campaign for a Tobin tax on global financial speculation, have been relatively successful in shaping global institutional agendas (Risse 2000b). Among the more radical critics of liberal global governance, however, such activities are considered more cosmetic than substantive. Rather than reform, Tormey describes the aims of these critics as principally post-ideological, seeking an alternative system of global governance which privileges people over profits, and the local over the global (Tormey 2004). Delegitimizing and contesting the existing order, by highlighting its contradictions through local struggles at multiple points in the global system and bringing to public attention its lack of legitimacy, are central to the autonomist or molecular political strategy adopted by these more revolutionary segments of the anti-capitalist movement (Tormey 2004).

Understood as key agents of progressive global change, the constellation of new social movements and anti-capitalist protests plays a critical role in radical accounts of the politics of liberal global governance. These agents represent a historically distinctive form of the global politics of contention as the liberal global governance complex increasingly becomes the focus of global collective claim-making by agencies of transnational civil society, from the Jubilee 2000 Campaign to the campaign for Global Trade Justice (Tilly 2004). A global redistributive politics is in the making. In this redistributive politics, states, as Onora O'Neill

149

(2001) has written, are no longer the sole or primary agents of justice in the global arena. Huge amounts of humanitarian aid and assistance of all kinds is channelled through NGOs, while the powerful advocacy networks promoting the duties of global social justice represent a form of practical political cosmopolitanism. Where they can exploit international public opinion, divisions within the G8, and between the G8 leaders and their publics, significant advances can be made in promoting a progressive political agenda.

However, the divisions within the anti-capitalist movement, and the structural constraints on suprastate agencies resulting from global markets and the US as super-hegemon, necessarily limit the prospects for fundamental or structural change. Such change is therefore much more likely to result, in the assessment of many radical thinkers, from some form of global crisis, whether a severe financial shock, economic depression, war, the growing gap between rich and poor, or ecological disaster, precipitating the failure of existing liberal global governance mechanisms to cope effectively (Callinicos 2003; Tormey 2004). In these circumstances, a more progressive agenda and alternatives to liberal global governance may acquire strategic influence, depending on the particular historical configuration of global social forces. Since economic crisis and poverty are endemic to global capitalism, as with all varieties of capitalism, the conditions for fundamental change are inherent in the contradictions of the liberal global governance complex. Globalization and liberal global governance are, according to this line of reasoning, historically unsustainable in their present form, not least because of the growing political backlash. As Mittleman observes, the contradictions and tensions within the prevailing order are becoming 'engines of change [that] may eventually transform or even destroy the system, inaugurating a period of post-globalization' (2000: 242).

In contrast to this radical account of global governance, more orthodox interpretations place greater emphasis on its institutional dynamics and potential to regulate or manage the forces of globalization. Rather than privileging the path-dependent logics of global capitalism, the institutionalist account explores how the contentious politics of global governance shapes global policy outcomes: who makes the rules, how, and to what purposes?

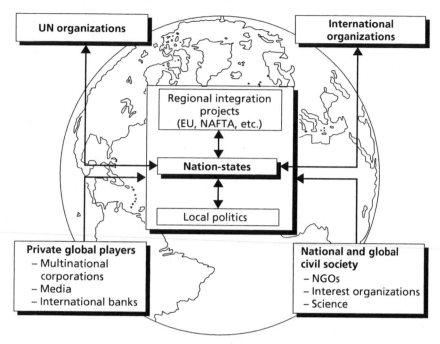

Figure 7.3 Levels of action in the architecture of global governance

Source: Kennedy, Messner and Nuscheler 2002.

Institutionalist analysis emphasizes complexity and polyarchy: global governance as a *multilayered, multisectoral* and *multi-actor* system in which institutions and politics matter a great deal to the determination of global policy outcomes, that is, to who gets what, when and why.

Global governance is multilayered in so far as the making and implementation of global policies involve a process of political coordination and cooperation between suprastate, national, transnational, and often substate agencies (see figure 7.3). Humanitarian relief operations, for instance, require the coordinated efforts of global, regional, national and local agencies. In this respect, the process of global governance is not so much hierarchical (command and control from the top) as horizontal: a process which involves coordination and cooperation between agencies across various levels, from the local to the global, involving a globalization of politics and rule making (Rosenau 2000a). However, the configuration of power and politics differs from sector to sector and issue to issue, such that policy outcomes are not readily controlled by the dominant powers, whose interests and influence may vary from issue to issue. On trade issues, for instance, it does make a difference that China is a bigger exporter than the US. Outcomes therefore tend to be more contingent on bargaining, coalition politics, consensus and compromise than deference to hegemonic power, significant though that may be (Keohane 2001). The politics of global governance is, thus, significantly differentiated; the politics of global financial regulation is quite distinct from the politics of peacekeeping. Rather than being monolithic or unitary, the system is best understood as multi-sectoral or segmented.

Finally, many of the agencies of, and participants in, the global governance complex are no longer purely intergovernmental bodies. There is considerable involvement of representatives of transnational civil society, from Greenpeace to Jubilee 2000 and an array of NGOs; of the corporate sector, from Monsanto to the International Chamber of Commerce and other trade or industrial associations; and of mixed public–private organizations, such as the International Organization of Securities Commissions (IOSCO) or the Global AIDS Fund (Scholte 2000a). At the 1995 WTO ministerial conference in Hong Kong some 846 NGOs attended, far outnumbering state delegates and representing geographically and socially diverse interests, from the Africa Trade Network, Genewatch and the Korean Fisheries Association to the Consumers Union of Japan and the American Potato Trade Alliance. In addition to being multilayered and multisectoral, global governance is a multi-actor complex in which diverse agencies participate in the formulation and conduct of global public policy.

A polyarchic conception of global governance does not imply that all states or agencies have an equal voice or input into, let alone an equal influence over, its agenda or programmes. On the contrary, there is a recognition that the system is institutionally biased or distorted in favour of the most powerful states and vested interests: it is not by chance that in recent years the promotion of the global market has taken priority over 'making poverty history' (Whitman 2005). Yet the very nature of globalization is such that in weaving, however unevenly, thickening webs of worldwide interconnectedness, hierarchical and hegemonic forms of governance become more costly and demanding to pursue and less effective and legitimate (Rosenau 2000b; Ikenberry 2001; Keohane 2001; Ferguson and Mansbach 2004). A notion of shared or over-lapping fates ensures that multilateralism works to moderate (though not to eliminate) power asymmetries (Ikenberry 2001). Even the most powerful recognize that without, at the least, the formal participation and tacit agreement of the weak or marginal-ized, effective and especially legitimate solutions to global prob-lems – whether terrorism or money laundering – which directly impinge on their own welfare would be impracticable. In these new circumstances of 'complex interdependence', in which the returns to hierarchy are outweighed generally by the benefits of multilat-eral cooperation, traditional 'hard' power instruments – military force or economic coercion – have a more circumscribed influence. This too creates new political opportunities for the forces of transnational civil society, which can mobilize considerable 'soft power' resources in the pursuit of their diverse objectives (Risse 2000a).

Associated with the global communications revolution, citizens' groups, NGOs and social movements have acquired new and more effective ways of organizing and mobilizing across national fron-tiers to participate in the governance of global affairs (see figure 7.4 and chapter 2; also Scholte 2000a; Edwards and Gaventa 2001; Tarow 2005). Whereas for much of the twentieth century interna-tional diplomacy was essentially an activity conducted between consenting states, the existence of suprastate organizations, such as the UN and the WTO, has created new arenas in which the voice of peoples – as opposed to simply governments – is increasingly heard. Some view this as a global associational revolution in which citizens, communities and private interests organize to influence the conduct and content of global governance (Rosenau 1990). Across the entire global agenda, on issues from the ecological to the ecumenical, NGOs and transnational movements give expres-sion to the concerns and interests of an emerging transnational civil society.

For the most part, however, by far the majority of transnational movements and NGOs lack the kinds of economic, financial or political resources available to most states (except the least devel-oped) and multinational companies. Accordingly their influence and political impact are best measured not in terms of 'hard power'

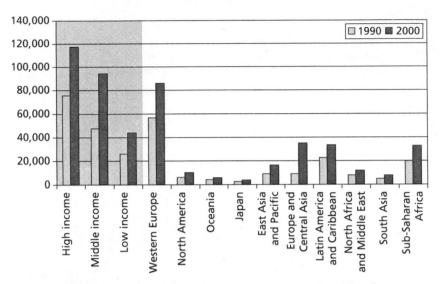

Figure 7.4 Growth of transnational civil society: membership of international non-governmental organizations, 1990–2000

Source: Anheier, Glasius and Kaldor 2001.

but rather in respect of their 'soft power', that is, not in terms of their capacity to coerce or induce others to change their ways but rather in terms of their capacity to shape others' interests, attitudes, agendas and identities (Nye 2004). In a media-saturated global environment, the communicative or discursive power of transnational civil society – the capacity to reach a global audience and shape international public opinion and the way issues are perceived and discussed – is considerable (Dryzek 2006). Witness, for instance, the primacy of ecological issues on the global agenda, such as global warming, and how these have moved from the edges to the centre of political debate. This is manifest in the ways in which transnational movements and organizations exert influence by exploiting distinct political strategies. These include:

- influencing public attitudes, interests and identities;
- redefining the agendas of local, national and global politics;
- providing communities and citizens with channels to global and regional decision-making forums;
- exercising moral, spiritual or technical authority; and

- seeking to make governments, international bodies and corporations accountable for their actions and decisions.

Among the more recent and successful campaigns of transnational civil society are Make Poverty History, the Jubilee 2000 'drop the debt' campaign, the international coalition for the establishment of the International Criminal Court, the campaign against the Multilateral Agreement on Investment, and the Ottawa Convention banning landmines.

Beyond transnational civil society, other more powerful non-state forces represent the interests of global corporate capital and business more generally. With enormous resources at their disposal, multinational corporations and the plethora of transnational business associations which represent corporate interests – for example, the World Business Council and the International Chamber of Commerce – have acquired a privileged position, most especially in the governance of the global economy. But their influence extends well beyond the economic domain, since few issues, whether global warming or human rights in Chile, can be divorced from economic interests and calculations.

A central characteristic of global governance is a redrawing of the boundaries between public authority and private power. There has been a significant privatization of aspects of global governance, from the establishment of technical standards to the disbursement of humanitarian assistance and official aid through NGOs. The International Accounting Standards Board establishes global accounting rules, while the major bond rating agencies make critical judgements about the credit status of governments and public authorities around the globe, and the Voluntary Principles on Security and Human Rights establish standards for corporate security activities in the extractive industries, which tend to operate in the most volatile regions of the world. Much of this privatized governance occurs in the shadow of global public authorities, but to the extent to which corporate and private interests influence the agendas of bodies such as the WTO and IOSCO there is a fusion of public and private power. The current salience of public–private partnerships, such as the Global AIDS Fund and the Global Compact, highlights the expanding influence and role of private interests in the formulation as well as the delivery of global policies.

Of course, this does not work simply in one direction, since there is considerable variation between different policy sectors, with deregulation in some areas, such as trade and finance, being accompanied by reregulation in others (intellectual property rights, nuclear safety). To the extent to which the corporate community has divergent interests, there are more strategic opportunities for suprastate bodies and civil society forces to advance a progressive agenda. In this context, suprastate agencies are not preordained to be instruments of global domination but, according to the institutionalist account, have the potential for enhancing the global public interest or social justice. What is required is a more transparent and democratic system of global governance.

Much of the formal business of global governance is conducted beyond the public gaze. Indeed (as noted in chapter 2), significant aspects of the formulation and implementation of global public policy occur within an expanding array of transgovernmental networks (such as the Financial Action Task Force), trisectoral networks (public, corporate and NGOs: for instance, the World Commission on Dams Forum, and the Roll Back Malaria Initiative) and transnational networks (such as the IASB, formerly IASC). These networks – which can be ad hoc or institutionalized – have become increasingly important in coordinating the work of experts and functionaries within governments, international organizations and the corporate and the NGO sector (examples are the Global Water Partnership and the Global Alliance for Vaccines and Immunization). They function to set policy agendas, disseminate information, formulate rules and establish and implement policy programmes – from money laundering measures in the FATF to global initiatives to counter AIDS. Many of these networks are of a purely bureaucratic nature, but they have also become primary mechanisms through which civil society and corporate interests are effectively embedded in the global policy process. In part, the growth of these networks is a response to the overload and politicization of multilateral bodies, but it is also an outcome of the growing technical complexity of global policy issues and the communications revolution. These developments raise critical questions concerning the democratic credentials of global rule-making.

Those globalists who adopt an institutionalist position tend to argue that the lack of transparency and accountability of suprastate governance is one of the crucial factors in limiting its effectiveness and legitimacy (Keohane 2001). Rather than its abolition, they advocate its democratic reform (see chapter 9). Institutionalists consider that governance beyond the state is a chronic feature of modern political life, since it arises from the functional benefits which, in an interdependent world, states and communities can realize through the strategic coordination of their policies and activities (Keohane 1984). Suprastate institutions matter a great deal because they deliver important benefits to states and their citizens – and their absence would undermine the achievement of human welfare and security (see table 7.3 above). Accordingly, they 'empower governments rather than shackle them' (Keohane 1984: 13). Crucially, they also moderate the effects of power politics by generating distinctive forms of multilateral, transgovernmental and transnational politics. The latter can help not only to restrain the powerful but also to create the possibilities of a more progressive global politics through which globalization can be governed in the interests of all, not simply of the few.

Reform of liberal global governance is a key theme in institutionalist studies. In part, this is because of growing political awareness that the prevailing system, as anti-globalization protests attest, is widely perceived as having limited political legitimacy and limited effectiveness. Among its key defects is the structural dominance of the most powerful states in shaping the institutions, patterns and outcomes of global governance. Important aspects of global governance are also distorted by the imperatives of nurturing, legitimizing and sustaining the global market. Furthermore, the technocratic nature of global institutions removes many issues from public scrutiny and thus creates a growing backlash against globalization. These distortions are reinforced by several critical gaps in the governance capacity of the system, most especially in respect of its welfare, human security and poverty reduction functions (UNDP 1999). The most strategically important of these gaps is its democratic deficit (Commission on Global Governance 1995; General 2000; Keohane 1998, 2001). Creating more representative, responsive, transparent and accountable international institutions by widening the participation of states and NGOs in key global fora and strengthening existing lines of accountability are central to this reformist vision (Commission on Global

Governance 1995). As Keohane (1998) asserts, global governance requires an enhanced system of 'voluntary pluralism under conditions of maximum transparency'. A more pluralistic system of global governance, in this view, implies more democratic global governance.

In effect, liberal reformists advocate the reconstruction of aspects of liberal-pluralist democracy at the international level shorn of the requirements of electoral politics. Accordingly 'accountability will be enhanced not only by chains of official responsibility but also by the requirement of transparency. Official actions, negotiated amongst state representatives in international organizations, will be subject to scrutiny by transnational networks' (Keohane 1998). Democratizing global governance is conceived principally in rather limited terms as enhancing the procedures for making and legitimizing global public policy (see chapter 10).

Intrinsic to this reformism is a deeply rooted liberal anxiety, which has some rational basis in the events of the 1930s, that '[international] institutions, especially those created to tackle the problems of globalism, come at particular moments of crisis under strains that are so great as to preclude their effective operation. They become the major channels through which the resentments against globalization work their destruction' (James 2001: 5). Saving globalization as a valid ethical aspiration is a matter with which more radical globalists would take fundamental issue. For they tend to advocate either its transformation or alternatively its delegitimation (see chapter 10).

Part II

Remaking Globalization

8

Beyond Globalization/Anti-Globalization

There is some validity in the phrase 'globalization is what is made of it'. How globalization is constructed, in the media and academic discourse, frames, if not constrains, its meaning for both academics and activists alike. Contemporary discourses of globalization commonly interpret it as a titanic struggle between its advocates and its opponents, between the forces of globalization and those of anti-globalization, between globalists and sceptics, between the global and the particular. These antinomies certainly have heuristic value in helping define what is at stake – in the intellectual and political realms – given the enormous complexity of the subject matter. Hence, we have followed this framework. However, too often, these antinomies can slip into a reification of the academic and political contestation about the nature and significance of globalization. If taken too literally, they can readily tend towards the substitution of rhetoric for rigorous analysis. At this stage it is important to reflect on the current controversies and some of the emerging complexities in the globalist and sceptical analyses.

The making and unmaking of globalization: deconstructing the academic controversy

As Holton, among others, has suggested, globalization scholarship has come in three overlapping but distinctive waves: the hyperglobalist, the sceptical, and the post-sceptical (Holton 2005: 5; Bruff 2005; cf. Held et al. 1999). The wave analogy is useful in so far as it alludes to the successive diffusion and churning over of

161

distinct research programmes in which core research problematics come to be reappropriated and redefined by new research agendas. Significantly, too, it does not imply a simple notion of cumulative knowledge or linear progress. Building on Holton's schema while modifying it in a number of respects, four successive waves of globalization scholarship can be identified and roughly labelled as the theoretical, the historical, the institutional, and the deconstructive. As with all such schemata, this one is neither definitive nor exhaustive, but rather should be understood as a heuristic for organizing a highly complex field of study.

As manifest in the works of Giddens (1990), Robertson (1992), Rosenau (1990), Albrow (1996), Ohmae (1995), Harvey (1989) and Lawrence (1996), among others, the initial theoretical wave was generally concerned with debates about the conceptualization of globalization, its principal dynamics and its systemic and structural consequences as a secular process of worldwide social change. By contrast, the historical wave, drawing on the historical sociology of global development, was principally concerned with exploring in what ways, if any, contemporary globalization could be considered novel or unique – whether it defined a new epoch, or transformation, in the socio-economic and political organization of human affairs – and, if so, what the implications were for the realization of progressive values and projects of human emancipation (see, among others, Held et al. 1999; Hirst and Thompson 1999; Frank 1998; Castells 1996; Bordo, Taylor and Williamson 2003; Dicken 1998; Baldwin 1999; Gilpin 2002b; Gill 2003; Mann 1986, 2001; Hopkins 2002; Sassen 1996; Hardt and Negri 2000; Hoogvelt 1997; O'Rourke and Williamson 1999; Boyer and Drache 1996; Appadurai 1998; Amin 1997; Taylor 1995; and Tomlinson 2007).

Sceptical of these arguments about structural transformation, the third (institutional) wave sought to assess claims about global convergence (and divergence) by concentrating on questions of institutional change and resilience, whether in national models of capitalism, state restructuring or cultural life (see among others here Garrett 1998, 2001; Swank 2002a; Held 2004; Keohane and Nye 2003; Campbell 2004; Mosley 2003; Cowan 2003; Hay 2000; Pogge 2001). Finally, the fourth and most recent wave reflects the influence of poststructuralist and constructivist thinking across the social sciences, from Open Marxism to postmodernism. As a consequence, there is an emphasis on the importance of ideas, agency, communication, contingency and normative change to any convincing analysis of the making, unmaking and remaking of globalization understood both as a historical process and a hegemonic discourse. Central to this literature is a debate about whether the current historical conjuncture is best understood as an epoch of competing and alternative globalizations (in the plural), what Stanley Hoffmann has referred to as the 'clash of globalizations', or one of imperialism and empire (although these may not be incompatible) (S. Hoffmann 2002; Rosenberg 2005; Hay 2005; Urry 2003; Bello 2002; Held and McGrew 2002a; Callinicos 2003; Keohane and Nye 2003; Rosamond 2003; Wolf 2004; Saul 2005; Harvey 2003).

These four broad approaches frame contemporary globalization scholarship. Returning to the initial heuristic in chapter 1 (figure 1.1 on p. 5) it is now appropriate to map these four waves of scholarship in relation to the normative (cosmopolitan or communitarian) and explanatory (globalist or sceptic) dimensions of contention. As with figure 1.1 the vertical scale in figure 8.1 represents the contest over the intellectual hegemony of globalization characterized by a privileging either of globalist forms of analysis (the globalists) or alternatively statist or societal forms of analysis (the sceptics). The horizontal scale represents the normative domain, differentiating between cosmopolitan and communitarian forms of ethical reasoning: that is, an attachment to some ideal of the 'good global community' as opposed to the advocacy of a plurality of coexisting 'good national or local communities'. Figure 8.1 constructs the intellectual terrain identifying at least four distinct modes of analysis:

- globalization is taken to be a really existing condition and considered to be amenable to either political reform or transformation (the transformationalists);
- globalization is taken seriously but as a new form of domination to be resisted along with any grand political projects for remaking the world according to cosmopolitan universal principles (the critical globalists);
- the idea of globalization, or its presumed benign nature, is regarded with deep scepticism, and instead the emphasis is on the continued centrality of state power to the improvement of the human condition (the statists);

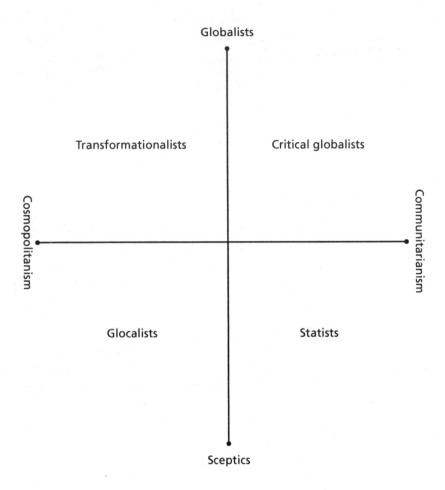

Figure 8.1 The great globalization controversy: the intellectual terrain

- the privileging of the global is rejected and the intermeshing of processes of globalization and localization is emphasized, but with a normative attachment to 'rooted cosmopolitanism' (the glocalists).

Clearly these positions themselves conceal interesting overlaps, not to mention significant differences (of interpretation and ethical commitment) within the globalist and sceptic camps. Nonetheless, figure 8.1 usefully maps the spectrum of contention, demonstrating a complexity and diversity of views and thereby moving beyond the antinomies of the globalization/anti-globalization heuristic.

The unmaking of globalization: the sceptics' case

Sceptical scholarship echoes Joseph Stiglitz's quip referred to above that 'globalization today has been oversold' (2005: 229). As noted in chapter 1, it is oversold in at least three senses: as a description of social reality (a social ontology); as an explanation of social change (an explanans); and as an ideology of social progress (a political project). In all these respects, most particularly in the wake of 9/11, globalist rhetoric increasingly appears rather hollow. This scepticism comes in two forms: the statist and the localist. Central to statist scepticism is the work of, among others, Hirst and Thompson (1999), Hay (2005); Rugman (2001) and Gilpin (2002b). This broadly realist and historical materialist scholarship holds that contemporary globalization is not historically unprecedented, that the dominant economic trends are towards internationalization and regionalization, and that the idea of globalization has been much more significant than its descriptive or explanatory utility. In effect they argue that critical and transformationalist scholarship significantly exaggerates globalization's empirical and normative significance, arguing that the world remains principally one of discrete national societies or states.

These sceptical arguments have acquired particular force in the current context. For today borders and boundaries, nationalism and protectionism, localism and ethnicity appear to define an epoch of radical de-globalization, the disintegration of the liberal world order and the demise of globalism. Ferguson (2005) suggests that the current epoch has many similarities with the 'sinking' of the 'last age of globalization', which ended in the destruction of the First World War and the subsequent world depression. Saul (2005), in similar vein, argues that the ideology or discourse of globalism, upon which globalization as a 'social fact' or social ontology depends, is rapidly receding in the face of the resurgence of nationalism, ethnicity, religious fundamentalism, and geopolitics. As

Rosenberg (2005) concludes, the current conjuncture demonstrates the follies of globalization theory, not to mention just how far its proponents misread and misunderstood the 1990s period in the context of world historical development. Rather than globalization, the current world order is defined by the reassertion of US hegemony, the rise of a new mode of Western imperialism, interventionism, geopolitics and intercapitalist rivalry. Historical materialist and realist theories of imperialism or geopolitics provide more accurate descriptions and explanations of the current conjuncture than does any transformationalist or critical globalist scholarship (Harvey 2003; Rosenberg 2005; Kennedy-Pipe and Rengger 2006; Kiely 2006; Callinicos 2007). Indeed Rosenberg goes so far as to suggest that the existence of the new imperialism demonstrates not only the intellectual bankruptcy of globalization as description, explanation and ideology, but also paradoxically that ' "globalization" did not even exist' (2005: 65).

These sceptics, on the whole, do not mourn the passing of the discourse of globalization. On the contrary, for many of them it constitutes a welcome return to grounded historical critique, to understanding both the real possibilities and real obstacles to the construction of a better world. For those of a historical materialist persuasion, this requires capturing state power democratically, building a post-capitalist society and developing a progressive internationalism as opposed to the utopia of global democracy; more anti-capitalism perhaps than anti-globalism per se (Tormey 2004). Among those of realist persuasion it means using state power to create the conditions of a more just international order – a form of liberal internationalism. What both share is a commitment to the state as the principal, but not the sole, agent of social and political progress, which is building a better world from the inside out rather than the outside in.

Poststructuralism in the social sciences has encouraged a shift away from macro-social analysis to a concern with the particular, the local, and the micro-social. 'Glocalist' scholarship takes this shift seriously. It seeks to problematize the local-global complex rather than a priori to assert, or presume, the causal primacy of either or to conceive them as in a structurally contradictory relationship. In simple terms, glocalist analysis, which inherits much from third and fourth wave thinking, takes both globalization and

166

localization seriously without necessarily privileging either in explanations of the social. Holton refers to this as 'methodological glocalism', because it is an approach whose 'defining characteristic . . . is to observe the interpenetration of the two [local and global]' and to 'recognize the co-existence and inter-relations between these various layers of social life', acknowledging that such interrelations 'are not necessarily corrosive or incompatible' since 'the global and the national or local may under certain circumstances depend on each other' (Holton 2005: 191). Glocalist scholarship charts a third course between globalism and statism.

Some of the more influential work in this genre is located within cultural studies, anthropology, and social and urban geography. Brenner (2004), for example, argues that capitalism has always operated at different spatial scales, from the local to the global, but that the restructuring of capitalism in the 1990s brought with it a more complex spatiality. Social relations are increasingly articulated and rearticulated simultaneously across a multiplicity of spatial scales, from the sublocal to the local, national, transnational, regional and global. Thus much of the work on global cities illuminates how they are simultaneously local, national, transnational, regional and global centres of power (Smith 2001; P. Taylor 1995). Rather than conceiving this multiplicity of spatial scales as necessarily organized in a hierarchical or contradictory fashion, Brenner argues that they are mutually constitutive. By this he does not mean that the global and local can simply be dissolved into one another, for they retain their distinctive forms, but rather that explanation of one necessarily requires an account of the other. Brenner's work is a critique of that globalization scholarship which privileges any particular spatial scale: in other words, that suggests that social relations are becoming increasingly deterritorialized, denationalized or alternatively regionalized or nationalized. On the contrary, he argues, the multiplicity of spatial scales are relational, not containers of social relations. Territory still matters, but not in the way in which it is conventionally theorized – as deterritorialization or reterritorialization.

Similar arguments are made in many studies of cultural globalization. Hannerz (1992) and Appadurai (1998), among others, have argued that it is associated with cultural hybridization, fusion or creolism. Stressing the social construction, rather than primordial origins, of individual and collective identity, they point to ways in which local and global cultural resources are conjoined in the production of new kinds of identities and cultural communities, from the self-identification of Irish-Americans to the indigenization of world religions. To explain these processes of cultural hybridization requires moving beyond the antinomies of the global and the local to a recognition of their mutual imbrication.

Recognition of the complexity and contingency of this mutual imbrication informs the normative thinking of much glocalist scholarship. Although it is animated by a concern to identify the structures and processes of domination which range in, across and through societies, it necessarily rejects the crude binary division between the global as the principal source of domination and the local as the principal source of resistance or emancipation. This produces an interesting blurring of ethical attachments between ethical cosmopolitanism and communitarianism: a rooted cosmopolitanism (Appiah 2005). Such a rooted cosmopolitanism seeks the 'furthering of cosmopolitan norms through rather than beyond the nation-state' (Eckersley 2005). Some emphasize a new localism through which regimes of urban governance harness local, national and global social forces to the realization of cosmopolitan social purposes (Brenner 2004; Smith 2001). Tarrow (2005) highlights the growing significance of rooted cosmopolitanism in the context of growing transnational activism, which blends together local and global struggles. And still others emphasize the strategies of autonomous development as articulated by the Zapatista movement, which, Olesen notes, relies on 'a growing imbrication of local, national and transnational levels of interaction rather than their increasing disconnection'. As with critical globalism, there is no singular normative vision of a better world, only an aspiration for 'a world in which many worlds fit' (Olesen 2005: 54, 12).

The making and remaking of globalization: the globalists

There are broadly two main strands of globalist scholarship: the transformationalist and the critical globalist. Transformationalist scholarship presents a far from benign or economistic reading of globalization. Among the principal works which share such a perspective, although rooted within different theoretical and methodological traditions, are those of Castells (1997), Rosenau (1990, 2003), Giddens (1990), Held and McGrew (2002a); Held et al. (1999); and Scholte (2000b). They present a rich account of the distinctive features of contemporary globalization from within a broadly historical sociology tradition. They map the scale and complexity of worldwide social relations across all dimensions, from the economic to the cultural, arguing that their historically unprecedented extensity and intensity represents a significant 'global shift' in the social organization of human affairs.

Contrary to an economistic analysis, globalization is conceived as operating across different domains, from the cultural to the political. Nor does it display a simple logic of global integration or convergence. On the contrary, it is considered dialectical, integrating and fragmenting, uniting and dividing the world by creating winners and losers, and by including and excluding locales, as it proceeds. While it generates pressures for socio-economic convergence, these are mediated by domestic factors so that significant divergence, whether in levels of national social spending or economic growth, may often be the result. Rather than imposing a 'golden straitjacket' on all states, its consequences are significantly differentiated. Yet increasingly states and societies confront similar problems of boundary control as the separation of the global and the domestic becomes less tenable. Political problems, from people trafficking to the management of the national economy, are simultaneously both domestic and global matters. This erosion of the internal and external, domestic and international, articulates the growing compression of time and space in an epoch of instant global communications. A resulting structural consequence is that the relationships between territory, economy, society, identity, sovereignty and the state no longer appear as historically fixed and congruent – even if this was imaginary – but rather as relatively fluid and disjointed. For the transformationalists, it is this apparent dislocation or destabilizing of the institutional coordinates of modern social life that is the source of both heightened conflict and insecurity, at all levels, from the local to the global. This dislocation takes many forms, from the political to the cultural. It finds, for example, particular expression in the political domain in the apparent disjuncture between national sovereignty and the suprastate locus of many aspects of the actual business of contemporary government.

Transformationalist accounts do not imbue globalization with any particular telos, neither an inevitably more prosperous or peaceful world, nor an inevitable emergence of a singular world society or a coming anarchy. However, there is broad agreement that its structural consequences do much to multiply the complexity of modern societies and thereby their governance, while simultaneously creating a range of new transnational problems, from global warming to global financial instability, which are hugely difficult to resolve. One consequence is the restructuring of the state evidenced in the shift from government to governance. Furthermore, since decisions in one country can directly impact on the interests of citizens of other societies, a whole new range of transboundary problems are generated which challenge the efficacy of national democracy. Beyond the political domain, the consequences of globalization present comparable challenges to the organization and functioning of modern societies.

In addition to the structural consequences of globalization, the transformationalist literature has much to say about its distributional consequences. In particular, Castells, among others, argues (contra the Washington Consensus and liberal accounts) that economic globalization is associated with a polarizing and divided world, as the gap between rich and poor widens while much of humanity remains on the margins or is excluded from its benefits (Castells 2000). This structural exclusion and structural inequality, it is argued, is an inevitable consequence of market-led globalization. However, this need not be the case if globalization could be harnessed to the ideals of social justice. The cosmopolitan normative thrust of the transformationalist analysis is thus an argument for ethical or humane globalization, combining economic efficiency with equity or social justice. This is a demand for nothing less than the reform or transformation of actually existing globalization. For Held, Castells and others, this takes the form of variations on a project for global democracy and global justice (Held 2004; Castells 2005; Scholte 2005). It is a project which, building on the reform of existing infrastructures of global governance and civil society, seeks the democratic regulation of globalization in order to address its more socially malignant structural and distributional consequences.

By contrast critical globalism is perhaps best described as encompassing that 'engaged' scholarship which takes globalization seriously because it is constitutive of new global structures and systems of transnational domination (Mittleman 2000; Rupert and Solomon 2004; Gill 2003; Hardt and Negri 2000; Eschele 2005; Petersen 2004). As such, critical globalist scholarship not only acknowledges the ways in which the organization and exercise of social power is being radically extended and transnationalized by the social forces of globalization, but also how, in the process, new subjectivities and transnational collectivities of resistance are formed. Variously referred to as the 'global matrix', 'global market civilization', or 'Empire', a new globalized social formation is held to be in the making which, according to critical globalist theory, requires new ways of thinking about and acting in the world (James and Nairn 2005; Gill 2003; Hardt and Negri 2000). Issuing principally from poststructural and post-Marxist scholarship, this approach seeks to understand the making and unmaking of these new globalized structures of domination, as well as the possibilities for their remaking or progressive transformation.

Among the more influential of this scholarship is the work of Hardt and Negri. In *Empire* they theorize and explain the emergence of a historically unique form of global domination with globalization at its core. Though they refer to this as Empire, it is distinguished from classic imperialism:

> By 'Empire' . . . we understand something altogether different from 'imperialism'. . . . Imperialism was really an extension of the sovereignty of the European nation-states beyond their own boundaries. . . . In contrast to imperialism, Empire establishes no territorial center of power and does not rely on fixed boundaries or barriers. It is a decentered and deterritorializing apparatus of rule that progressively incorporates the entire global realm within its open, expanding frontiers . . . (Hardt and Negri 2000: Introduction)

Central to the making of Empire, they argue, are processes of globalization which they consider enduring rather than contingent. These same processes, however, engender projects of transnational

171

resistance which create the social basis for alternative globalizations in opposition to the totalizing logic of Empire:

> The passage to Empire and its processes of globalization offer new possibilities to the forces of liberation. Globalization, of course, is not one thing, and the multiple processes that we recognize as globalization are not unified or univocal. Our political task, we will argue, is not simply to resist these processes but to reorganize them and redirect them toward new ends. The creative forces of the multitude that sustain Empire are also capable of autonomously constructing a counter-Empire, an alternative political organization of global flows and exchanges. The struggles to contest and subvert Empire, as well as those to construct a real alternative, will thus take place on the imperial terrain itself – indeed, such new struggles have already begun to emerge . . . (Hardt and Negri 2000: Introduction)

Hardt and Negri's 'Empire' has much in common with other neo-Gramscian accounts of the hegemony of a globalized capitalist order (Gill 2003). Both consider globalization as a historically distinctive mode of domination which is not only economic but cultural, social, ideological and political. Both also emphasize the highly contested nature of this domination, articulated in diverse local and transnational struggles of resistance and recognition, from the Zapatistas in Mexico to the World Social Forum, which constitute the solidarist networks of alternative globalizations.

Agency, subjectivity and social struggle are thus vital expository concepts in the critical globalist lexicon. As Evans, among many others, observes, globalization is associated with the emergence of a globalized contentious politics in which local and global struggles are conjoined, since 'the defence of difference and quests for local power require global strategies and connections, likewise transnational social movements must have local social roots' (Evans 2005: 7). These alternative globalizations, which are not necessarily progressive, partly reflect the simultaneous rise of identity politics and of global consciousness, constituting new subjectivities and ways of thinking about and acting in the world. The sources of alternative globalizations are thus to be located not simply in distributional struggles but also in struggles over recognition, whether of indigenous peoples or gender discrimination. This 'globalization from below' perspective focuses attention on the significance of individual and collective agency, from fair trade consumerism to G8 protests, in the making and remaking of global society.

In certain respects, as with the transformationalists, there is an assumption that, irrespective of its particular form, globalization per se is integral to (post)modernity or (post)modern social life. Corporate globalization is not its sole face and it is not inevitably hegemonic. Nor is globalization per se inherently malign, but rather harbours progressive potential. The principal normative and political question is whether and how that potential is to be realized. In this regard, critical globalism resists the valorization of any singular normative vision of ethical globalization or its institutionalization, whether global democracy or a post-capitalist order, in favour of a radical communitarianism; that is, the positive prospect of coexisting alternative globalizations: a peculiar multiplicity of local and globalized communities (Tormey 2004).

Since all explanatory theories of globalization are implicitly, if not explicitly, normative, disagreement about its essential nature is, in part at least, often rooted in different ethical outlooks. Indeed the most contentious aspect of the study of contemporary globalization concerns the ethical and the political: whether it hinders or assists the pursuit of a better world and whether that better world should be defined by cosmopolitan or communitarian principles, or both.

9

World Orders, Ethical Foundations

Throughout the modern period concepts of the political good have generally been elaborated at the level of state institutions and practices; the state has been at the intersection of intellectually and morally ambitious conceptions of political life (Dunn 1990: 142–60). Political theory, by and large, has taken the nation-state as a fixed point of reference and has sought to place the state at the centre of interpretations of the nature and proper form of the political good. Relations among states have of course been analysed; but they have rarely been examined, especially in recent times, as a central element of political theory and political philosophy. The central element has been the territorial political community and its many possible relations to what is desirable or politically good.

The ethically bounded political community

The theory and practice of liberal democracy has added important nuances to this position. For within the framework of liberal democracy, while territorial boundaries and the nation-state demarcate the proper spatial limits of the political good, the articulation of the latter is directly linked to the citizenry. Theories of the modern state tend to draw a sharp contrast between the powers of the state and the power of the people (Skinner 1989). For early theorists of the state such as Thomas Hobbes, the state is the supreme political reference point within a specific community and territory; it is independent of subjects and rulers, with distinctive political properties of its own (1968: chs 16–19). By

174

contrast, theorists of democracy tend to affirm the idea of the people as the active sovereign body, with the capacity, in principle, to make or break governments. As John Locke bluntly put it in 1690, 'the *Community* perpetually *retains a Supreme Power*' over its lawmakers and legislature (1963: 413, see also 477). The political good inheres in, and is to be specified by, a process of political participation in which the collective will is determined through the medium of elected representatives (Bobbio 1989: 144). Rightful power or authority, that is, sovereignty, is vested in the people, subject to various entrenched rules, procedures and institutions which constitute national constitutional agreements and legal traditions. The democratic good unfolds in the context of these delimiting or self-binding mechanisms (Holmes 1988; Dahl 1989).

The theory of the political good in the modern territorial polity (nation-state) rests on a number of assumptions which repay an effort of clarification (see Miller 1995, 1999; Held 1995: ch. 10). These are that a political community is properly constituted and bounded when:

1 Its members have a common socio-cultural identity; that is, they share an understanding, explicit or implicit, of a distinctive culture, tradition, language and homeland, which binds them together as a group and forms a (if not the) basis (acknowledged or unacknowledged) of their activities.
2 There is a common framework of 'prejudices', purposes and objectives that generates a common political ethos; that is, an imagined 'community of fate' which connects them directly to a common political project – the notion that they form a people who should govern themselves.
3 An institutional structure exists – or is in the process of development – which protects and represents the community, acts on its behalf and promotes the public interest.
4 'Congruence' and 'symmetry' prevail between a community's 'governors' and 'governed', between political decision-makers and those the decisions affect. That is to say, national communities exclusively 'programme' the actions, decisions and policies of their governments, and the latter determine what is right or appropriate for their citizens.

5 Members enjoy, because of the presence of conditions 1–4, a common structure of rights and duties; that is, they can lay claim to, and can reasonably expect, certain kinds of equal treatment, that is, certain types of egalitarian principles of justice and political participation (citizenship).

According to this account, which in this context can be referred to as the sceptical analysis of the political good, appropriate conceptions of what is right for the political community and its citizens follow from its cultural, political and institutional roots, traditions and boundaries. These generate the resources – conceptual, ethical and organizational – for the determination of its fate and fortunes. Underpinning this understanding of the bounded community is a principle of justification which involves a significant communitarian line of thought: ethical discourse cannot be detached from the 'form of life' of a community; the categories of political discourse are integral to a particular tradition; and the values of such a community take precedence over individual or global requirements (Walzer 1983; Miller 1988, 1995; MacIntyre 1981, 1988).

A cosmopolitan global ethic

Globalists take issue with each of the above propositions, concluding that the political good today can only be disclosed by reflection on the diversity of the 'communities of fate' to which individuals and groups belong, and the way in which this diversity is reinforced by the political transformations globalization has brought in its wake. According to this globalist interpretation, the political good is entrenched in overlapping communities, and in an emergent transnational civil society and global polity. Disputes about the political good should be disputes about the nature and proper form of the developing global order. The basis of this globalist view can be grasped from a critique of the above five points.

First, shared identity in political communities historically has been the result of intensive efforts of political construction; it has never been a given (see chapter 3 above; cf. Gellner 1983; B. Anderson 1983; A. Smith 1986, 1995). Even within the boundaries of long-established communities, cultural and political identity is often disputed by and across social classes, gender divisions, local allegiances, ethnic groupings and the generations. The existence of a shared political identity cannot simply be read off vociferously proclaimed symbols of national identity. The meaning of such symbols is contested and the 'ethos' of a community frequently debated. The common values of a community may be subject to intense dispute. Justice, accountability, the rule of law and welfare are just a few terms around which there may appear to be a shared language, and yet fiercely different conceptions of these may be present (Held 1991: 11–21). In fact, if by a political consensus is meant normative integration within a community, then it is all too rare (Held 1996: part 2; and see below). Political identity is only by exception, for instance during wars, a singular, unitary phenomenon. Moreover, contemporary reflexive political agents, subject to an extraordinary diversity of information and communication, can be influenced by images, concepts, values, lifestyles and ideas from well beyond their immediate communities, and can come to identify with groupings beyond their borders – ethnic, religious, social and political (J. B. Thompson 1995; Held et al. 1999: ch. 8; Keck and Sikkink 1998). And while there is no reason to suppose that they will uncritically identify with any one of these, some people may well find self-chosen ideas, commitments or relations more important for their identity than 'membership in a community of birth' (J. Thompson 1998: 190; cf. Giddens 1991; Tamir 1993). Cultural and political identity today is constantly under review and reconstruction at both individual and collective levels (see Held and Moore 2007).

Second, the argument that locates the political good firmly within the terrain of the nation-state fails to consider or properly appreciate the diversity of political communities individuals can value, and the fact that individuals can involve themselves coherently in different associations or collectivities at different levels and for different purposes (J. Thompson 1998). It is perfectly possible, for example, to enjoy membership and voting rights in Scotland, the UK and Europe without there necessarily being a threat to one's identification or allegiances to any one of these three political entities (see Archibugi, Held and Köhler 1998). It is perfectly possible, in addition, to identify closely with the aims and ambitions of a transnational social movement – concerned, for instance, with environmental, gender or human rights issues – without compromising other more local political commitments. Such a pluralization of political orientations and allegiances can be linked to the erosion of the state's capacity to sustain a singular political identity in the face of globalization. In the first instance, globalization can weaken the state's ability to deliver certain goods to its citizens, for example, security, job protection (versus outsourcing) and environmental sustainability, thus eroding its legitimacy and the confidence of its citizens in its historic legacy. At the same time, the globalization of cultural processes and communications can stimulate new images of community, new avenues of political participation and new discourses of identity. Globalization is helping to create novel communication and information patterns and a dense network of relations linking particular groups and cultures to one another, transforming the dynamics of political relations, above, below and alongside the state. Increasingly, successful political communities have to work with, not against, a multiplicity of identities, cultures and ethnic groupings. An overlapping consensus which might underpin such communities is often fragile and based purely on a commitment to common procedures – for instance, procedural mechanisms for the resolution of conflict – not a set of substantive, given values. A national political ethos may, at best, be skin-deep.

Third, globalization can 'hollow out' states, weakening their sovereignty and autonomy. State institutions and political agents are, some globalists maintain, increasingly like 'zombies', acting out the motions of politics but failing to determine any substantive, welfare-enhancing public good (Beck 1992, 1997). Contemporary political strategies involve easing adaptation to world markets and transnational economic flows (see chapter 5). Adjustment to the international economy – above all, to global financial markets – becomes a fixed point of orientation in economic and social policy. The 'decision signals' of these markets, and of their leading agents and forces, become a vital standard of national decision-making. This position is linked, moreover, to the pursuit of distinctive supply-side measures – above all, to the use of education and training as tools of economic policy. Individual citizens must be empowered with cultural and educational capital to meet the challenges of increased (local, national, regional, global) competition and the greater mobility of industrial and financial capital. States no longer have the capacity and policy instruments they require to contest the imperatives of global economic change; instead, they must help individual citizens to go where they want to go through the provision of social, cultural and educational resources. The terms of reference of public policy are set by global markets and corporate enterprise. The pursuit of the public good becomes synonymous with enhancing adaptation to this private end. Accordingly, the roles of the state as protector and representative of the territorial community, as a collector and (re)allocator of resources among its members, and as a promoter of an independent, deliberatively tested shared good are all in decline.

Fourth, the fate of a national community is no longer in its own hands. Regional and global economic, environmental and political processes profoundly redefine the content of national decision-making. In addition, decisions made by quasi-regional or quasi-supranational organizations such as the EU, WTO or the World Bank diminish the range of political options open to given national 'majorities'. In a similar vein, decisions by particular states – not just the most economically or militarily powerful nations – can ramify across borders, circumscribing and reshaping the political terrain. National governments by no means determine what is right or appropriate for their own citizens (Offe 1985). National policies with respect to interest rates, the harvesting of rainforests, the encouragement or restriction of the growing of genetically modified food, arms procurement and manufacture, and incentive provisions to attract inward investment by multinational companies, along with decisions on a huge range of additional public matters from AIDS to the problems faced by a post-antibiotic culture (when antibiotics cease to be effective on a mass scale because of prior overprescription), can have major consequences for those in neighbouring and distant lands. Political communities are thus embedded in a substantial range of processes which connect them in complex configurations.

Fifth, national communities are locked into webs of regional and global governance which alter and compromise their capacity to provide a common structure of rights, duties and welfare for their citizens (see chapter 7). Regional and global processes, organizations and institutions expand, circumscribe and delimit the kinds of entitlements and opportunities national states can offer and deliver. From human rights to trade regimes, political power is being rearticulated and reconfigured. Increasingly, contemporary patterns of globalization are associated with a multilayered system of governance, the diffusion of political power, and a widening gap between the influence of the richest and poorest communities. A complex constellation of 'winners' and 'losers' emerges (see chapter 6). Locked into an array of geographically diverse forces, national governments are having to reconsider their roles and functions. Although the intensification of regional and global political relations has diminished the powers of national governments, it is recognized ever more that the nurturing and enhancement of the public good requires coordinated multilateral action; for instance, to prevent global recession and enhance sustainable growth, to protect human rights and intercede where they are grossly violated, and to act to avoid environmental catastrophes such as ozone depletion or global warming. A shift is taking place from government to multilayered global governance. Accordingly, the institutional nexus of the political good is being reconfigured.

Each of the five propositions set forth by the sceptics – the theorists and advocates of the modern nation-state – can be contrasted with positions held by the globalists. Thus the political community and the political good need, on the globalists' account, to be understood as follows:

1 Individuals increasingly have complex loyalties and multilayered identities, corresponding to the globalization of economic and cultural forces and the reconfiguration of political power. The movements of cultural goods across borders, hybridization and the intermingling of cultures create the basis of a transnational civil society with overlapping identities – which progressively finds expression in, and binds people together into, transnational movements, agencies and legal and institutional structures.

2 The continuing development of regional, international and global flows of resources and networks of interaction, along with the recognition by growing numbers of people of the increasing interconnectedness of political communities in diverse domains

180

(including the social, cultural, economic and environmental), generates an awareness of overlapping 'collective fortunes' which require collective solutions. Political community begins to be reimagined in both regional and global terms.

3 An institutional structure exists comprising elements of local, national, regional and suprastate governance. At different levels, individual communities are protected and represented (albeit often imperfectly); their collective interests require both multilateral advancement and domestic (local and national) adjustment if they are to be sustained and promoted.

4 Complex economic, social and environmental processes, shifting networks of regional and international agencies, and the decisions of many states and private organizations cut across spatially delimited national locales, with determinate consequences for their political agendas and strategic choices. Globalization decisively alters what it is that a national community can ask of its government, what politicians can promise and effectively deliver, and the range of people(s) affected by governmental actions. Political communities are 'reprogrammed'.

5 The rights, duties and welfare of individuals can only be adequately entrenched if, in addition to their proper articulation in national constitutions, they are underwritten by regional and global regimes, laws and institutions. The promotion of the political good and of egalitarian principles of justice and political participation are rightly pursued at regional and global levels. Their conditions of possibility are inextricably linked to the establishment and development of robust transnational organizations and institutions of regional and suprastate governance. In a global age, the latter are the necessary basis of cooperative relations and just conduct.

In contradistinction to the conception of the political good promulgated by advocates of the modern nation-state, what is right for the individual political community and its citizens, in the globalists' account, must follow from reflection on the processes which generate an intermingling of national fortunes and fates. The growing fusion of worldwide economic, social, cultural and environmental forces requires a rethinking of the politically and philosophically 'isolationist' position of the communitarians and sceptics. For the contemporary world 'is not a world of closed communities with mutually impenetrable ways of thought, self-sufficient economies and ideally sovereign states' (O'Neill 1991: 282). Not only is ethical discourse separable from forms of life in a national community, but it is developing today at the intersection and interstices of overlapping communities, traditions and languages. Its categories are increasingly the result of the mediation of different cultures, communication processes and modes of understanding. There are not enough good reasons for allowing, in principle, the values of individual political communities to trump or take precedence over global principles of justice and political participation.

Of course, the globalists, like the sceptics, often have very different conceptions of what exactly is at stake here; that is, they hold very different views of what the global order should be like and the moral principles which might inform it. But they draw a clear-cut distinction between their conception of where the political good inheres and that of the sceptics. While for the latter ethical discourse is, and remains, firmly rooted in the bounded political community, for the former it belongs squarely to the world of 'breached boundaries' – the 'world community' or global order, the cosmopolitan human association.

Universal values and cultural diversity after 9/11

The question of cultural diversity, value pluralism and the pluralization of identities is at the heart of liberalism and the liberal polity, and the increasing global contest between liberal principles and identity or faith-based politics. The core claim of liberalism and its democratic child, liberal democracy, is that citizenship is the medium to ensure the necessary political conditions for equal membership in a polity, and within that framework the possibility of people living together peacefully despite plural values, cultural diversity and different faiths and traditions. Liberalism defends an institutional order that seeks, in principle, to enable citizens as individuals to go about their business and pursue their chosen beliefs and ends. Only polities, the argument goes, that acknowledge the equal status of all persons, that seek neutrality with respect to personal ends, hopes and aspirations, and that pursue the public justification of social economic and political arrangements can ensure a basic or common structure of political action which allows individuals to pursue their projects – both individual and collective – as free and equal agents. Liberalism, thus understood, is compatible with a version of the sceptical analysis of the political good.

Yet liberal principles have a universal component, often referred to as cosmopolitanism (see Held 2007). Cosmopolitanism defends, and is the root of, attempts at the global level since 1945 to check and place limits on sovereignty while creating spaces for humans to flourish independently of state control, tradition or particular faiths. Many global governance institutions were founded on these concerns, including the UN Charter system, the human rights regime, and the International Criminal Court. The embrace of universal principles by such institutions was always partial and one-sided and, from the beginning, in tension with the countervailing values of the primacy of statehood, also embedded in these same structures. Despite this, the challenge to them today goes much deeper than the charge of hypocrisy or double standards; for they are often criticized and condemned for simply pursuing Western agendas and being at the mercy of the big powers, or for doing too little, too late, or for doing nothing at all. The dominance of the US after the end of the Cold War reinforced this sense; 9/11 and the US-led reaction magnified it further. The start of the twenty-first century has witnessed an intensification of geopolitics, conflicts, violence, territorial struggle and the clash of identities in many parts of the world. As a result, the foundations of the liberal world order are being questioned, internally as a result of the difficulties of assimilationist and multicultural policies in many countries (and not just in the West), and externally as a result of the 'war on terror' and the backlashes it has provoked (see chapters 2, 3 and 4).

Tensions between national identity and cosmopolitan identity are marked, and the debate about the nature and legitimate role of the 'great powers', and in particular the role of the US, is worldwide (see chapters by Nye, Slaughter and Hale, Cox and Quinn, in Held and Moore 2007). The US remains simultaneously a much criticized and sometimes reviled country while remaining the most attractive destination for migrants the world over. At the global level, politics is now an arena in which liberalism, secularism and Westernism are being challenged by a diverse array of political projects, some of which aim to destroy them. There are grave dangers here, as well as political and cultural opportunities, for instance to reconstitute elements of democratic life itself (see Held 2006).

The rise of fundamentalism in recent years – Muslim, Christian, Jewish and Hindu, among other forms – is one response to the complex and sometimes unwelcome and bewildering impacts of globalization, and the way they have been mediated by great power politics. Fundamentalism is, on the one side, a call for a return to the codes and principles of basic scriptures and texts, and, on the other side, an expression of 'beleaguered tradition' – tradition under pressure from modernity, given greater force and shape by contemporary globalization (Giddens 1999a: 48–50). Fundamentalism is less about what people believe and more about why they believe it and how they justify it, rejecting a world that asks for reasons and public justification (see Habermas 2001: 126–9). It has no time for multiple identities, complex allegiances and cultural ambiguity. In the contemporary world, fundamentalism can be uncovered not just among religious groupings but also among many different kinds of community – political, economic, ethnic, and environmental, among others. The fault line running through contemporary global society divides those who call for the guardians of tradition to reassert themselves, and those who accept and welcome cultural diversity and seek dialogue and the minimum rules of coexistence so that all can live peacefully without resort to violence and coercion. It is a deep fault line, and testifies to people's remarkable capacities, under changing conditions, to hold tight to traditional values and practices, to forge new ones, and to be able, sometimes, to reason from the point of view of others. The debate about the nature and form of the political good after 9/11 highlights the shifting grounds on which the sceptical analysis of the political is defended and challenged anew.

10

The Contentious Politics of Globalization: Mapping Ideals and Theories

The intensity of the debate about the nature, extent and impact of globalization, explored in the previous chapters, is matched by the reinvigoration of political debate about whether, or how, to resist, contest, manage or adapt to new global conditions. It is immediately apparent that far from 'globalization' bringing about the death of politics, as some fear, it is reilluminating the political terrain. In this chapter, we explore the new terrain by mapping the principal normative visions and theories concerning the proper nature and desirable form of globalization and governance in the twenty-first century. Put simply, the discussion examines the new politics of globalization: what can, and should, be done? Figure 10.1 identifies six leading positions in the debate, although it will become apparent that, as well as marked differences of view, there are some areas of common ground.

One way of understanding the contentious positions in the politics of globalization is to draw on the earlier distinctions between cosmopolitan and communitarian, and globalist and sceptical, thinking. Figure 10.2 seeks to do this by locating them according to their underlying cosmopolitan or communitarian sensibilities and the extent to which they coalesce around a globalist or sceptical argument. The political projects listed differ not only in substantive terms but also with respect to their radicalism (from reform to rejection) and political strategies (from lobbying to protest). Here the focus is necessarily limited to a brief overview of each and how they define the parameters of a politics of globalization. Moreover, while there remain avid defenders of a free market globalized capitalism or, alternatively, a radical relocalization of

185

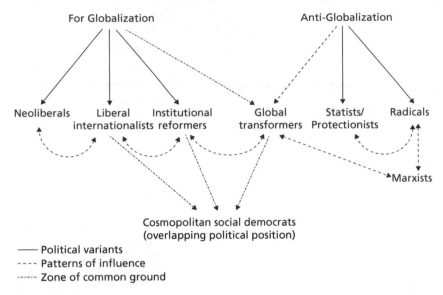

For Globalization   Anti-Globalization

Neoliberals   Liberal   Institutional   Global   Statists/   Radicals
internationalists reformers   transformers Protectionists

Marxists

Cosmopolitan social democrats
(overlapping political position)

—— Political variants
- - - - Patterns of influence
······ Zone of common ground

Figure 10.1   Variants in the politics of globalization

social life, the locus of contention has come to revolve increasingly around the questions of how contemporary globalization can be regulated, or transformed, or alternative types of globalization pursued. The discussion starts with the neoliberals.

Neoliberals

Advocates of neoliberalism have, in general, been committed to the view that political life, like economic life, is (or ought to be) a matter of individual freedom and initiative (see Hayek 1960, 1976; Nozick 1974). Accordingly, a laissez-faire or free market society is the key objective, along with a 'minimal state'. The political programme of neoliberalism includes the extension of the market to more and more areas of life; the creation of a state unburdened by 'excessive' intervention in the economy and social life; and the curtailment of the power of certain groups (for instance, trade unions) to press their aims and goals. A free order, in this view, is incompatible with the enactment of rules which specify how people should use the means at their disposal (Hayek

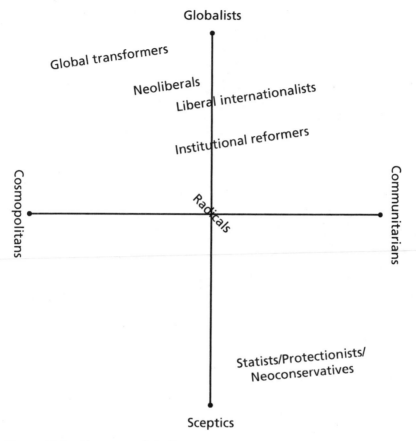

Figure 10.2 The great globalization controversy: political configurations

1960: 231–2). Governments become coercive if they interfere with people's own capacity to determine their interests. Moreover, there is only one sufficiently sensitive mechanism for determining 'collective' choice on an individual basis: the free market itself. When protected by a constitutional state upholding the rule of law, no system provides a mechanism of collective choice as dynamic, innovative and responsive as the operations of the free market (see Held 2006: ch. 7).

The project of neoliberalism has been pursued, first and foremost, through a powerful agenda of economic reform, commonly referred to as the 'Washington Consensus'. This agenda is focused on free trade, capital market liberalization, flexible exchange rates,

Table 10.1 The original and augmented Washington Consensus

The original Washington Consensus
- Fiscal discipline
- Reorientation of public expenditures
- Tax reform
- Financial liberalization
- Unified and competitive exchange rates
- Trade liberalization
- Openness to foreign direct investment
- Privatization
- Deregulation
- Secure property rights

The augmented Washington Consensus: the original list plus:
- Legal/political reform
- Regulatory institutions
- Anti-corruption
- Labour market flexibility
- WTO agreements
- Financial codes and standards
- 'Prudent' capital-account opening
- Non-intermediate exchange rate regimes
- Poverty reduction

Source: Rodrik 2001: 51.

market-determined interest rates, the transfer of assets from the public to the private sector, the tight focus of public expenditure on well-directed social targets, balanced budgets, tax reform, secure property rights and the protection of intellectual property rights (see the top half of table 10.1). It has been the economic orthodoxy for a significant period of the last twenty years in leading OECD countries and in the international financial institutions. It has been prescribed, in particular, by the IMF and World Bank as the policy basis for developing countries.

The 'Washington Consensus' was first set out authoritatively by John Williamson (1990, 1993). While Williamson endorsed most of the policies listed above, he did not advocate free capital mobility (Williamson 2003). Subsequently, the term acquired a very particular conservative connotation as it became linked to the economic agenda of Ronald Reagan and Margaret Thatcher, with their emphasis on free capital movements, monetarism and a minimal state that does not accept responsibility for correcting income inequalities or managing serious externalities (i.e.

domestically generated cross-border problems). We use the term Washington Consensus in this latter sense, although it is important to note that in recent years the original Washington Consensus has been augmented by policies designed to improve public and private institutional effectiveness and competence (see the bottom half of table 10.1).

For the advocates of a neoliberal world order, globalization defines a new epoch in human history in which traditional nation-states are becoming unnatural, even impossible, business units in a global economy (Ohmae 1995: 5). In the view of these thinkers, we are witnessing the emergence of a single global market alongside the principle of global competition as the harbinger of human progress. Economic globalization is leading to the denationalization of economies through the establishment of transnational networks of production, trade and finance. In this increasingly 'borderless' economy, successful national governments are becoming flexible transmission belts for global market forces. Those states that fail to make this adaptation will fall behind and stagnate, eroding the opportunities of their peoples.

For the elites in this new global economy, tacit transnational 'class' allegiances have evolved, cemented by an attachment to neoliberal economic orthodoxy. Even among the marginalized and dispossessed, the worldwide diffusion of a consumerist ideology also imposes a new sense of identity, slowly displacing traditional cultures and ways of life. The global spread of Western liberal democracy further reinforces the sense of an emerging civilization defined by universal standards of economic and political organization. Governance of this order is conducted principally through the disciplines of the world market combined with minimal forms of international governance designed to promote global economic integration through the dismantling of barriers to commerce and investment. Economic power and political power are becoming effectively denationalized and diffused (Ohmae 1995: 149). As a result, globalization embodies the potential for creating a radically new world order which, according to neoliberals, will encourage human freedom and prosperity unencumbered by the dictates of stifling public bureaucracy and the power politics of states. This state of affairs represents nothing less than the fundamental re-formation of world order to fit with the enduring logic of human freedom.

Liberal internationalists

Recognizing the challenges posed by growing global interconnect-edness – as opposed to a world shaped ever more harmoniously by global competition and global markets – liberal internationalists consider that political necessity requires, and will help bring about, a more cooperative world order. Three factors are central to this position: growing interdependence, democracy and global institutions. Leading liberal internationalists of the nineteenth century argued that economic interdependence generates propitious conditions for international cooperation between governments and peoples (see Hinsley 1986). Since their destinies are bound together by many serious economic and political issues, states, as rational actors, come to recognize that international cooperation is essential to managing their common fate. Secondly, the spread of democracy establishes a foundation for international peace. Democracies are constrained in their actions by the principles of openness and accountability to their electorates. In these conditions, governments are less likely to engage in secretive politics, to pursue manipulative geopolitics or to go to war (Howard 1981). Thirdly, through the creation of international law and institutions to regulate international interdependencies, greater harmony between states can be maintained. Moreover, in an increasingly interdependent world the political authority and jurisdiction of these international institutions has a natural tendency to expand, as the welfare and security of domestic society becomes increasingly bound up with the welfare and security of global society.

In the twentieth century, liberal internationalist views played a leading role in the aftermath of both the First and Second World Wars. The creation of the League of Nations, with its hope for a 'world safe for democracy', was infused with such ideology, as was the foundation of the UN system. In the context of the New World Order after the Cold War, liberal internationalist ideas have acquired renewed vitality but have been adapted to fit new circumstances (Long 1995). One of the most systematic statements of this position can be found in the report of the Commission on Global Governance, *Our Global Neighbourhood* (1995). The report recognizes the profound political impact of globalization: 'The shortening of distance, the multiplying of links, the deepening of interdependence: all these factors, and their interplay, have been transforming the world into a neighbourhood' (1995: 43). Its main concern is to address the problem of democratic governance in this new 'global neighbourhood'. As the report asserts:

> It is fundamentally important that governance should be under-pinned by democracy at all levels and ultimately by the rule of enforceable law . . . As at the national level, so in the global neigh-bourhood: the democratic principle must be ascendant. The need for greater democracy arises out of the close linkage between legitimacy and effectiveness . . . as the role of international institutions in global governance grows, the need to ensure that they are democratic also increases. (1995: 48, 66)

But the report is emphatic that global governance 'does not imply world government or world federalism' (1995: 336). Rather, it understands global governance as a set of pluralistic arrangements by which states, international organizations, international regimes, non-governmental organizations, citizen movements and markets combine to regulate or govern aspects of global affairs. This position is also advanced in the recent report for the UN High-Level Panel (2005).

To achieve a more secure, just and democratic world order *Our Global Neighbourhood* proposes a multifaceted strategy of international institutional reform and the nurturing of a new collaborative ethos 'based upon the principles of consultation, transparency, and accountability. . . . There is no alternative to working together and using collective power to create a better world' (Commission on Global Governance 1995: 2, 5). In key respects, the existing system of global governance cannot ensure this ambition without substantial reform; and reform must be based on a political strategy of international institutional transformation and the nurturing of a new global civic ethic. Central to this position is a reformed United Nations system buttressed by the strengthening of regional forms of international governance, such as the EU. Through the establishment of a peoples' assembly and a Forum of (Global) Civil Society, both associated with the UN General Assembly, the world's peoples are to be represented directly and indirectly in the institutions of global governance. Moreover, the Commission proposes that individuals and groups be given a right of petition to the UN through a Council of Petitions, which will recommend action to the appropriate agency. Combined with the deeper entrenchment of a common set of global rights and responsibilities, the aim is to strengthen notions of global citizenship. An Economic Security Council is proposed, to coordinate global economic governance, making it more open and accountable. Democratic forms of governance within states are to be nurtured and strengthened through international support mechanisms, while the principles of sovereignty and non-intervention are to be adapted 'in ways that recognize the need to balance the rights of states with the rights of people, and the interests of nations with the interests of the global neighbourhood' (Commission on Global Governance 1995: 337). Binding all these reforms together is a commitment to the nurturing of a new global civic ethic based on 'core values that all humanity could uphold: respect for life, liberty, justice and equity, mutual respect, caring, and integrity'. Central to this global civic ethic is the principle of participation in governance at all levels from the local to the global.

Institutional reformers

The management of the social, economic and political dislocation arising from contemporary processes of globalization is the starting point of a key strand of work focused on radical institutional reform, anchored in the United Nations Development Programme's initiative on providing global public goods (see Kaul, Grunberg and Stern 1999). Public goods, the UNDP programme maintains, can no longer be equated with state-provided goods alone. Diverse state and non-state actors shape and contribute to the resources and rule systems of public life – and they need to do so if some of the most profound challenges of globalization are to be met. Moreover, since these challenges reach across the public domain in all countries and regions, it is only through an extended public dialogue about the nature and provision of public goods that a new, more accountable and just global order can be built.

Advocates of this view argue that many of today's global public policy crises – from global warming to the spread of AIDS – can be understood best through the lens of public goods theory, and that

192

the common interest is often best protected by the provision of such goods at the global level. However, the existing institutions of global governance do not enable the effective provision of global public goods because they are weakened by three crucial gaps. In the first instance, there is a jurisdictional gap – the discrepancy between a globalized world and national, separate units of policy-making, giving rise to the problem of who is responsible for many pressing global issues, particularly externalities. Second, there is a serious participation gap – the failure of the existing international system to give adequate voice to many leading global actors, state and non-state. Civil society actors are too often excluded from the decision-making structures of leading states and IGOs, which resemble more the shape of 'silos', loaded from above, than a transparent and open system, accessible on all sides. Third, there is an incentive gap – the challenges posed by the fact that, in the absence of a supranational entity to regulate the supply and use of global public goods, many states will seek to free ride and/or fail to find durable collective solutions to pressing transnational problems.

In order to overcome these constraints, global public management theory advocates the buttressing and reform of the role of states and international institutions to enhance the supply of global public goods. The assumption is that, *pace* neoliberal thinkers, states remain the key agents through which public decisions are made and implemented, and that an effective continuum has to be created between national and international policy-making (Kaul, Grunberg and Stern 1999: xix–xxxviii). Addressing each of the three gaps provides an agenda for enhanced multilateral cooperation. The jurisdictional gap can be closed by extending cooperation among states through the establishment, for example, of clear 'externality profiles', which could become the basis for enhancing reciprocity between them and for the internalization of externalities by all parties (building back into national communities the external costs and benefits of a policy). If such initiatives could be linked to establishing clear maps of the jurisdictional challenges created by transnational public problems, then a basis might be established not only for holding states to account for the external problems they generate but also for gleaning where new institution building must take place, that is, where the existing states system needs development and supplementation.

The participatory gap can be addressed by adopting a tripartite approach to decision-making, in which governments share the opportunity for a voice with civil society and business. 'All actors must have a voice, have an appropriate opportunity to make the contribution expected of them and have access to the goods that result' (Kaul, Grunberg and Stern 1999: xxix). Leading agents of politics, business and civil society must become active participants in the setting of public agendas, in the formulation of policy ideas and in deliberations on them.

Finally, the incentive gap can be closed by creating explicit incentives and disincentives to overcome the frictions of international cooperation, through the full provision of information, effective surveillance to reduce cheating and ensure compliance, an equitable distribution of the benefits of collaboration, a strengthening of the role of epistemic communities as providers of 'objective' knowledge and information, and through encouraging the activities of NGOs as mechanisms of accountability when they name and shame weak or failing policies. No one incentive package will fit all issue areas, but without such mechanisms global policy problems will be much harder to solve (see also Kaul et al. 2003; Held 2004: ch. 6).

Global transformers

There is considerable overlap between some of the principles and objectives of the liberal internationalists and institutional reformers and the fourth position to be set out here, referred to as that of the global transformers. This position accepts that globalization, as a set of processes which alter the spatial organization of socio-economic relations and transactions, is neither new nor inherently unjust or undemocratic (see Held et al. 1999). Rather, the issue it poses is one about its desirable *form* and distributional consequences. The argument is that there is nothing inevitable or fixed about its current form, marked by huge asymmetries of power, opportunity and life chances. Globalization can be better and more fairly governed, regulated and shaped. This distinguishes the global transformers from those who argue for alternatives to globalization – whether protectionism or localism – and those who simply seek to manage it more effectively. In this sense, their position is neither straightforwardly for nor against globalization; at issue here are its core organizational principles and institutions.

Advocates of the transformationalist position maintain that recasting globalization needs to be conceived as a 'double-sided process' (see Held 1995; Linklater 1998; Archibugi, Held and Köhler 1998; Held 2004). By a double-sided process – or process of double democratization – is meant not just the deepening of political and social reform within a national community, involving the democratization of states and civil societies over time, but also the creation of greater transparency, accountability and democracy across territorial borders. Democracy in the new millennium must allow citizens to gain access to, and render accountable, the social, economic and political processes which cut across and transform their traditional community boundaries. Each citizen of a state will have to learn to become a 'cosmopolitan citizen' as well; that is, a person capable of mediating between national traditions and alternative forms of life. Citizenship in a democratic polity of the future, it is argued, is likely to involve a growing mediating role: a role which encompasses dialogue with the traditions and discourses of others with the aim of expanding the horizons of one's own framework of meaning and prejudice, and increasing the scope of mutual understanding. Political agents who can 'reason from the point of view of others' will be better equipped to resolve, and resolve fairly, the new and challenging transboundary issues that create overlapping communities of fate. In addition, the global transformers maintain that, if many contemporary forms of power are to become accountable and if many of the complex issues that affect us all – locally, nationally, regionally and globally – are to be democratically regulated, people will have to have access to, and membership in, diverse political communities.

The core of this project involves reconceiving legitimate political activity in a manner which emancipates it from its traditional anchor in fixed borders and delimited territories and, instead, articulates it as an attribute of basic democratic arrangements or basic democratic law which can, in principle, be entrenched and drawn on in diverse self-regulating associations – from cities and subnational regions to nation-states, supranational regions and wider global networks. It is argued that such a process of emancipation has already begun as political authority and legitimate forms of governance are diffused 'below', 'above' and 'alongside' the nation-state. But this 'cosmopolitan' political project is in favour of a radical extension of this process so long as it is circumscribed and delimited by a commitment to a far-reaching cluster of democratic rights and duties. It proposes a series of short- and long-term measures in the conviction that, through a process of progressive, incremental change, geopolitical forces will come to be socialized into democratic agencies and practices (Held 1995: part III; 2002b).

At stake, in the first instance, is the reform of the UN system. Reform in this context means the dislodging of the geopolitical settlement of 1945 which shapes the distribution of power and authority throughout the UN today. Altering the veto and voting structure in the Security Council is a pressing issue for the impartial generation, application and administration of international rules and regulations. The creation of a UN second chamber would aid this outcome if it were modelled not on principles of geopolitical representation, as found in the UN General Assembly, but on stakeholding and deliberative lines. A second chamber of this kind could stand as a microcosm of global society and represent the deliberations of leading parties. The creation of effective public assemblies at the global and regional level must complement those at local and national levels. In addition, IGOs need to be opened up to public examination and agenda-setting by key stakeholders. Not only should such bodies be transparent in their activities, requiring, for example, an international freedom of information treaty, but they should be accessible and open to public scrutiny in all aspects of their affairs. The establishment of new global governance structures with responsibility for addressing global poverty, welfare and related issues is also vital to offset the power and influence of the predominantly market-oriented agencies such as the IMF and WTO (even if the latter are reformed, as they must be in due course).

Alongside new ways of fostering democracy and social justice beyond borders, the global transformers argue that there is a need for new modes of administering and implementing international agreements and international law, including an enhanced capacity for peacekeeping and peace-making. Ideally, such a capacity could be built by creating a permanent independent military force

196

recruited directly from among individuals who volunteer from all countries. Finally, none of this can be effective without new income streams to both fund these developments and create the basis, in principle, for autonomous and impartial political authority at the global level. New resource flows are indispensable, whether in the form of a Tobin tax on global financial speculation, a resource use tax or parallel mechanisms. The advocacy of new cosmopolitan institutions would descend into high-mindedness without a commitment to addressing the desperate conditions of the worst off, by cancelling the debt of the poorest countries, by reversing the net outflow of capital from the South to the North, and by generating new means to invest in the infrastructure of human autonomy – health, education, welfare and so on (see Held 2006: ch 11).

Statists/Protectionists/Neoconservatives

The position referred to here as statist/protectionist is, of course, very different from the above. Moreover, more than the other political positions discussed so far, it is best seen as representing a range of views, only aspects of which overlap. In the first instance, many strong arguments for the primacy of national communities, nation-states and multinational states in the world order are not necessarily protectionist in the sense of being hostile to an open world economy and free trade. These arguments are often more about the essential means, that is, strong state structures, to ensure successful participation in open markets and good governance arrangements than about withdrawal or delinking from the rest of the world (Cattaui 2001). Second, these arguments are frequently associated with a marked scepticism about the globalization thesis (a scepticism explored in chapters 2–7 of this book). This scepticism concludes that the extent of contemporary 'globalization' is wholly exaggerated (Hirst 1997; Hirst and Thompson 1999). Moreover, it holds that the rhetoric of globalization is seriously flawed and politically naive since it underestimates the enduring power of national governments to regulate international economic activity. Rather than being out of control, the forces of internationalization themselves depend on the regulatory power of national governments to ensure continuing economic liberalization.

Hand in hand with this view is an emphasis on the necessity of enhancing or reinforcing the capacities of states to govern – to help organize, in other words, the security, economic well-being and welfare of their citizens. The priority is to build competent state capacity; that is, to deepen it where it already exists in the developed world and to nurture it where it is most urgently needed – in the poorest countries. Without a monopoly of the means of violence, disorder cannot be checked, and the welfare of all in a political community is likely to be threatened. But even with a monopoly of violence, good government does not necessarily follow: corruption has to be checked, political skills acquired, human rights upheld, accountability assured, and investment in the infrastructure of human development – health, education and welfare – maintained. Without strong national governing capacities, little can be achieved in the long run. In this regard, the economic success of the developmental states of East Asia is a telling example, since their success was the product of government-inspired, and not laissez-faire, policies (Cattaui 2001; see Leftwich 2000). Nurturing domestic industries, limiting foreign competition, and restricting cross-border capital flows are symptomatic of new forms of statism which have some aspects in common with old-style mercantilism (see chapter 11).

Statist and protectionist positions become more closely connected when the politics of national communities is associated with a hostility to, or outright rejection of, global links and institutions, especially when they are perceived to be driven by American, Western or foreign commercial interests.* Aspects of the latter are often thought of as posing a direct threat to local or national identities or to religious traditions. What is uppermost here is the protection of a distinctive culture, tradition, language or religion, which binds people together and offers a valued common ethos and sense of common fate. If the latter is tied to a political structure which defends and represents a community, it can clearly have huge symbolic and national significance. This can give rise to a spectrum of political positions, from the secular nationalist (represented by

---

* There were elements of this in the 'no' votes in France and Holland in 2005 concerning whether to adopt a new European constitution, which was proposed in the hope of streamlining EU decision-making.

strong national cultural traditions) to fundamentalist religious groupings (such as radical Islam). It is important to stress that a significant diversity of political projects can be located along this spectrum. While some reinforce the politics of the primacy of the national interest, and lead to an emphasis on geopolitics or geoeconomics as the inevitable struggle of warring states and communities, others pose a fundamental challenge to all political structures, national or global, which do not conform to a particular identity (Huntington 1996). Neoconservatives in the US thus advocate the unilateral exercise of US power to expand the reach of 'democratic capitalism' and to prevent the rise of non-liberal or non-Western powers which may challenge US global primacy.

But even if a clash of cultures or civilizations is not behind antipathy to global forces, statist/protectionist positions can be linked to deeply rooted scepticism or antipathy to Western power and dominance. In this respect, the argument tends to interpret global governance and economic internationalization as primarily Western projects, the main object of which is to sustain the primacy of the West in world affairs. As one observer put it, 'international order and "international solidarity" will always be slogans of those who feel strong enough to impose them on others' (Carr 1981: 87). According to this view, only a fundamental challenge to dominant geopolitical and geoeconomic interests will produce a more pluralist and legitimate world order in which particular identities, traditions and worldviews can flourish unhindered by hegemonic forces. In this regard, it has much in common with the last set of positions to be explored below.

Radicals

While the advocates of liberal internationalism, institutional reform and global democratic transformations emphasize the necessity of strengthening and enhancing global governance arrangements, proponents of the radical project stress the need for governance mechanisms based on the establishment of accountable and self-governing communities (cf. Burnheim 1985; Walker 1994; Falk 1995b; Beetham 2005: ch. 6). The radical project is concerned to establish the conditions necessary to empower people to take

199

control of their own lives and to create communities based on participation, the common good and sustainability. For many radicals, the agents of change are to be found in existing civil society movements.

In the last few decades, new regional and global transnational actors have emerged, contesting the terms of globalization – including new social movements such as the environmental movement, the women's movement and the anti-globalization or Social Justice movement. These are the 'new' voices of an emergent transnational public domain, heard, for instance, at the Rio Conference on the Environment, the Cairo Conference on Population Control, the Beijing Conference on Women, the Johannesburg Conference on Sustainable Development, and on the streets in Seattle, Prague, Genoa and London. Some hold that these developments indicate the beginnings of 'globalization from below' – the 'coming out' of global activism and global civil society.

According to Mary Kaldor (2003), 'global civil society' emerged against the backdrop of the spread of demands for democratization around the world after the end of the Cold War and with the intensifying process of global interconnectedness. It reflects a demand for greater personal autonomy and self-organization in highly complex and uncertain societies, where power and decision-making increasingly escape national boundaries. Kaldor interprets this not as a call to abolish states or the state system per se, but rather as an aspiration to extend the impact and efficacy of human rights, to deepen the international rule of law guaranteed by a range of interlocking institutions, and to develop citizen networks which might monitor, contest and put pressure on these institutions. She summarizes the point thus: 'what we might describe as global civil society would be the interaction of those groups, networks and movements who provide a voice for individuals in global arenas and who act as . . . the transmission belts between the individual and global institutions'. Kaldor sees global civil society as 'a contested process, in which different views about the world's future can be expressed' (2003: 560, 561).

Other radical thinkers find in the emergence of global activism a firmer attachment to the achievement of social and economic equality, the establishment of the necessary conditions for self-development, and the creation of self-governing political structures

200

(Klein 2002). The radical model, thus understood, is less about (as Kaldor conceives it) 'pressuring' the states system to open up and change, and more about a 'bottom up' vision of civilizing world order. It represents a conception of 'humane governance' which is grounded in the existence of a multiplicity of communities and movements, as opposed to the individualism and appeals to rational self-interest of neoliberalism and of current voting systems. Features of this model can be found in experiments in many countries devolving decision-making to local people. Examples which have attracted much attention include the system of participatory budgeting in the city of Porto Alegre in southern Brazil, and the campaign for decentralized planning in the state of Kerala in southern India (see Beetham 2005: 134–6).

Radical thinkers in general are reluctant to prescribe substantive constitutional or institutional blueprints for a more democratic world order, since this represents the centralized, modern, 'top down' statist approach to political life which they reject. Accordingly, the emphasis is typically on identifying the principles on which politics might be constructed irrespective of the particular institutional forms it might take. Through a programme of resistance and the 'politicization' of social life, the view is that social movements are defining a 'new progressive politics' which involves 'explorations of new ways of acting, new ways of knowing and being in the world, and new ways of acting together through emerging solidarities' (Walker 1994: 147–8). As Walker suggests, 'one lesson . . . is that people are not as powerless as they are made to feel. The grand structures that seem so distant and so immovable are clearly identifiable and resistible on an everyday basis. Not to act is to act. Everyone can change habits and expectations or refuse to accept that the problems are out there in someone else's backyard' (1994: 159–60). Underlying this radical model of change is an attachment to normative theories of direct democracy and participatory democracy (Held 2006).

There are echoes here of Rousseau's 'republican vision' and New Left ideals of community politics and participatory democracy. But the radical model also draws on Marxist critiques of liberal democracy, as is evident in the language of equality, solidarity, emancipation and the transformation of existing power relations. The achievement of 'real democracy' is, thus, sometimes conceived as inseparable from the achievement of social and economic equality, the establishment of the conditions for self-governance, and the creation of strong political communities (see Callinicos 2002). Encouraging and developing in citizens a sense of simultaneous belonging to local and global communities of interest is also central to the search for new models of social, political and economic organization consonant with the principle of self-government. However, it is recognized that 'self-government today . . . requires a politics that plays itself out in a multiplicity of settings, from neighbourhoods to nations to the world as a whole. Such a politics requires citizens who can think and act as multiply situated selves' (Sandel 1996: 351).

While the politics of radicalism is rooted in protest-driven concerns and, frequently, in single-issue campaigns, there are signs that elements of contemporary protest movements are moving beyond this agenda, and developing institutional reform programmes not unlike those found among the institutional reformers and global transformers. At the recent meetings of the World Social Forum in Porto Alegre, for instance, several recommendations for restructuring aspects of globalization were put on the agenda, from improving corporate governance and placing limits on the freedom of capital, to measures to protect core labour standards and safeguard the environment. The focus of attack of these proposals is 'unfettered globalization' and 'unrestricted corporate power', rather than globalization per se. A new emphasis on working with, and the reform of, the UN system creates other fruitful avenues of overlap with elements of some of the other positions set out above. However, overlap in this regard will never be complete, since some radical positions – for instance, various anarchist groupings and those notorious for attacking Starbucks at the 1999 Seattle WTO meeting – do not seek common ground or a new reconciliation of views. In this respect, they are no different from the more extreme neoliberalizers who put their faith first and foremost in deregulated markets.

The different normative conceptions of global politics and its possible future trajectories are summarized in table 10.2. The table sets out the main variants in the politics of globalization and identifies each position's conception of guiding ethical principles, who should govern, the most urgent global reforms, the proper form of

Table 10.2 Models of global politics: a summary and comparison

	1 Neoliberals	2 Liberal internationalists	3 Institutional reformers
Guiding ethical principle(s)	Individual liberty	Human rights and shared responsibilities	Collaborative ethos built on the principles of transparency, consultation and accountability
Who should govern?	Individuals through market exchanges and 'minimum' states	The people through governments, accountable international regimes and organizations	The people through civil society, effective states and international institutions
Key reforms	Dismantling of bureaucratic state organizations and deregulation of markets	International free trade, and the creation of transparent and open international governance arrangements	Widening political participation, tripartite approach to national and international decision-making, secure provision of global public goods
Desired form of globalization	Global free markets, rule of law, with 'safety net' for worst off	Accelerating interdependence through free trade, embedded in cooperative forms of intergovernmentalism	Regulated global processes alongside democratic global governance
Mode of political transformation	Effective political leadership, minimizing bureaucratic regulation and creating international free-trade order	Strengthening of human rights regime, environmental regulation along side reform of global governance	Buttressing role of state and civil society to enhance scope for collective action, and reform of governance, from the local to global level

(continued)

Table 10.2 (continued)

	4 Global transformers	5 Statists/Protectionists/ Neoconservatives	6 Radicals
Guiding ethical principle(s)	Political equality, social equal liberty, justice and shared responsibilities	National interest, shared socio-cultural identity and common political ethos	Equality, the common good, environmental sustainability
Who should govern?	The people through multilayered governance arrangements from local to global	States, peoples and national markets	The people through self-governing communities
Key reforms	Strengthening of diverse membership in overlapping political communities, development of stakeholder and deliberative forums from local to global levels, buttressing role of international law	Strengthened state capacity to govern, international political cooperation (where necessary)	Self-managed enterprises, workplaces and communities, alongside democratic governance arrangements
Desired form of globalization	Multilevel democratic cosmopolitan polity, regulating global processes to ensure the equal autonomy of all	Reinforced capacity of national states, effective geopolitics	Localization, subnational regionalization, deglobalization
Mode of political transformation	Reconstruction of global governance through democratization of states, civil society and transnational institutions	State reform and geopolitics	Social movements, non-governmental organizations, 'bottom up' social change

globalization, and how and with what means that desirable form might be achieved. What is striking about the table is both the obvious differences of position found in columns 1, 5 and 6 and the areas of overlap between positions 2, 3 and 4. We return to the significance of this overlap in the next two chapters.

11

Reconstructing World Order: Towards Cosmopolitan Social Democracy

The 'great globalization debate' identifies some of the most fundamental issues of our time. It poses key questions about the organization of human affairs and the trajectory of global social change. It also raises matters which go to the centre of political discussion, illuminating the strategic choices societies confront and the constraints which define the possibilities of plausible political action.

Are the principal accounts of globalization elaborated here fundamentally at odds and contradictory in all respects, or is a productive synthesis possible? In order to address this question, it is important to separate out the clash of views between the globalists and sceptics (explored in chapters 2–7), and between the leading positions in respect of the politics of globalization (examined in chapter 10). While the issues raised in the debate among the globalizers and their critics cut across both the analytical and political, it is important to separate them in order to make an initial assessment. It is not the purpose of this volume to address these matters at length and, indeed, we have done this elsewhere (see Held et al. 1999; Held and McGrew 2000, 2002a, 2002b). But a number of points are worth emphasizing by way of a conclusion, starting with the exchange between the globalizers and sceptics. These points indicate that there is more to say about globalization and its limits than has been said in the debate so far.

In the first instance, the debate between the globalizers and sceptics raises profound questions of interpretation (see chapter 8). It demonstrates that facts do not speak for themselves, and depend for their meaning on complex interpretative frameworks. There are clashes involving the conceptualization and interpretation of some of the most critical evidence. However, it would be wrong to conclude from this that the marshalled evidence is of secondary importance; often the kind of evidence proffered by both sides differs markedly. For example, sceptics put primary emphasis on the organization of production and trade (stressing the geographical rootedness of MNCs and the marginal changes in trade–GDP ratios over the course of the twentieth century), while globalists tend to focus on financial deregulation and the explosive growth of global financial markets over the last twenty-five years. Sceptics stress the continuing primacy of the national interest and the cultural traditions of national communities, while globalists point to the growing significance of transnational political problems – such as worldwide pollution, global warming and world trade disputes – which create a growing sense of the common fate of humankind. A considered response to the debate must weigh all these considerations before coming to a settled view.

Secondly, the debate demonstrates that there is something to be learned from both sides; it is implausible to maintain that either side comprises mere rhetoric or ideology. The sceptical case has significant historical depth and needs to be carefully dissected if the globalists' position is to be adequately defended. Many of the empirical claims raised by the sceptics' arguments, for example concerning the historical significance of contemporary trade and direct investment flows, require detailed examination. But having said this, the globalist interpretation in its various forms does illuminate important transformations going on in the spatial organization of power – the changing nature of communication, the diffusion and speeding up of technical change, the spread of capitalist economic development, the extension of global governance arrangements – even if its understanding of these matters sometimes exaggerates their scale and impact.

Thirdly, each position has different strengths and weaknesses. The leading claims of the globalists are at their strongest when focused on institutional and processual change in the domains of economics (the establishment of a global trading system, the integration of financial markets, and the spread of transnational production systems), politics (the development of global political processes and the entrenchment of layers of governance across political boundaries) and security (the changing nature of warfare and the challenge of environmental degradation, particularly climate change). But they are at their most vulnerable when considering the movements of people, their allegiances and their cultural and moral identities. For the available evidence suggests that migration is only just reaching the levels today that it attained in the late nineteenth century (measured in terms of extent and intensity); that the role of national (and local) cultures remains central to public life in nearly all political communities; and that imported foreign products are constantly read and reinterpreted in novel ways by national audiences, that is, they become rapidly indigenized (Miller 1992; Liebes and Katz 1993; J. B. Thompson 1995). Given the deep roots of national cultures and ethnohistories, and the many ways they are often refashioned, the fact that there is no common global way of thinking can hardly be a surprise (see chapter 3). Despite the vast flows of information, imagery and people around the world, there are only a few signs, at best, of a universal or global history in the making, and few signs of a decline in the importance of nationalism.

There has been a shift, as the globalists argue, from government to global governance, from the modern state to a multilayered system of power and authority, from relatively discrete national communication and economic systems to their more complex and diverse enmeshment at regional and global levels (see chapters 2 and 5; Held et al. 1999: chs 2–3). On the other hand, there are few grounds for thinking that a concomitant widespread pluralization of political identities has taken place. One exception to this is to be found among the elites of the global order – the networks of experts and specialists, senior administrative personnel and transnational business executives – and those who track and contest their activities, the loose constellation of social movements, trade unionists and (a few) politicians and intellectuals. However, even the latter groups have a significant diversity of interest and purpose, a diversity clearly manifest in the broad range of those who constitute the 'anti-globalization' protesters of Seattle, Genoa and elsewhere. The globalists' emphasis on the transformation of political identities is overstated. What one commentator noted about the European Union can be adapted to apply, in many respects, to the rest of the world: the central paradox is that governance is becoming increasingly a multilevel, intricately institutionalized and spatially dispersed activity, while representation, loyalty and identity remain stubbornly rooted in traditional ethnic, regional and national communities (Wallace 1999: 21).

One important qualification needs to be added to the above argument, one which focuses on generational change. While those who have some commitment to the global order as a whole and to the institutions of global governance constitute a distinct minority, a generational divide is evident. Compared to the generations brought up in the years prior to 1939, those born after the Second World War are more likely to see themselves as internationalists, to support the UN system and to be in favour of the free movement of migrants and trade. Examining Eurobarometer data and findings from the World Values Survey (involving over seventy countries), one observer concludes that 'cohort analysis suggests that in the long term public opinion is moving in a more international direction' (Norris 2000: 175). Generations brought up with Yahoo, MTV and CNN affirm this trend and are more likely to have some sense of global identification, although it remains to be seen whether this tendency crystallizes into a majority position and whether it generates a clearly focused political orientation.

Fourthly, while there are very significant differences between the globalists and sceptics, it is important to note some common ground. The debate, as chapter 8 shows, does not simply comprise ships passing in the night. Indeed, both sides would accept that

1 There has been marked growth in recent decades in economic interconnectedness within and among regions, albeit with multifaceted and uneven consequences across different communities.
2 Interregional and global (political, economic and cultural) competition challenges old hierarchies and generates new inequalities of wealth, power, privilege and knowledge.
3 Transnational and transborder problems, such as the spread of genetically modified foodstuffs, money laundering and global terrorism, have become increasingly salient, calling into question aspects of the traditional role, functions and institutions of accountability of national government.
4 There has been an expansion of international governance at regional and global levels – from the EU to the WTO – which

poses significant normative questions about the kind of world order being constructed and whose interests it serves.

5 These developments require new modes of thinking about politics, economics and cultural change. They also require imaginative responses from politicians and policy-makers about the future possibilities and forms of effective political regulation and democratic accountability.

All sides would accept that there has been a significant shift in the links and relations among political communities. That is to say, that there has been a growth in economic and political communications within and across states and regions; that transnational and transborder problems have become pressing across the world; that there has been an expansion in the number and role of intergovernmental organizations, international non-governmental organizations and social movements in regional and global affairs; and that existing political mechanisms and institutions, anchored in nation-states, will be insufficient in the future to handle the pressing challenges of regional and global problems, centred, for instance, on global inequalities and social injustice. In order to draw out the significance of these points of agreement, it is helpful to focus on the challenges to traditional conceptions of political community posed by global social, economic and political change.

The new context of political community

Political communities can no longer be considered (if they ever could with any validity) simply as 'discrete worlds' or as self-enclosed political spaces; they are enmeshed in complex structures of overlapping forces, relations and networks. Clearly, these are structured by inequality and hierarchy, as the sceptics insist. However, even the most powerful among them – including the most powerful states – do not remain unaffected by the changing conditions and processes of regional and global entrenchment. A few points can be emphasized to clarify further the changing relations between modern nation-states. All indicate an increase in the extensiveness, intensity, velocity and impact of international and transnational relations, and all suggest important questions about the evolving character of political community.

The locus of effective political power can no longer be assumed to be simply national governments – effective power is shared and bartered by diverse forces and agencies at national, regional and international levels. All parties agree on this. Furthermore, the idea of a political community of fate – of a self-determining collectivity – can no longer meaningfully be located within the boundaries of a single nation-state alone. Some of the most fundamental forces and processes which determine the nature of life chances – from the organization of world trade to global warming – are now beyond the reach of individual nation-states to resolve by themselves. The political world at the start of the twenty-first century is marked by a significant series of new types of political externalities or 'boundary problems'. In the past, of course, nation-states principally resolved their differences over boundary matters by pursuing 'reasons of state' backed by diplomatic initiatives, and ultimately by coercive means. But this power logic is singularly inadequate and inappropriate to resolve the many complex issues, from economic regulation to resource depletion and environmental degradation, which engender – at seemingly ever greater speeds – an intermeshing of 'national fortunes'. In a world where powerful states make decisions not just for their peoples but for others as well, and where transnational actors and forces cut across the boundaries of national communities in diverse ways, the questions of who should be accountable to whom, and on what basis, do not easily resolve themselves. Political space for the development and pursuit of effective government and the accountability of power is no longer coterminous with a delimited political territory. Forms of political organization now involve a complex deterritorialization and reterritorialization of political authority (see chapter 2; Rosenau 1997).

Contemporary global change is associated with a transformation of state power as the roles and functions of states are rearticulated, reconstituted and re-embedded at the intersection of regionalizing and globalizing networks and systems. The simple formulations of the loss, diminution or erosion of state power can misrepresent this change. Indeed, such a language involves a failure to conceptualize adequately the nature of power and its complex manifestations, since it represents a crude zero-sum view of power. The latter conception is particularly unhelpful in attempting to understand the apparently contradictory position of states under contemporary conditions. For while global economic change is engendering, for instance, a reconfiguration of state–market relations, states and international public authorities are deeply implicated in this very process (for example, through the weakening or removal of national capital controls). Global economic change by no means necessarily translates into a diminution of state power; rather, it is altering the conditions under which state power can be exercised. In other domains, such as the military, states have adopted an activist posture through the creation of alliances and coalitions, while in the political domain they have been central to the explosive growth and institutionalization of regional and global governance. These are not developments which can be explained convincingly in the language of the decline, erosion or loss of state power per se. In addition, such formulations mistakenly presume that state power was much greater in previous epochs; and states, especially in the developed world, on almost every measure, are far more powerful than their predecessors (Mann 1997). The apparent simultaneous weakening and expansion of state power is symptomatic of an underlying structural transformation – a global shift in the organization of power and authority. This is nowhere so evident as in respect of state sovereignty and autonomy, which constitute the very foundations of the modern state.

There are many good reasons for doubting the theoretical and empirical basis of the claim that states are being eclipsed by contemporary patterns of globalization. The position we wish to develop is critical of many of the arguments of both the globalists and the sceptics. While regional and global interaction networks are developing and strengthening, they have variable and multiple impacts across different countries. Moreover, national sovereignty today, even in regions with intensive overlapping and divided authority structures, has not been wholly subverted. Rather, it is the case that, in such areas and regions, sovereignty has been transformed. It has been displaced as an illimitable, indivisible and exclusive form of public power, embodied in an individual state, and embedded in a system of multiple, often pooled, power centres and overlapping spheres of authority (see Held

212

2002b). There has been, in other words, a reconfiguration of political power.

We call this interpretation of shifts in relations of power neither globalist nor sceptic but transformationalist. It accepts a modified version of the globalization argument, emphasizing that while contemporary patterns of global political, economic and communication flows are historically unprecedented, the direction of these remains uncertain, since globalization is a contingent historical process replete with conflicts and tensions. At issue is a dynamic and open-ended conception of where globalization might be leading and the kind of world order it might prefigure. In comparison with the sceptical and globalist accounts, the transformationalist position makes no claims about the future trajectory of globalization; nor does it evaluate the present in relation to some single, fixed ideal-type 'globalized world', whether a global market or a global civilization. Rather, the transformationalist account emphasizes that globalization is a long-term historical process which is inscribed with challenges and significantly shaped by conjunctural factors.

At the core of the transformationalist case is a belief that contemporary globalization is reconstituting or 're-engineering' the power, functions and authority of national governments. While not disputing that many states still retain the ultimate legal claim to effective supremacy over what occurs within their own territories, the transformationalist position holds that this should be juxtaposed with, and understood in relation to, the expanding jurisdiction of institutions of international governance and the constraints of, as well as the obligations derived from, international law. This is especially evident in the EU, where sovereign power is divided between international, national and local authorities, but it is also evident in the operation of IGOs such as the WTO (Goodman 1997). However, even where sovereignty still appears intact, states no longer, if they ever did, retain sole command of what transpires within their own territorial boundaries. Complex global systems, from the financial to the ecological, connect the fate of communities in one locale to the fate of communities in distant regions of the world. Furthermore, global infrastructures of communication and transport support new forms of economic and social organization which transcend national boundaries. Sites of power and the subjects of power may be literally, as well as metaphorically, oceans apart. In these circumstances, the notion of the nation-state as a self-governing, autonomous unit appears to belong more to the category of normative claims than to that of descriptive statements. The modern institution of territorially circumscribed sovereign rule appears somewhat anomalous juxtaposed with the transnational organization of many aspects of contemporary economic and social life (Sandel 1996). Globalization, in this account, is associated with a transformation or an 'unbundling' of the relationship between sovereignty, territoriality and political power (Ruggie 1993a; Sassen 1996).

While for many people – politicians, political activists and academics – contemporary globalization is associated with new limits to politics and the erosion of state power, the argument developed here is critical of such political fatalism. For contemporary globalization has not only triggered or reinforced the significant politicization of a growing array of issue areas, but it has been accompanied by an extraordinary growth of institutionalized arenas and networks of political mobilization, surveillance, decision-making and regulatory activity which transcend national political jurisdictions. This has expanded enormously the capacity for, and scope of, political activity and the exercise of political authority. In this sense, globalization is not beyond regulation and control. Globalization does not prefigure the 'end of politics' so much as its continuation by new means. Yet this is not to overlook the profound intellectual, institutional and normative challenges which it presents to the existing organization of political communities, highlighted in the previous chapters.

At the heart of these challenges lies the expansion in transborder political issues which erode clear-cut distinctions between domestic and foreign affairs. In nearly all major areas of government policy, the enmeshment of national political communities in regional and global processes involves them in intensive issues of transboundary coordination and control. Moreover, the extensity, intensity and impact of a broad range of processes and issues (economic, political and environmental) raise questions about where those issues are most appropriately addressed. If the most powerful geopolitical forces are not to settle many pressing matters simply in terms of their own objectives and by virtue of their

214

power, then existing structures and mechanisms of accountability need to be reconsidered. Environmental issues illuminate this matter well.

In response to the intensification of, and public awareness of, environmental issues, there has been an interlinked process of cultural and political globalization. This can be exemplified by the emergence of new scientific and intellectual networks; new environmental movements organized transnationally with transnational concerns; and new international institutions, regimes and conventions such as those agreed in 1992 at the Earth Summit in Brazil and in subsequent follow-up meetings. Unfortunately, none of the latter have as yet been able to acquire sufficient political power, domestic support or international authority to do more than (at best) limit the worst excesses of some of the worst global environmental threats.

Not all environmental problems are, of course, global; such a view would be highly misleading. Nonetheless, there has been a striking shift in the physical and environmental conditions – that is, in the extent, intensity and rapid transmission of environmental problems – affecting human affairs in general. These processes have moved politics dramatically away from an activity which crystallizes first and foremost around state and interstate concerns. It is clearer than ever that the fortunes of political communities and peoples can no longer be simply understood in exclusively national or territorial terms. In a world in which global warming connects the long-term fate of many Pacific islands to the actions of tens of millions of private motorists across the globe, the conventional territorial conception of political community appears profoundly inadequate. Globalization weaves together, in highly complex and abstract systems, the fates of households, communities and peoples in distant regions of the globe (McGrew 1997: 237). While it would be a mistake to conclude that political communities are without distinctive degrees of division or cleavage at their borders, they are clearly shaped by multiple cross-border interaction networks and power systems. Thus questions are raised both about the fate of the idea of political community, and about the appropriate level for the effective governance of human affairs: the national, the regional or the global. The proper locus of politics and the articulation of the public interest becomes a puzzling matter.

Towards a new politics of globalization

The contemporary phase of global change is transforming the very foundations of world order by reconstituting traditional forms of sovereign statehood, political community and international governance. But these processes are neither inevitable nor by any means fully secure. Globalization involves a shift away from a purely state-centric politics to a new and more complex form of multilayered global politics. This is the basis on and through which political authority and mechanisms of regulation are being articulated and rearticulated. As a result, the contemporary world order is best understood as a highly complex, interconnected and contested order in which the interstate system is increasingly embedded within an evolving system of multilayered regional and global governance. There are multiple, overlapping political processes at work at the present historical conjuncture.

At the beginning of the twenty-first century, there are strong reasons for believing that the traditional international order of states, in E. H. Carr's words, 'cannot be restored, and a drastic change of outlook is unavoidable' (1981: 237). Such changes of outlook are clearly delineated in the contest between what, in chapter 10, were identified as the principal variants or cleavages in the politics of globalization. The extreme ends of the political spectrum are deeply problematic. Whereas neoliberalism simply perpetuates existing economic and political systems and offers no real solutions to the problems of market failure, the radical position appears wildly optimistic about the potential for localism to resolve, or engage with, the governance agenda generated by the forces of globalization. How can such a politics cope with the challenges posed by overlapping communities of fate? But the discussion in chapter 10 did more than highlight these two positions; it disclosed important points of overlap between liberal internationalist, institutional reformist, and global transformist thought.

We wish to refer to this overlapping ground as the domain of cosmopolitan social democracy (see figure 8.1 on p. 164). This is because it seeks to nurture some of the most important values of social democracy – the rule of law, political equality, democratic

216

politics, social justice, social solidarity and economic effectiveness – while applying them to the new global constellation of economics and politics. Accordingly, the project of cosmopolitan social democracy can be conceived as a basis for uniting around the promotion of the impartial administration of law at the international level; greater transparency, accountability and democracy in global governance; a deeper commitment to social justice in the pursuit of a more equitable distribution of the world's resources and human security; the protection and reinvention of community at diverse levels (from the local to the global); and the regulation of the global economy through the public management of global financial and trade flows, the provision of global public goods, and the engagement of leading stakeholders in corporate governance. This common ground in global politics contains clear possibilities of dialogue and accommodation between different segments of the 'globalization/anti-globalization' political spectrum, although this is clearly contested by opinion at either end of the spectrum. In addition, some of the positions represented by the statists/protectionists (see column 5 of table 10.2 on p. 203) could be part of the dialogue; for clearly 'cosmopolitan social democracy' requires strong competent governance at all levels – local, national, regional and global. Table 11.1 summarizes the project of cosmopolitan social democracy. It does not present an all-or-nothing choice, but rather lays down a direction of change with clear points of orientation, in the short and long term.

The common ground represented by cosmopolitan social democracy provides a basis for a little optimism that global social justice is not simply a utopian goal. Moreover, it can be conceived as establishing the necessary ethical and institutional foundations for a progressive shift in the direction of a more cosmopolitan world order. In a world of overlapping communities and power systems, global issues are an inescapable element of the agenda of all polities and many organizations. The principal political question of our times is how these issues are best addressed or governed, and how global justice and security can best be provided. Cosmopolitan social democracy provides a framework for progressive thinking and political action on these questions, in a context of shared global concerns which unite a diverse array of political opinion.

217

Table 11.1 Towards cosmopolitan social democracy

Guiding ethical principles/core values	Rule of law, human security, global social justice, universal human rights, democracy, legitimacy.
Short-term measures	*Governance* • Reform of global governance: representative UN Security Council; establishment of a Human Security Council; strengthened systems of global accountability; enhancement of national and regional governance infrastructures and capacities; enhanced parliamentary scrutiny of development and foreign policy. *Security* • Strengthening global humanitarian protection capacities; implementation of the UN's existing Millennium Development Goals; strengthening of arms control and arms trade regulation. *Economy* • Regulating global markets: selective capital controls; regulation of offshore financial centres; voluntary codes of conduct for MNCs. • Promoting development: abolition of debt for highly indebted poor countries (HIPCs); meeting UN aid targets of 0.7% GNP; fair trade rules; removal of EU and US subsidies of agriculture and textiles.
Long-term transformations	*Governance* • Double democratization (national to suprastate governance); enhanced global public goods provision; global citizenship. *Security* • Global social charter; permanent peacekeeping and humanitarian emergency forces; regional security arrangements; social exclusion and equity impact reviews of all global development policies.

(continued)

218

Table 11.1 (*continued*)

	Economy <ul><li>Taming global markets: World Financial Authority; codes of conduct for MNCs; global tax mechanism; global competition authority.</li><li>Market correcting: mandatory global labour and environmental standards; foreign investment codes and standards; redistributive and compensatory measures; commodity price and supply agreements.</li><li>Market promoting: privileged market access for developing countries; convention on global labour mobility and migration.</li></ul>
Institutional/political conditions	Activist states, global progressive coalition (involving key democratic and developing states and civil society forces), strong multilateral institutions, open regionalism, global civil society, redistributive regimes, regulation of global markets, transnational public sphere.

12

Implementing Cosmopolitan Social Democracy: The Challenge of 9/11 and Global Economic Governance

This chapter elaborates the notion of cosmopolitan social democracy by testing it against pressing global issues, and by showing how it can generate more convincing policy prescriptions than current orthodoxies. It begins by evaluating those policies that have largely set the global political agenda in recent years – broadly, the Washington security doctrine and Washington economic consensus – and argues that they are failing. Alternatives rooted in cosmopolitan social democracy are then proposed. In particular, a transformation in security doctrines allied to a change of direction in the governance of the world economy would, it is contended, buttress international law and multilateral institutions, and help entrench the guiding principles at the heart of cosmopolitan social democracy.

The policies of what can be called the 'old order' have not fulfilled expectations (Held 2004; Barnett, Held and Henderson 2005). The most successful developing countries in the world (China, India, Vietnam, Uganda, among them) are successful because they have not followed the Washington Consensus agenda (see Rodrik 2005), and the conflicts that have been diffused most successfully (the Balkans, Sierra Leone, Liberia, Sri Lanka, among others) are ones that have benefited from multilateral support and a human security agenda (see the Human Security Centre, 2005). Here are clear clues as to how to proceed, and to build alternatives to both the Washington Consensus and the Washington security doctrine.

9/11, the war in Iraq and human security

If 9/11 was not a defining moment in human history, it was for today's generations. The terrorist attack on the World Trade Center and the Pentagon was an atrocity of immense proportions. Yet, after 9/11, the US and its allies could have decided that the most important things to do were to strengthen international law in the face of global terrorist threats, and to enhance the role of multilateral institutions. They could have decided it was important that no single power or group should act as judge, jury and executioner. They could have decided that global hotspots like the Middle East which help feed global terrorism should be the main centre of international attention. They could have decided to be tough on terrorism and tough on the conditions which lead people to imagine (falsely) that al-Qaeda and similar groups are agents of justice in the modern world. But they have systematically failed to pursue this agenda. In general, after 9/11 the world has become more polarized, international law weaker, and multilateral institutions more vulnerable.

The war in Afghanistan in 2002 and Iraq in 2003 gave priority to a narrow security agenda which is at the heart of the Bush administration's security doctrine. This doctrine contradicts many of the core tenets of the post-1945 world order (Ikenberry 2002). It sets out a policy which is essentially unilateral, which seeks order through primacy, which pursues the pre-emptive and preventive use of force, which relies on a conception of leadership based on a coalition of the willing and which aims to make the world safe for freedom and democracy – by globalizing American rules and conceptions of justice. The doctrine has been enacted as the global War on Terror. The language of interstate warfare was preserved intact and projected onto a new enemy. As a result, the terrorists of 9/11 were dignified as soldiers and war prosecuted against them. But this strategy was a distortion and simplification of reality and a predictable failure. In pursuing dominance through force, the War on Terror has created numerous innocent victims, and acted as a spur to terrorist recruitment (see Soros 2006). It has shown little, if any, understanding of the grievances, dignity, pride and fears of others, and of the way the fate and fortune of all peoples are increasingly tied together in our global age. Instead of seeking to extend the rule

221

of law, ensuring that no party – terrorist or state – acts as judge, jury and executioner, seeking dialogue with the Muslim world, strengthening the multilateral order, and developing the means to deal with the criminals of 9/11, the US and its allies (notably the UK) pursued old-war techniques and fuelled global insecurity.

The new doctrine has many serious implications (Hoffmann 2003, 2006). Among these are a return to geopolitics – to an understanding of international relations as a sphere of competition for power through territorial and political control unencumbered by attempts to establish internationally recognized limits (self-defence, collective security) on their ambitions. Yet if this 'freedom' is (dangerously) granted to the US, why not also to Russia, China, India, Pakistan, Israel, Iran and so on? It cannot be consistently argued that all states bar the most powerful accept limits on their self-defined goals. The flaws of international law and the UN Charter can either be addressed, or taken as an excuse for further weakening international institutions and legal arrangements.

Today, the attempt to develop international law and to enhance the capacity of international institutions for peacekeeping and peace-making is threatened not just by the dangers posed by transnational terrorist networks, but also by the deeply misguided responses to them. There are a number of very pressing issues which need to be addressed if we are to salvage the achievements of the post-1945 world – above all, the development of global governance institutions hedged, in principle, by the universal human rights regime – and build on them in a manner that provides not just security in the narrowest sense – protection from the immediate threat of coercive power and violence – but security in the broadest sense: protection for all those whose lives are vulnerable for whatever reason to global economic, political or environmental forces. The way forward involves advocacy of a human security agenda that is based on multilateralism and impartial rules, which seeks order through law and social justice, which seeks to re-link security and the human rights agenda, which seeks to strengthen representative and responsible global governance, and which aims to make the world safe for humanity, with global justice and democratic values.

A human security agenda requires three things of governments and international institutions – all currently missing (Held and

Kaldor 2001). First, there must be a commitment to the rule of law and the development of multilateral institutions – not the prosecution of war as the first response. Civilians of all faiths and nationalities need protection. Terrorists and all those who systematically violate the sanctity of life and human rights must be brought before an international criminal court that commands cross-national support. This does not preclude internationally sanctioned military action to arrest suspects, dismantle terrorist networks and deal with aggressive rogue states – far from it (see Hoffmann 2004). But such action should always be understood as a robust form of international law enforcement, above all as a way, as Mary Kaldor (1988) has most clearly put it, of protecting civilians and bringing suspects to trial. In short, if justice is to be dispensed impartially, no power can arrogate to itself the global role of setting standards, weighing risks and meting out justice. What is needed is momentum towards global, not American or Russian or Chinese or British or French, justice. We must act together to sustain and strengthen a world based on common principles and rules (Solana 2003).

Second, a sustained effort has to be undertaken to generate new forms of global political legitimacy for international institutions responsible for global security, governance and peace building. This must include the condemnation of systematic human rights violations wherever they occur, and the establishment of new forms of political and economic accountability. This cannot be equated with an occasional or one-off effort to create a new momentum for peace and the protection of human rights, as is all too typical.

And, finally, there must be a head-on acknowledgement that the global polarization of wealth, income and power, and with it the huge asymmetries of life chances, cannot be left to markets to resolve alone. Those who are poorest and most vulnerable, linked into geopolitical situations where their economic and political claims have been neglected for generations, may provide fertile ground for terrorist recruiters. The project of economic globalization has to be connected to manifest principles of social justice; the latter need to frame global market activity (see below).

Of course, terrorist crimes of the kind witnessed on 9/11 and on many occasions since (in Chechnya, Saudi Arabia, Pakistan, Morocco, Spain, the UK and elsewhere) may often be the work of the simply deranged and the fanatic and so there can be no

223

guarantee that a more just and institutionally stable world will be a more peaceful one in all respects. But if we turn our back on this project, there is no hope of ameliorating the social basis of disadvantage often experienced in the poorest and most dislocated countries. Gross injustices, linked to a sense of hopelessness born of generations of neglect, feed anger and hostility. Popular support against terrorism depends on convincing people that there is a legal and peaceful way of addressing their grievances. Without this sense of confidence in global public institutions and processes, the defeat of terrorism becomes a hugely difficult task.

Elsewhere, this agenda has been set out at length (Held 2004; Barnett, Held and Henderson 2005). Here we will simply list some of the steps which could be taken to implement a human security agenda which is at the heart of public discussion in many parts of the world today ('old Europe', Latin America, Africa and Asia). These include:

- Relinking the security and human rights agendas in international law – the two sides of international humanitarian law which, together, specify what is counted as grave and systematic abuses of human security and well-being, and the minimum conditions required for the development of human agency.
- Reforming UN Security Council procedures to improve the specification of, and legitimacy of, credible reasons for, credible threshold tests for, and credible promises in relation to, armed intervention in the affairs of a state – the objective being to link these directly to a set of conditions which would constitute a severe threat to peace, and/or a threat to the minimum conditions for the well-being of human agency, sufficient to justify the use of force, and which would lock the deployment of force into a clear framework of international humanitarian law.
- Recognizing the necessity to dislodge and amend the now outmoded 1945 geopolitical settlement as the basis of decision-making in the Security Council, and to extend representation to all regions on a fair and equal footing.
- Expanding the remit of the Security Council, or creating a parallel Human Security Council, to examine and, where necessary, intervene in the full ambit of human crises – physical, social, biological, environmental – which can threaten human agency.

- Founding a World Environmental Organization to promote the implementation of existing environmental agreements and treaties, whose main mission would be to ensure that the development of world trading and financial systems are compatible with the sustainable use of the world's resources.

In order to reconnect the security and human rights agendas and to bring them together into a coherent framework of law, it would be necessary to hold an international or global constitutional convention. Rather than set out a blueprint of what the outcomes of such a convention should be, it is important to stress the significance of a legitimate process that reviews the security and human rights sides of international law and seeks to reconnect them in a global legal framework, and builds a global discourse both against terrorism and for the peaceful development of each and all. For too long, security and development, and the security and the human rights agendas, have been treated as separate intellectual and foreign policy domains, but they should not have been, and they cannot be any longer.

If the developed world wants rapid movement to the establishment of global legal codes and mechanisms to enhance security and ensure action against the threats of terrorism, then they need to be part of a wider process of reform that addresses the insecurity of life experienced in developing societies. Across the developing or majority world, issues of justice with respect to government and terrorism are not widely regarded as a priority on their own, and are rarely perceived as legitimate unless they are connected with fundamental humanitarian issues rooted in social and economic well-being, such as education, clean water and threats to public health.

To address these problems requires not just a shift in how security is conceived and pursued, but also in how economic development is elaborated and managed. The narrow liberal economic agenda dominant in recent years needs to be recast and economic strategy linked to a larger socio-economic framework of global economic governance, setting fundamental standards for all human life and rethinking the economic tools available to global economic policy. A broader human security agenda needs to be matched by a broader programme of economic development.

The contested nature of global economic governance

For the last two to three decades, the agenda of economic liberal-ization and global market integration – or the Washington Consensus, as it is sometimes called – has been the mantra of many leading economic powers and international financial institutions. The standard view of economic development has maintained that the path to economic and social well-being is economic liberaliza-tion and international market integration (see chapters 6 and 10). As Martin Wolf put it, 'all else is commentary' (2004: 144). But is this true? There are strong grounds for doubting that the standard liberal economic approach delivers on promised goals and that global market integration is the indispensable condition of devel-opment. Moreover, their forceful implementation by the World Bank, IMF and leading economic powers has often led to counter-productive results.

Developing countries that have benefited most from globaliza-tion are those that have not played by the rules of the standard liberal market approach, including China, India and Vietnam (Rodrik 2005). In addition, those that have, for example the Latin American and the Caribbean countries, have done worse judged by the standards of East Asia and their own past. In other words, the link between growth, economic openness and liberalization is weaker than the standard liberal argument suggests. The wide-spread shift among developing countries to greater openness has coincided with a slowdown in the rate of world economic growth compared to earlier in the postwar period, from 2.7 per cent in 1960–78 to 1.5 per cent from 1979–2000 (Milanovic 2005).

The link between growth and poverty reduction is also not as close as the liberal argument would predict (see chapter 6). Accounts of this type generally assume a catch-up or convergence story whereby poorer countries, opening their markets and liber-alizing, are expected to grow faster and richer so that income dif-ferentials narrow over time. However, the evidence to support this is controversial, at best. In the first instance, excluding the phe-nomenal development of China and to some extent India, the reported number of people living below the World Bank poverty line of $1 a day (see chapter 6) has actually risen in the two decades since 1981 (see Wade 2006). Moreover, the World Bank's measure of absolute poverty, based on $1 a day, is to a large extent arbitrary. If you take the figure of $2 a day the trend in poverty (including China and India) is upward (see Held and Kaya 2006). In addition, there is a near perfect correlation between a group's relative standing at the beginning of the 1990s and its real cumulative income gains in the years that followed (see Pogge 2006). The evidence shows that gains at the bottom of the global income hierarchy were minimal or even negative, as the first, that is to say, bottom, percentile, lost 7.3 per cent and the second gained only 1 per cent.

Examining and evaluating trends in income inequality between countries, it is clear that much depends again on how China's economic success and subsequent reduction in poverty is treated. If China is excluded from consideration, inequality between countries can be shown to have increased since 1980. The date of 1980 is important because it is often claimed to be the moment when income inequality between countries reached its historic peak. Of course, there is much to be said for including China in the account, but then it has to be borne in mind that China's success has depended significantly on a host of factors, not all of which fit neatly into the neoliberal argument. For example, China has staggered and regulated its entry into the global market; tariffs have been cut, but only after economic take-off, particularly heavily in the last ten to twelve years; capital movements have remained tightly regulated; FDI is locked into partnerships, often with significant political controls; and crucially its currency (to date) remains non-convertible.

None of this is to argue that trade and international capital flows do not provide important potential gains to many countries. The question, rather, is under what conditions trade and capital flows (and what kinds of trade and capital flows) are introduced to maximize benefit. Thinking of globalization as either an inextricably positive force or the opposite is likely to miss the core conditions for successful development and political change. The choice is not between globalization in its liberal free market form, on the one hand, and no globalization, on the other. Rather, what is at issue is the proper form globalization should take.

This critical issue cannot be resolved within the terms of the Washington Consensus because the thrust of the latter is to enhance economic liberalization and to adapt public policy and the public domain to market-leading institutions and processes. It thus bears a heavy burden of responsibility for the common political resistance or unwillingness to address significant areas of market failure, including:

- the problem of externalities, such as the environmental degradation exacerbated by current forms of economic growth;
- the inadequate development of *non*-market social factors, which alone can provide an effective balance between 'competition' and 'cooperation' and thus ensure an adequate supply of essential public goods such as education, effective transportation and sound health; and
- the underemployment of productive resources in the context of the demonstrable existence of urgent and unmet need.

The Washington Consensus has weakened confidence in public authority and in that authority's ability – locally, nationally and globally – to govern and provide urgent public goods. Economic freedom is championed at the expense of social justice and environmental sustainability, with damage to both. There is a confusion, moreover, between economic freedom and economic effectiveness. The question (and it is, of course, a big question) is one of how markets, democratic choices about public goods, and a concern with basic universal standards such as human rights and environmental protection can be pursued systematically and simultaneously. What follows constitutes some first steps in addressing this question.

To begin with, bridges have to be built between international economic law and human rights law, between commercial law and environmental law, between state sovereignty and transnational law (Chinkin 1998). It is as if all these things refer to separate domains and do not speak to each other, with the consequence that entrenched interests trump social and environmental considerations, among other urgent matters. What is required is not only the firm enactment of existing human rights and environmental agreements, and the clear linking of these with the ethical codes of particular industries, but also the introduction of new terms of reference into the ground rules or basic laws of the free market and trade system. Helpful precedents exist in the social chapter of the

228

Maastricht Agreement and in the attempt to attach labour and environmental conditions to the NAFTA regime.

At stake, ultimately, are three interrelated transformations. The first would involve engaging companies in the promotion of core universal principles, as the UN's Global Compact does at present. To the extent that this led to the entrenchment of human rights and environmental standards in corporate practices, that would be a significant step forward. But if this is to be something other than voluntary, vulnerable to being ignored, then it needs to be elaborated in due course into a set of more codified and mandatory rules. Thus the second set of transformations would involve the entrenchment of revised rules and codes on health, child labour, trade union activity, environmental protection, stakeholder consultation and corporate governance in the articles of association of economic organizations and trading agencies. The key groups and associations of the economic domain would have to adopt in their very modus operandi a structure of rules and procedures compatible with universal social requirements if these requirements are to prevail. Now, of course, it can be countered that poorly designed regulatory structures can harm employment levels, but Scandinavian countries show that it is possible to be both business friendly and welfare orientated.

There are several possible objections to the scheme set out. However, most of these are misplaced. The framework of human rights and environmental values is sound because it is preoccupied with the equal liberty and equal development possibilities of all human beings, and is consistent with the universal principles enshrined in the post-1945 multilateral order. But it has to be conceded that without a third set of changes the advocacy of such standards descends into high-mindedness because it fails to pursue the socio-economic changes that are a necessary part of such a commitment.

At a minimum, this means that development policies must be linked to:

- promoting the development space necessary for national trade and industrial incentives, including infant industry protection;
- building robust public sectors nurturing political and legal reform;
- developing transparent, accountable political institutions;

229

- ensuring long-term investment in health care, human capital and physical infrastructure;
- challenging the asymmetries of access to the global market which are often hypocritical and indefensible;
- ensuring the sequencing of global market integration into a framework of fair rules for trade and finance;
- eliminating odious unsustainable debt, and creating new finance facilities for development purposes.

In addition, if such measures were combined with a Tobin tax on the turnover of financial markets, and/or a consumption tax on fossil fuels, and/or a shift of the priorities from military expenditure, now running at $900 billion per annum globally, towards the alleviation of severe need (direct aid amounts to only some $50 billion dollars per annum globally), then the development context of the Western nations and Northern nation-states could begin to be accommodated more adequately to those nations struggling for survival and minimum welfare.

The UN budget is $3.8 billion per annum plus peacekeeping, but the US and Europe each spend vastly more annually on chocolate and bubble gum, alcohol, cars, pet food and so on. The expenditure on each of these items dwarfs the amounts available for direct poverty alleviation and for dealing with urgent diseases. The US and its allies went to war after 9/11; 9/11 was a serious matter, a crime against the United States and a crime against humanity. But every day ten times as many people as were lost on 9/11 die of poverty, malnutrition and poverty-related diseases – and, yet, there is no war or, better still, decisive social change in relation to these life and death issues. The resources are available, but the question is political will and choice. Figures 12.1–5 and table 12.1 disclose some interesting detail in this regard.

Political challenges and progressive coalitions

Surprisingly perhaps, it is an opportune moment to pursue cosmopolitan social democracy. With the resurgence of nationalism and unilateralism in US foreign policy, uncertainty over the future of Europe after the 'no' votes in France and Holland, the crisis of

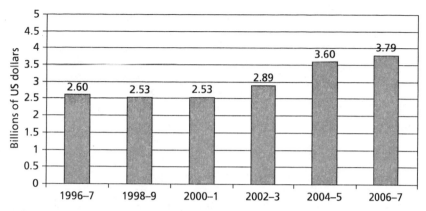

All figures exclude peacekeeping budgets and extrabudgetary UN expenses.

Figure 12.1 UN core budget 1996–1997 to 2006–2007

Source: Data for 1996–2005 drawn from UN 2005; data for 2006–7 from UN 2006.

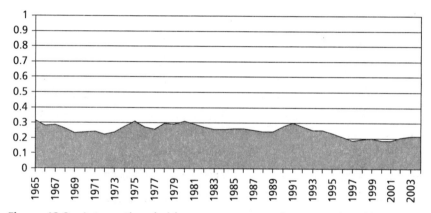

Figure 12.2 International aid as a percentage of gross national income (world), 1965–2003

Source: Data drawn from the World Bank's World Development Indicators database.

global trade talks and development strategies, the growing confidence of China, India and Brazil in world economic fora (especially in relation to world trade negotiations), and the unsettled relations between Islam and the West, the political tectonic plates appear to be shifting. It is highly unlikely that the multilateral order can survive for much longer – a decade or two perhaps – in its current form. Something is surely going to give.

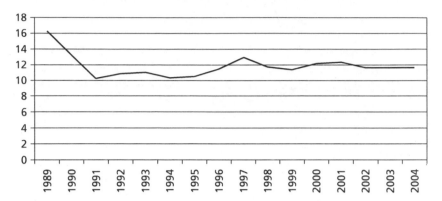

Figure 12.3 The amount by which world official development assistance as a percentage of gross national income would have to be multiplied to equal world military expenditure as a percentage of gross national product, 1989–2004

Source: Data drawn from the World Bank's World Development Indicators database.

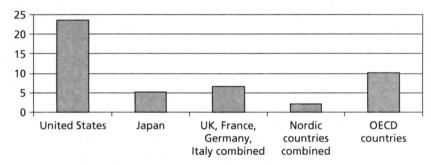

Figure 12.4 Ratio of military expenditure to official development assistance, selected countries, 2004

Source: Data and chart adapted from Worldwatch Institute 2006, with figures from SIPRI 2005 and OECD 2005.

The political space for the development of cosmopolitan social democracy has to be made, and advances are being realized through the activities of all those social forces that are engaged in the pursuit of the rule of law at all levels of governance and pressing for greater coordination and accountability of the leading forces of globalization; the opening up of IGOs to key stakeholders and participants; greater equity in the distribution of the world's resources; the protection of human rights and fundamental freedoms; sustainable

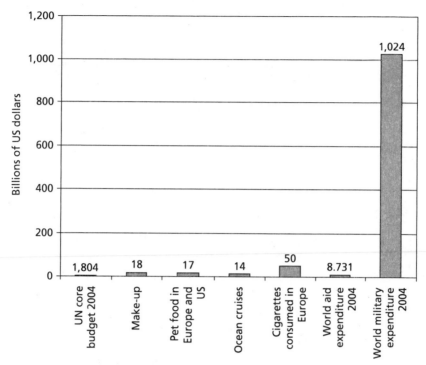

Figure 12.5 Global consumption priorities

Source: UN core budget: UN 2005; make-up, pet food, ocean cruises: Worldwatch Institute 2004; cigarettes: Shah 2006, with figures from UNDP 1998b; world aid expenditure: World Bank's World Development Indicators database; world military expenditure: SIPRI 2004.

development across generations; and peaceful dispute settlement in leading geopolitical conflicts. This is not a political project that starts from nowhere. It is, in fact, deeply rooted in the political world shaped and formed after the Holocaust and the Second World War. Moreover, it can be built on many of the achievements of multilateralism (from the founding of the UN system to the development of the EU), international law (from the human rights regime to the establishment of the International Criminal Court) and multilayered governance (from the development of local government in cities and subnational regions to the dense web of international policy-making fora), while also recasting them for the global age we are in.

The story of our increasingly global order is not a singular one. Globalization is not, and has never been, a one-dimensional

Table 12.1 Comparisons of annual expenditure on luxury items compared to estimated funding needed to meet selected basic needs

Product	Annual expenditure	Social or economic goal	Additional annual investment needed to achieve goal
Make-up	$18 billion	Reproductive health care for all women	$12 billion
Pet food in Europe and United States	$17 billion	Elimination of hunger and malnutrition	$19 billion
Perfumes	$15 billion	Universal literacy	$5 billion
Ocean cruises	$14 billion	Clean drinking water for all	$10 billion
Ice cream in Europe	$11 billion	Immunizing every child	$1.3 billion

Source: Worldwatch Institute 2004: table 1–6; figures drawn from UNDP 1998.

phenomenon. While there has been a massive expansion of global markets which has altered the political terrain, increasing exit options for capital of all kinds and adding to the relative power of corporate interests (see Held et al. 1999: chs 3–5; Held and McGrew 2000: ch. 25), the story of globalization is far from simply economic. Since 1945 there has been a significant entrenchment of cosmopolitan values concerning the equal dignity and worth of all human beings in international rules and regulations; the reconnection of international law and morality, with sovereignty no longer cast merely as effective power but increasingly as legitimate authority defined in terms of the maintenance of human rights and democratic values; the establishment of complex governance systems, regional and global; and the growing recognition that the public good – whether conceived as financial stability, environmental protection or global egalitarianism – requires coordinated multilateral action if it is to be achieved in the long term (see Held 2002b). These developments need to be and can be built on. The present world order combines elements of both paradise and power: of power politics and cosmopolitan values.

A coalition of political groupings could emerge to push these achievements further, comprising European countries with strong liberal and social democratic traditions; liberal groups in the US polity which support multilateralism and the rule of law in international affairs; developing countries struggling for freer and fairer trade rules in the world economic order; non-governmental organizations, from Amnesty International to Oxfam, campaigning for a more just, democratic and equitable world order; transnational social movements contesting the nature and form of contemporary globalization; and those economic forces that desire a more stable and managed global economic order.

Europe could have a special role in advancing the cause of cosmopolitan social democracy (McGrew 2001, 2002). As the home of both social democracy and a historic experiment in governance beyond the state, Europe has direct experience in considering the appropriate designs for more effective and accountable suprastate governance. It offers novel ways of thinking about governance beyond the state which encourage a (relatively) more democratic – as opposed to more neoliberal – vision of global governance. Moreover, Europe is in a strategic position (with strong links west and east, north and south) to build global constituencies for reform of the architecture and functioning of global governance. Through interregional dialogues, it has the potential to mobilize new cross-regional coalitions as a countervailing influence to those constituencies that oppose reform, including unilateralist forces in the US.

Of course, this is not to suggest that the EU should broker a crude anti-US coalition of transnational and international forces. On the contrary, it is crucial to recognize the complexity of US domestic politics and the existence of progressive social, political and economic forces seeking to advance a rather different kind of world order from that championed by the Republican right of the political spectrum (Nye 2002). Despite its unilateralist inclinations, it is worth noting that public opinion in the US (especially the younger generation) has been quite consistently in favour of the UN and multilateralism, and slightly more so than European publics (Norris 2000). Any European political strategy to promote a broad-based coalition for a new global covenant must seek to enlist the support of these progressive forces within the US polity, while it must resist within its own camp the siren voices now calling with renewed energy for the exclusive re-emergence of national identities, ethnic purity and protectionism.

Although some of the interests of those groupings which might coalesce around a movement for cosmopolitan social democracy would inevitably diverge on a wide range of issues, there is potentially an important overlapping sphere of concern among them for the strengthening of multilateralism, building new institutions for providing global public goods, regulating global markets, deepening accountability, protecting the environment and urgently ameliorating social injustices that kill thousands of men, women and children daily. Of course, how far they can unite around these concerns – and can overcome fierce opposition from well-entrenched geopolitical and geoeconomic interests – remains to be seen. The stakes are very high, but so too are the potential gains for human security and development if the aspirations for global democracy and social justice can be realized.

References

Abbott, A. J. and De Vita, G. (2003) Another piece in the Feldstein-Horoika puzzle. *Scottish Journal of Political Economy* 50(1): 68–89.

Ahmed, A. S. and Donnan, H. (1994) *Islam, Globalization and Post-modernity*. New York: Routledge.

Albrow, M. (1996) *The Global Age*. Cambridge: Polity.

Altvater, E. and Mahnkopf, B. (1997) The world market unbound. *Review of International Political Economy* 4(3).

Amin, S. (1996) The challenge of globalization. *Review of International Political Economy* 3(2).

Amin, S. (1997) *Capitalism in the Age of Globalization*. London: Zed Press.

Amin, S. (2004) *The Liberal Virus*. London: Zed Press.

Anderson, B. (1983) *Imagined Communities: Reflections on the Origins and Spread of Nationalism*. London: Verso.

Anderson, K. and Blackhurst, R. (eds) (1993) *Regional Integration and the Global Trading System*. Brighton: Harvester.

Anderson, K. and Norheim, H. (1993) Is world trade becoming more regionalized? *Review of International Economics* 1(2).

Anderson, P. (1974) *Lineages of the Absolutist State*. London: New Left Books.

Anheier, H., Glasius, M. and Kaldor, M. (eds) (2001) *Global Civil Society 2001*. Oxford: Oxford University Press.

Appadurai, A. (1990) Disjuncture and difference in the global cultural economy. *Theory, Culture and Economy* 7: 295–300.

Appadurai, A. (1998) *Modernity at Large*. Minneapolis: University of Minnesota Press.

Appiah, K. A. (2005) *The Ethics of Identity*. Princeton: Princeton University Press.

Archibugi, D., Held, D. and Köhler, M. (eds) (1998) *Re-imagining Political Community: Studies in Cosmopolitan Democracy*. Cambridge: Polity.

References

Ashford, D. (1986) *The Emergence of the Welfare State*. Oxford: Blackwell.

A.T. Kearney/Foreign Policy (2003, 2005, 2006) A.T. Kearney/Foreign Policy Globalization Index (annual). At www.atkearney.com.

Avant, D. (2004) The privatization of security and change in the control of force. *International Studies Perspectives* 5: 153–7.

Avant, D. (2005) *The Market for Force: The Consequences of Privatizing Security*. Cambridge: Cambridge University Press.

Axford, B. (1995) *The Global System*. Cambridge: Polity.

Baldwin, R. (2006) Multilateralizing regionalism: spaghetti bowls as building blocs on the path to global free trade. Working Paper, National Bureau of Economic Research, New York.

Baldwin, R. E. and Martin, P. (1999) Two waves of globalisation: superficial similarities, fundamental differences. Working Paper 6904, National Bureau of Economic Research, New York.

Banerjee, A. and Zanghieri, P. (2003) A new look at the F-H puzzle using an integrated panel. CEPII Working Paper, Centre d'Études Prospectives et d'Informations Internationales, Paris.

Barkawi, T. and Laffey, M. (1999) The imperial peace: democracy, force and globalization. *European Journal of International Relations* 5(4): 403–34.

Barnett, A., Held, D. and Henderson, C. (eds) (2005) *Debating Globalization*. Cambridge: Polity.

Barnett, T. P. (2004) *The Pentagon's New Map: War and Peace in the Twenty-First Century*. New York: Putnam.

Barry, B. (1998a) International society from a cosmopolitan perspective. In D. Mapel and T. Nardin (eds), *International Society: Diverse Ethical Perspectives*, Princeton: Princeton University Press.

Barry, B. (1998b) The limits of cultural politics. *Review of International Studies* 24(3).

Barry, Brian (1999) Statism and nationalism: a cosmopolitan critique. In I. Shapiro and L. Brilmayer (eds), *Global Justice*, New York: New York University Press.

Bhattcharya, G. (2005) *Traffick: The Illegal Movement of People and Things*. London: Pluto 3Press.

Baxter, M. and Crucisi, M. J. (1993) Explaining savings-investment correlations. *American Economic Review* 83(3): 416–36.

Baylis, J. and Smith, S. (eds) (2005) *The Globalization of World Politics*. Oxford: Oxford University Press.

Bayly, C. A. (2004) *The Birth of the Modern World*. Cambridge: Cambridge University Press.

Beck, U. (1992) *Risk Society: Towards a New Modernity*. London: Sage.

References

Beck, U. (1997) *The Reinvention of Politics*. Cambridge: Polity.

Beck, U. (1999a) *What is Globalization?* Cambridge: Polity.

Beck, U. (1999b) *World Risk Society*. Cambridge: Polity.

Beck, U. (2001) Power in the global economy. Lecture delivered at the London School of Economics and Political Science, 22 Feb.

Beetham, D. (1995) What future for economic and social rights? *Political Studies* 48 (special issue).

Beetham, D. (1998) Human rights as a model for cosmopolitan democracy. In Archibugi, Held and Köhler 1998.

Beetham, D. (2005) *Democracy*. Oxford: OneWorld.

Bekaert, G. and Hodrick, R. J. (2005) International stock market return comovements. Working Paper, National Bureau of Economic Research, New York.

Bello, W. (2002) *Deglobalization: Ideas for a New Global Economy*. London: Zed Press.

Bentley, J. H. (1996) Cross-cultural interaction and periodization in world history. *American Historical Review* 101(3).

Bhagwati, J. (2004) *In Defense of Globalization*. Oxford: Oxford University Press.

Bhattcharya, G. (2005) *Traffick: The Illegal Movement of People and Things*. London: Pluto Press.

Birdsall, N. (1998) Life is unfair: inequality in the world. *Foreign Policy* 111 (Summer).

BIS (Bank for International Settlements) (2001) *BIS Quarterly Review* (Basel) (Dec.).

BIS (Bank for International Settlements) (2003) *BIS Quarterly Review* (Basel) (Dec.).

BIS (Bank for International Settlements) (2004) *BIS Quarterly Review* (Basel) (Dec.).

BIS (Bank for International Settlements) (2005a) *Triennial Central Bank Survey*. Basel: BIS.

BIS (Bank for International Settlements) (2005b) *BIS Quarterly Review* (Basel) (Sept.).

BIS (Bank for International Settlements) (2006) *OTC Derivatives Activity in the First Half of 2006*. Basel: BIS.

Bitzinger, R. A. (2003) *Towards a Brave New Arms Industry?* Adelphi Paper 356. London: International Institute for Strategic Studies and Oxford University Press.

Black, J. (2004) *War and the New Disorder in the Twenty First Century*. London: Continuum.

Bobbio, N. (1989) *Democracy and Dictatorship*. Cambridge: Polity.

Bordo, M. D. and Helbling, T. (2003) Have national business cycles become synchronized? Working Paper, National Bureau of Economic Research, New York.

Bordo, M. D., Eichengreen, B. and Irwin, D. A. (1999) Is globalization today really different than globalization a hundred years ago? Working Paper 7195, National Bureau of Economic Research, New York.

Bordo, M. D., Taylor, A. M. and Williamson, J. G. (eds) (2003) *Globalization in Historical Perspective*. Chicago: Chicago University Press.

Bourguignon, F. and Morrisson, C. (2002) Inequality among world citizens, 1820–1992. *American Economic Review* 4 (Sept): 727–44.

Bourguignon, F. et al. (2002) Making sense of globalization: a guide to the economic issues. CEPR Policy Paper 8, Centre for Economic Policy Research, London. At www.cepr.org.

Boyer, R. and Drache, D. (eds) (1996) *States against Markets*. London: Routledge.

Bozeman, A. B. (1984) The international order in a multicultural world. In H. Bull and A. Watson (eds), *The Expansion of International Society*, Oxford: Oxford University Press.

Bradshaw, Y. W. and Wallace, M. (1996) *Global Inequalities*. London: Pine Forge Press/Sage.

Braithwaite, J. and Drahos, P. (1999) *Global Business Regulation*. Cambridge: Cambridge University Press.

Braudel, F. (1984) *The Perspective of the World*. New York: Harper and Row.

Bray, D. (2005) *The Not So Clear Consensus on Climate Change*. Geesthacht: GKSS Forschungszentrum. At http://w3g.gkss.de/G/Mitarbeiter/bray.html/BrayGKSSsite/BrayGKSS/WedPDFs/Science2.pdf.

Brenner, N. (2004) *New State Spaces: Urban Governance and the Rescaling of Statehood*. Oxford: Oxford University Press.

Breuilly, J. (1992) *Nationalism and the State*. Manchester: Manchester University Press.

Brewer, A. (1980) *Marxist Theories of Imperialism: A Critical Survey*. London: Routledge and Kegan Paul.

Brown, C. (1995) International political theory and the idea of world community. In K. Booth and S. Smith (eds), *International Relations Theory Today*, Cambridge: Polity.

Bruff, I. (2005) Making sense of the globalization debate when engaging in political economy analysis. *British Journal of Politics and International Relations* 7(3): 261–80.

Bryant, R. C. (2003) *Turbulent Waters: Cross-Border Finance and International Governance*. Washington DC: Brookings Institution.

Buhaug, H. and Gleditsch, N. P. (2006) The death of distance? The globalization of armed conflict. In M. Kahler and B. F. Walter (eds), *Territoriality and Conflict in an Era of Globalization*, Cambridge: Cambridge University Press.

Bull, H. (1977) *The Anarchical Society*. London: Macmillan.

Burbach, R., Nunez, O. and Kagarlitsky, B. (1997) *Globalization and its Discontents*. London: Pluto Press.

Burnheim, J. (1985) *Is Democracy Possible?* Cambridge: Polity.

Burtless, G. et al. (1998) *Globaphobia: Confronting Fears about Open Trade*. Washington DC: Brookings Institution.

Buzan, B. (1991) *People, States and Fear*. Brighton: Harvester.

Buzan, B., Little, R. and Jones, C. (1993) *The Logic of Anarchy*. New York: Columbia University Press.

Cable, V. (1996) Globalization: can the state strike back? *The World Today* (May).

Cai, F. and Warnock, F. F. (2006) International diversification at home and abroad. Working Paper, National Bureau of Economic Research, New York.

Callinicos, A. (2002) Marxism and global governance. In Held and McGrew 2002.

Callinicos, A. (2003) *An Anti-Capitalist Manifesto*. Cambridge: Polity.

Callinicos, A. (2007) Globalization and imperialism. In D. Held and A. McGrew (eds), *Globalization Theory: Approaches and Analysis*, Cambridge: Polity.

Callinicos, A., Rees, J., Harman, C. and Haynes, M. (1994) *Marxism and the New Imperialism*. London: Bookmarks.

Cammack, P. (2002) Attacking the global poor. *New Left Review*, series II, no. 13.

Cammilleri, J. F. and Falk, J. (1992) *The End of Sovereignty*. Brighton: Edward Elgar.

Campbell, J. (2004) *Institutional Change and Globalization*. Princeton: Princeton University Press.

Caney, S. (2005) *Justice beyond Borders*. Oxford: Oxford University Press.

Carr, E. H. (1981) *The Twenty Years' Crisis 1919–1939*. London: Papermac.

Carrere, C. and Schiff, M. (2003) On the geography of trade: distance is alive and well. Working Paper, World Bank, Washington DC.

Castells, M. (1996) *The Rise of the Network Society*. Oxford: Blackwell.

Castells, M. (1997) *The Power of Identity*. Oxford: Blackwell.

Castells, M. (1998) *End of Millennium*. Oxford: Blackwell.

Castells, M. (2000) *The Rise of the Network Society*. Oxford: Blackwell.

Castells, M. (2005) Global governance and global politics. The 2004

References

Ithiel De Sola Pool Lecture. *PS Online*. At www.apsanet.org/imgtest/2005Global-Castellas.pdf.

Castles, S. and Miller, M. (2002) *The Age of Global Migration*. London: Palgrave.

Cattaui, M. L. (2001) Making, and respecting, the rules. 25 Oct. At www.openDemocracy.net

Cavaglia, S., Brightman, C. and Aked, M. (2000) The increasing importance of industrial factors. *Financial Analyst Journal* (Sept.–Oct.): 41–54.

Chang, H. J. (2003) *Globalization and the Economic Role of the State*. London: Zed Books.

Chinkin, C. (1998) International law and human rights. In T. Evans (ed.), *Human Rights Fifty Years On: A Reappraisal*, Manchester: Manchester University Press.

Chiswick, B. R. and Hatton, T. J. (2003) International migration and integration of labor markets. In Bordo, Taylor and Williamson 2003.

Chortoreas, G. E. and Pelagidis, T. (2004) Trade flows: a facet of regionalism or globalization? *Cambridge Journal of Economics* 28: 253–71.

Clark, I. (1989) *The Hierarchy of States: Reform and Resistance in the International Order*. Cambridge: Cambridge University Press.

Clark, I. (1999) *Globalization and International Relations Theory*. Oxford: Oxford University Press.

Clark, I. (2001) *The Post Cold War Order*. Oxford: Oxford University Press.

Clark, R. P. (1997) *The Global Imperative*. Boulder: Westview Press.

Coakley, J., Fuertes, A.-M. and Spagnolo, F. (2004) Is the Feldstein-Horioka puzzle history? *The Manchester School* 72(5): 569–89.

Coakley, J., Kulasi, F. and Smith, R. (1998) The Feldstein-Horioka puzzle and capital mobility: a review. *International Journal of Finance and Economics* 3(2): 169–88.

Coe, D. et al. (2002) The missing globalization puzzle. IMF Working Papers WP/02/171, International Monetary Fund, Washington DC.

Cohen, S. (2003) *Geopolitics of the World System*. New York: Rowman and Littlefield.

Colas, A. (2006) *Empire*. Cambridge: Cambridge University Press.

Commission on Global Governance (1995) *Our Global Neighbourhood*. Oxford: Oxford University Press.

Cooper, R. N. (1986) *Economic Policy in an Interdependent World*. Cambridge, Mass.: MIT Press.

Cortell, A. P. and Davies, J. W. (1996) How do international institutions matter? The domestic impact of international rules and norms. *International Studies Quarterly* 40.

Cowan, T. (2004) *Creative Destruction: How Globalization is Changing the World's Cultures*. Princeton: Princeton University Press.

Cox, R. (1996) Globalization, multilateralism and democracy. In R. Cox (ed.), *Approaches to World Order*, Cambridge: Cambridge University Press.

Cox, R. (1997) Economic globalization and the limits to liberal democracy. In McGrew 1997.

Crafts, N. and Venables, A. J. (2003) Globalization in history: a geographical perspective. In Bordo, Taylor and Williamson 2003.

Crawford, J. and Marks, S. (1998) The global democracy deficit: an essay on international law and its limits. In Archibugi, Held and Köhler 1998.

Crawford, J.-A. and Fiorentino, R. V. (2005) The changing landscape of regional trade agreements. Discussion Paper, World Trade Organization, Geneva.

Creveld, M. van (1989) *Technology and War: From 2000 BC to the Present*. New York: Free Press.

Creveld, M. van (1991) *The Transformation of War*. New York: Free Press.

Cutler, A. C. (2003) *Private Power and Global Authority*. Cambridge: Cambridge University Press.

Dahl, R. A. (1989) *Democracy and its Critics*. New Haven: Yale University Press.

Davies, J. B. et al. (2006) The world distribution of household wealth. WIDER Research Paper, 5 Dec., UNU-WIDER, New York.

Deacon, B. (2003) Global social governance reform: from institutions and policies to networks, projects and partnerships. In B. Deacon et al. (eds), *Global Social Governance*, Helsinki: Ministry for Foreign Affairs of Finland.

Deibert, R. (1997) *Parchment, Printing and the Hypermedia*. New York: Cornell University Press.

Desai, P. (2003) *Financial Crisis, Contagion, and Containment*. Princeton: Princeton University Press.

Desai, M. and Said, Y. (2001) The anti-capitalist movement. In H. Anheier, M. Glasius and M. Kaldor (eds), *Global Civil Society 2001*, Oxford: Oxford University Press.

Devereux, M., Lockwood, B. and Redoano, M. (2003) Capital account liberalization and corporate taxes. IMF Working Paper. At www.imf.org/external/pubs/ft/wp/2003/wp03180.pdf.

Dicken, P. (1998) *Global Shift*. London: Paul Chapman.

Dicken, P. (2003) *Global Shift*, 3rd edn. London: Sage.

243

References

Dickson, A. (1997) *Development and International Relations*. Cambridge: Polity.

Dollar, D. (2005) Globalization, poverty and inequality. In M. M. Weinstein (ed.), *Globalization: What's New?* New York: Columbia University Press.

Dollar, D. and Kraay, A. (2001) Growth is good for the poor. At www.worldbank.org/research/growth (accessed Mar. 2005).

Dollar, D. and Kraay, A. (2002) Spreading the wealth. *Foreign Affairs* 81(1): 120–33.

Donahue, J. D. and Nye, J. S. (eds) (2001) *Governance amid Bigger, Better Markets*. Washington DC: Brookings Institution.

Dore, R. (ed.) (1995) *Convergence or Diversity? National Models of Production in a Global Economy*. New York: Cornell University Press.

Dowrick, S. and DeLong, J. B. (2003) Globalization and convergence. In M. D. Bordo, A. M. Taylor and J. G. Williamson (eds), *Globalization in Historical Perspective*, Chicago: Chicago University Press.

Dryzek, J. (2006) *Deliberative Global Politics*. Cambridge: Polity.

Duffield, M. (2001) *Global Governance and the New Wars*. London: Zed Press.

Dunn, J. (1990) *Interpreting Political Responsibility*. Cambridge: Polity.

Dunning, J. (1993) *Multinational Enterprises and the Global Economy*. Wokingham: Addison-Wesley.

Dunning, J. H. (2000) The new geography of foreign direct investment. In N. Woods (ed.), *The Political Economy of Globalization*, Basingstoke: Palgrave.

Eatwell, J. and Taylor, L. (2000) *Global Finance at Risk*. Cambridge: Polity.

Eckersley, R. (2005) Cosmopolitan nations, cosmopolitan states. Paper for Symposium on Human Rights, Global Justice and Cosmopolitan Democracy, University of Queensland.

Edwards, M. (2003) *Civil Society*. Cambridge: Polity.

Edwards, M. and Gaventa, J. (eds) (2001) *Global Citizen Action*. London: Earthscan.

Eichengreen, B. (1996) *Globalizing Capital: A History of the International Monetary System*. Princeton: Princeton University Press.

Eichengreen, B. (2002) *Financial Crises*. Oxford: Oxford University Press.

Ekins, P. (1992) *A New World Order: Grassroots Movements for Global Change*. London: Routledge.

Elkins, D. J. (1995) *Beyond Sovereignty: Territory and Political Economy in the Twenty First Century*. Toronto: University of Toronto Press.

244

References

Enders, W. and Sandler, T. (2006) *The Political Economy of Terrorism*. Cambridge: Cambridge University Press.

Eschele, C. (2005) Constructing the antiglobalization movement. In C. Eschele and B. Maiguashia (eds), *Critical Theories, International Relations and the 'AntiGlobalization Movement': The Politics of Resistance*, London: Routledge.

Evans, P. (2005) Counter hegemonic globalization: transnational social movements in the contemporary global political economy. At http://sociology.berkeley.edu/faculty/evans/evans_pdf/Evans%20Transnational_Movements.pdf (accessed Sept. 2005).

Falk, R. (1969) The interplay of Westphalian and Charter conceptions of the international legal order. In R. Falk and C. Black (eds), *The Future of the International Legal Order*, vol. 1, Princeton: Princeton University Press.

Falk, R. (1987) The global promise of social movements: explorations at the edge of time. *Alternatives* 12.

Falk, R. (1995a) Liberalism at the global level: the last of the independent commissions? *Millennium* 24(3).

Falk, R. (1995b) *On Humane Governance: Toward a New Global Politics*. Cambridge: Polity.

Feldstein, M. and Horioka, C. (1980) Domestic savings and international capital flows. *Economic Journal* 90(358).

Ferguson, N. (2005) Sinking globalization. *Foreign Affairs* 84(2): 64–77.

Ferguson, Y. H. and Mansbach, R. W. (2004) *Remapping Global Politics*. Cambridge: Cambridge University Press.

Fernández-Armesto, F. (1995) *Millennium*. London: Bantam.

Ferro, M. (1997) *Colonization: A Global History*. London: Routledge.

Fieldhouse, D. K. (1999) *The West and the Third World*. Oxford: Blackwell.

Firebaugh, G. (2003) *The New Geography of Global Income Inequality*. Cambridge, Mass.: Harvard University Press.

Frank, A. G. (1998) *Re-Orient: Global Economy in the Asian Age*. New York: University of California Press.

Frank, A. G. and Gills, B. K. (eds) (1996) *The World System*. London: Routledge.

Freedman, L. (2006) *The Transformation of Strategic Affairs*. Adelphi Paper 379. London: International Institute for Strategic Studies.

Freeman, R. B. (2006) People flows in globalization. Working Paper 12315, National Bureau of Economic Research, New York.

Frieden, J. (1991) Invested interests: the politics of national economic policies in a world of global finance. *International Organization* 45(4).

References

Frost, M. (1986) *Towards a Normative Theory of International Relations*. Cambridge: Cambridge University Press.

Fujii, E. and Chinn, M. (2001) Fin de siècle real interest parity. *Journal of International Financial Markets, Institutions and Money* 11(3–4): 289–308.

Fukao, M. (1993) International integration of financial markets and the costs of capital. *Journal of International Securities Markets* 7.

Gagnon, J. and Unferth, M. (1995) Is there a world real interest rate? *Journal of International Money and Finance* 14(6).

Galbraith, J. R. (2002) A perfect crime: inequality in an age of globalization. *Daedalus* (Winter): 11–25.

Gamble, A. and Payne, A. (1991) Conclusion: the new regionalism. In A. Gamble and A. Payne (eds), *Regionalism and World Order*, London: Macmillan.

Ganghof, S. (2000) Adjusting national tax policy to economic internationalization. In F. Scharpf and V. Schmidt (eds), *Welfare and Work in the Open Economy*, Oxford: Oxford University Press.

Garrett, G. (1996) Capital mobility, trade and the domestic politics of economic policy. In Keohane and Milner 1996.

Garrett, G. (1998) Global markets and national politics. *International Organization* 52(4).

Garrett, G. (2000) The causes of globalization. *Comparative Political Studies* 33(6): 945–91.

Garrett, G. (2001) The distributional consequences of globalization. At www.yale.edu/leitner/pdf/CPEDLDC-Garrett.pdf (accessed May 2007).

Garrett, G. and Lange, P. (1991) Political responses to interdependence: what's 'left' for the left? *International Organization* 45(4).

Garrett, G. and Lange, P. (1996) Internationalization, institutions and political change. In Keohane and Milner 1996.

Garrett, G. and Nickerson, D. (2003) Globalization, democratization and government spending in middle income countries. In M. Glatzer and D. Rueschemeyer (eds), *Globalization and the Future of the Welfare State*, Pittsburgh: University of Pittsburgh Press.

Gellner, E. (1983) *Nations and Nationalism*. Oxford: Blackwell.

General, S. (2000). Renewing the United Nations. United Nations, New York, at www.un.org.

Gereffi, G. and Korzeniewicz, M. (eds) (1994) *Commodity Chains and Global Capitalism*. Westport: Praeger.

Germain, R. (1997) *The International Organization of Credit*. Cambridge: Cambridge University Press.

Geyer, M. and Bright, C. (1995) World history in a global age. *American Historical Review* 100(4).

References

Giannone, D. and Lenza, M. (2004) The Feldstein-Horioka fact. Discussion Paper, Centre for Economic Policy Research, London.

Giddens, A. (1985) *The Nation-State and Violence*, vol. 2 of *A Contemporary Critique of Historical Materialism*. Cambridge: Polity.

Giddens, A. (1990) *The Consequences of Modernity*. Cambridge: Polity.

Giddens, A. (1991) *Modernity and Self-Identity*. Cambridge: Polity.

Giddens, A. (1999a) *Runaway World*. London: Profile.

Giddens, A. (1999b) *The Third Way*. Cambridge: Polity.

Gill, S. (1992) Economic globalization and the internationalization of authority: limits and contradictions. *GeoForum* 23(3).

Gill, S. (1995) Globalization, market civilization and disciplinary neoliberalism. *Millennium* 24(3).

Gill, S. (2003) *Power and Resistance in the New World Order*. Basingstoke: Palgrave.

Gilpin, R. (1981) *War and Change in World Politics*. Cambridge: Cambridge University Press.

Gilpin, R. (1987) *The Political Economy of International Relations*. Princeton: Princeton University Press.

Gilpin, R. (2001) *Global Political Economy*. Princeton: Princeton University Press.

Gilpin, R. (2002a) A realist perspective on international governance. In D. Held and A. McGrew (eds), *Governing Globalization*, Cambridge: Polity.

Gilpin, R. (2002b) *The Challenge of Global Capitalism*. Princeton: Princeton University Press.

Gilroy, P. (1987) *There Ain't No Black in the Union Jack*. London: Hutchinson.

Godement, F. (1999) *The Downsizing of Asia*. London: Routledge.

Goldberg, L., Lothian, J. and Kunev, J. (2003) Has international financial integration increased? *Open Economies Review* 14(3): 299–317.

Goldblatt, D., Held, D., McGrew, A. and Perraton, J. (1997) Economic globalization and the nation-state: shifting balances of power. *Alternatives* 22(3).

Goldeier, J. M. and McFaul, M. (1992) A tale of two worlds: core and periphery in the post-Cold War era. *International Organization* 46(2): 467–91.

Goodman, J. (1997) The European Union: reconstituting democracy beyond the nation-state. In McGrew 1997.

Gordon, D. (1988) The global economy: new edifice or crumbling foundations? *New Left Review* 168.

Gourevitch, P. (1986) *Politics in Hard Times*. New York: Cornell University Press.

References

Gowan, P. (2001) Neoliberal cosmopolitanism. *New Left Review*, series II, no. 11.

Graham, G. (1997) *Ethics and International Relations.* Oxford: Blackwell.

Gray, C. S. (2005) *Another Bloody Century.* London: Weidenfeld and Nicolson.

Gray, J. (1998) *False Dawn.* London: Granta.

Greider, W. (1997) *One World, Ready or Not: The Manic Logic of Global Capitalism.* New York: Simon and Schuster.

Grieco, J. M. and Ikenberry, G. J. (2003) *State Power and World Markets.* New York: Norton.

Guehenno, J. M. (1995) *The End of the Nation-State.* Minneapolis: Minnesota University Press.

Guibernau, M. (1995) *Nationalisms.* Cambridge: Polity.

Haass, R. N. and Liton, R. E. (1998) Globalization and its discontents. *Foreign Affairs* (May–June).

Habermas, J. (2001) *The Postnational Constellation.* Cambridge, Mass.: MIT Press.

Hafez, Kai (2007) *The Myth of Media Globalization.* Cambridge: Polity.

Haggard, S. (2000) *The Political Economy of the Asian Financial Crisis.* Washington DC: Institute for International Economics.

Hall, S. (1992) The question of cultural identity. In S. Hall, D. Held and A. McGrew (eds), *Modernity and its Futures*, Cambridge: Polity.

Handwerk, B. (2004) Global warming: fast facts. At http://news.nationalgeographic.com/news/2004/12/1206_041206_global_warming.html.

Hannerz, U. (1992) *Global Complexity.* New York: Columbia University Press.

Hanson, B. T. (1998) What happened to Fortress Europe? External trade policy liberalization in the European Union. *International Organization* 52(1) (Winter).

Hardt, M. and Negri, A. (2000) *Empire.* Cambridge: Harvard University Press.

Harkavy, R. E. (1989) *Bases Abroad: The Global Foreign Military Presence.* Oxford: Oxford University Press.

Harrison, A. and McMillan, M. S. (2006) Outsourcing jobs? Multinationals and US employment. Working Paper, National Bureau of Economic Research, New York.

Hart, J. (1992) *Rival Capitalists: International Competitiveness in the USA, Japan and Western Europe.* Princeton: Princeton University Press.

Harvey, D. (1989) *The Condition of Postmodernity.* Oxford: Blackwell.

References

Harvey, D. (2003) *The New Imperialism.* Oxford: Oxford University Press.

Harvey, D. (2006) *Neoliberalism.* Oxford: Oxford University Press.

Hasenclever, A., Mayer, P. and Rittberger, V. (1997) *Theories of International Regimes.* Cambridge: Cambridge University Press.

Hay, C. (2000) Contemporary capitalism, globalization, regionalization and the persistence of national variation. *Review of International Studies* 26(4): 509–32.

Hay, C. (2001) Globalization, economic change and the welfare state. In R. Sykes, B. Palier and P. Prior (eds), *Globalization and European Welfare States,* Basingstoke: Palgrave.

Hay, C. (2002) Globalisation, 'EU-isation', and the space for social democratic alternatives: pessimism of the intellect: a reply to Coates. *British Journal of Politics and International Relations* 4(3): 452–64.

Hay, C. (2005) Globalization's impact on states. In J. Ravenhill (ed.), *Global Political Economy,* Oxford: Oxford University Press.

Hay, C. (2006) What's globalization got to do with it? Economic globalization and the future of the European welfare state. *Government and Opposition* 41(1): 1–22.

Hayek, F. (1960) *The Constitution of Liberty.* London: Routledge and Kegan Paul.

Hayek, F. (1976) *The Road to Serfdom.* London: Routledge and Kegan Paul.

Held, D. (ed.) (1991) *Political Theory Today.* Cambridge: Polity.

Held, D. (1995) *Democracy and the Global Order: From the Modern State to Cosmopolitan Governance.* Cambridge: Polity.

Held, D. (1996) *Models of Democracy,* 2nd edn. Cambridge: Polity.

Held, D. (2002a) Globalization, corporate practice and cosmopolitan social standards. *Contemporary Political Theory* 1(1): 59–78.

Held, D. (2002b) Law of states, law of peoples: three models of sovereignty. *Legal Theory* 8(1).

Held, D. (2004) *Global Covenant.* Cambridge: Polity.

Held, D. (2006) *Models of Democracy,* 3rd edn. Cambridge: Polity.

Held, D. (2007) Cultural diversity, cosmopolitan principles and the limits of sovereignty. In Held and Moore 2007.

Held, D. and Kaldor, M. (2001) What hope for the future? At www.lse.ac.uk/depts/global/maryheld.htm.

Held, D. and Kaya, A. (eds) (2006) *Global Inequality: Patterns and Explanations.* Cambridge: Polity.

Held, D. and Koenig-Archibugi, M. (eds) (2004) *American Power in the Twenty-First Century.* Cambridge: Polity.

Held, D. and McGrew, A. G. (eds) (2000) *The Global Transformations Reader.* 2nd edn 2003. Cambridge: Polity.

249

References

Held, D. and McGrew, A. (2002a) *Globalization/Anti-Globalization*, 1st edn. Cambridge: Polity.

Held, D. and McGrew, A. G. (eds) (2002b) *Governing Globalization: Power, Authority and Global Governance*. Cambridge: Polity.

Held, D. and Moore, H. (eds) (2007) *Cultural Politics in a Global Age*. Oxford: OneWorld.

Held, D., McGrew, A. G., Goldblatt, D. and Perraton, J. (1999) *Global Transformations: Politics, Economics and Culture*. Cambridge: Polity.

Helleiner, E. (1997) Braudelian reflections on economic globalization: the historian as pioneer. In S. Gill and J. Mittleman (eds), *Innovation and Transformation in International Studies*, Cambridge: Cambridge University Press.

Herod, A., Tuathail, G. O. and Roberts, S. M. (eds) (1998) *Unruly World? Globalization, Governance and Geography*. London: Routledge.

Hertz, N. (2001) Decrying Wolf. *Prospect* (Aug–Sept.): 12–13.

Hettne, B. (1998) The double movement: global market versus regionalism. In R. W. Cox (ed.), *The New Realism: Perspectives on Multilateralism and World Order*, Tokyo: United Nations University Press.

Hettne, B. (2007) Globalism, regionalism and interregionalism. In A. McGrew and N. Poku (eds), *Globalization, Development and Human Security*, Cambridge: Polity.

Higgott, R. (2000) Contested globalization: the changing context and normative challenges. *Review of International Studies* 26 (special issue): 131–55.

Hinsley, F. H. (1986) *Sovereignty*, 2nd edn. Cambridge: Cambridge University Press.

Hirst, P. (1997) The global economy: myths and realities. *International Affairs* 73(3) (July).

Hirst, P. (2001) *War and Power in the 21st Century*. Cambridge: Polity.

Hirst, P. and Thompson, G. (1996) *Globalization in Question*. Cambridge: Polity.

Hirst, P. and Thompson, G. (1999) *Globalization in Question*, 2nd edn. Cambridge: Polity.

Hirst, P. and Thompson, G. (2003) Globalization: a necessary myth? In D. Held and A. McGrew (eds), *The Global Transformations Reader*, 2nd edn, Cambridge: Polity.

Hobbes, T. (1968) *Leviathan* (1691). Harmondsworth: Penguin.

Hobsbawm, E. (1994) *Age of Extremes: The Short Twentieth Century 1914–1991*. London: Michael Joseph.

Hodgson, M. G. S. (1993) The interrelations of societies in history. In E. Burke (ed.), *Rethinking World History: Essays on Europe, Islam and World History*, Cambridge: Cambridge University Press.

References

Hoffmann, M. (1998) Long-run capital flows and the Feldstein-Horoika puzzle. *EUI Working Paper*. Florence: European University Institute.

Hoffmann, S. (2002) The clash of globalizations. *Foreign Affairs* (July).

Hoffmann, S. (2003) America goes backward. *New York Review of Books*, 12 June, pp. 74–80.

Hoffmann, S. (2004) *Gulliver Unbound: The Imperial Temptation and the War in Iraq*. Rowman and Littlefield.

Hoffmann, S. (2006) The foreign policy the US needs. *New York Review of Books*, 10 Aug., pp. 60–4.

Holmes, S. (1988) Precommitment and the paradox of democracy. In J. Elster and R. Stagstad (eds), *Constitutionalism and Democracy*, Cambridge: Cambridge University Press.

Holton, R. (2005) *Making Globalization*. Basingstoke: Palgrave.

Hoogvelt, A. (1997) *Globalization and the Postcolonial World: The New Political Economy of Development*. London: Macmillan.

Hoogvelt, A. (2001) *Globalization and the Postcolonial World*, 2nd edn. Basingstoke: Palgrave.

Hopkins, A. (ed.) (2002) *Globalization in World History*. London: Pimlico.

Howard, M. (1981) *War and the Liberal Conscience*. Oxford: Oxford University Press.

Hu, W. (1992) Global corporations are national firms with international operations. *California Management Review* 34(2).

Hui, V. T. (2005) *War and State Formation in Ancient China and Early Modern Europe*. Cambridge: Cambridge University Press.

Human Security Centre (2005) *Human Security Report 2005: War and Peace in the 21st Century*. At www.humansecurityreport.info (accessed Feb. 2006).

Hummels, D. (2001) The nature and growth of vertical specialization in world trade. *Journal of International Economics* 54(1): 75–96.

Huntington, S. P. (1996) *The Clash of Civilizations and the Remaking of World Order*. New York: Simon and Schuster.

Hurrell, A. (1999) Security and inequality. In A. Hurrell and N. Woods, *Inequality, Globalization and World Politics*, Oxford: Oxford University Press.

Hurrell, A. (2001) Global inequality and international institutions. In T. W. Pogge (ed.), *Global Justice*, Oxford: Oxford University Press.

Hurrell, A. and Woods, N. (1995) Globalization and inequality. *Millennium* 24(3).

Idso, S. B., Idso, C. D. and Idso, K. E. (2003) Enhanced or impaired? Human health in a CO_2-enriched warmer world. Centre for the Study of Carbon Dioxide and Global Change, Tempe. At www. co2science.org/scrpits/Template/0_CO2ScienceB2C/pdf/health2pps.pdf.

Ikenberry, G. J. (2001) *After Victory*. Princeton: Princeton University Press.

Ikenberry, G. J. (2002) America's imperial ambition. *Foreign Affairs* 81(5): 44–60.

IMF (International Monetary Fund) (2002) *World Economic Outlook 2002*. Washington DC: IMF.

IMF (International Monetary Fund) (2003) *World Economic Outlook 2003*. Washington DC: IMF.

IPCC (2007) *Summary Report for Policymakers*, at www.ipcc.ch/ pub/wg2SPfinal.pdf.

Irwin, D. (2002) Long run trends in world income and trade. *World Trade Review* 1(1): 89–100.

ITU (International Telecommunication Union) (2005) *ITU Internet Reports 2005: The Internet of Things Executive Summary*. Geneva: International Telecommunication Union. At www.itu.int/dms_ pub/itu-s/opb/pol/S-POL-IR.IT-2005-SUM-PDF-E.pdf (accessed Aug. 2006).

IWG (Information Working Group of the Voluntary Principles) (2005) Five-year overview of the Voluntary Principles on Security and Human Rights. At www.voluntaryprinciples.org.

James, H. (2001) *The End of Globalization*. Princeton: Princeton University Press.

James, P. and Nairn, T. (2005) *Global Matrix: Nationalism, Globalization, and Terrorism*. London: Routledge.

Jameson, F. (1991) *Postmodernism: The Cultural Logic of Late Capitalism*. London: Verso.

Jayasuriya, K. (1999) Globalization, law and the transformation of sovereignty: the emergence of global regulatory governance. *Indiana Journal of Global Legal Studies* 6(2).

Jessop, B. (1997) Capitalism and its future: remarks on regulation, government and governance. *Review of International Political Economy* 4(3).

Jessop, B. (2002) *The Future of the Capitalist State*. Cambridge: Polity.

Johnston, R. J., Taylor, P. J. and Watts, M. J. (eds) (1995) *Geographies of Global Change*. Oxford: Blackwell.

Jones, R. J. B. (1995) *Globalization and Interdependence in the International Political Economy*. London: Pinter.

Julius, D. (1990) *Global Companies*. London: Pinter.

Kaldor, M. (1998) *New and Old Wars: Organized Violence in a Global Era*. Cambridge: Polity.

References

Kaldor, M. (2003) Global civil society. In D. Held and A. McGrew (eds), *The Global Transformations Reader*, 2nd edn. Cambridge: Polity.

Kaldor, M. (2004) American power: from 'compellance' to cosmopolitanism? In Held and Koenig-Archibugi 2004.

Kaplan, R. (1994) The coming anarchy. *Atlantic Monthly* 277: 44–76.

Kaplinsky, R. (2006) *Between a Rock and a Hard Place: Globalization, Poverty, and Inequality*. Cambridge: Polity.

Kapstein, E. B. (1994) *Governing the Global Economy: International Finance and the State*. Cambridge, Mass.: Harvard University Press.

Kapstein, E. B. (2000) Winners and losers in the global economy. *International Organization* 54(2): 359–84.

Kaul, I., Grunberg, I. and Stern, M. (eds) (1999) *Global Public Goods: International Cooperation in the Twenty-First Century*. Oxford: Oxford University Press.

Kaul, I., Conceição, P., Goulven, K., and Mendoza, R. (eds) (2003) *Providing Global Public Goods*. Oxford: Oxford University Press.

Keane, J. (2004) *Violence and Democracy*. Cambridge: Cambridge University Press

Keck, M. and Sikkink, K. (1998) *Activists beyond Borders*. New York: Cornell University Press.

Kennedy, P., Messner, D. and Nuscheler, F. (2002) *Global Trends and Global Governance*. London: Pluto Press.

Kennedy-Pipe, C. and Rengger, N. (2006) Apocalypse now? Continuities or disjunctions in politics after 9/11. *International Affairs* 82(3): 539–52.

Keohane, R. O. (1984) *After Hegemony*. Princeton: Princeton University Press.

Keohane, R. O. (1995) Hobbes's dilemma and institutional change in world politics: sovereignty in international society. In H.-H. Holm and G. Sorensen (eds), *Whose World Order?* Boulder: Westview Press.

Keohane, R. O. (1998) International institutions: can interdependence work? *Foreign Policy* (Spring).

Keohane, R. O. (2001) Governance in a partially globalized world. *American Political Science Review* 95(1): 1–13.

Keohane, R. O. (2002) The globalization of informal violence, theories of world politics, and the 'liberalism of fear'. In R. O. Keohane (ed.), *Power and Governance in a Partially Globalized World*, London: Routledge.

Keohane, R. O. and Milner, H. V. (eds) (1996) *Internationalization and Domestic Politics*. Cambridge: Cambridge University Press.

Keohane, R. O. and Nye, J. S. (1972) *Transnational Relations and World Politics*. Cambridge, Mass.: Harvard University Press.

References

Keohane, R. O. and Nye, J. (1977) *Power and Interdependence*. Boston: Little, Brown.

Keohane, R. and Nye, J. (2003) Globalization: What's new? What's not? (And so what?) In D. Held and A. McGrew (eds), *The Global Transformations Reader*, 2nd edn, Cambridge: Polity.

Kiely, R. (2006) *The New Political Economy of Development*. Basingstoke: Palgrave.

King, D. A. (2004) Climate change science: adapt, mitigate or ignore? *Science* 303: 176–7.

Klein, B. S. (1994) *Strategic Studies and World Order*. Cambridge: Cambridge University Press.

Klein, N. (2000) *No Logo*. London: Flamingo.

Klein, N. (2002) *Fences and Windows: Dispatches from the Front Lines of the Globalization Debate*. Toronto: Vintage.

Koenig-Archibugi, M. (2002) Mapping global governance. In Held and McGrew 2002b.

Kofman, E. and Youngs, G. (eds) (1996) *Globalization: Theory and Practice*. London: Pinter.

Korten, D. C. (1995) *When Corporations Ruled the World*. Hartford: Kumerian Press.

Krasner, S. D. (1985) *Structural Conflict: The Third World against Global Liberalism*. Los Angeles: University of California Press.

Krasner, S. D. (1993) Economic interdependence and independent statehood. In R. H. Jackson and A. James (eds), *States in a Changing World*, Oxford: Oxford University Press.

Krasner, S. D. (1995) Compromising Westphalia. *International Security* 20(3).

Krause, K. (1992) *Arms and the State: Patterns of Military Production and Trade*. Cambridge: Cambridge University Press.

Krugman, P. (1994) Does third world growth hurt first world prosperity? *Harvard Business Review* (July).

Krugman, P. (1995) Growing world trade: causes and consequences. *Brookings Papers on Economic Activity*, no. 1.

Ku, C. (2001) Global governance and the changing face of international law. The 2001 John W. Holmes Memorial Lecture, prepared for delivery at the annual meeting of the Academic Council in the United Nations System, 16–18 June, Puebla, Mexico. *ACUNS Reports and Papers Series*, 2001, no. 2.

Lacey, R. and Danziger, D. (1999) *The Year 1000*. London: Little, Brown.

Landes, D. S. (1989) *The Wealth and Poverty of Nations*. New York: Norton.

References

Lane, P. R. and Milesi-Ferretti, G. M. (2003) International financial integration. *IMF Staff Papers* 50: 82–100.

Lawrence, R. (1996) *Single World, Divided Nations? International Trade and OECD Labor Markets*. Washington DC: Brookings Institution.

Leander, A. (2002) Conditional legitimacy, reinterpreted monopolies: globalisation and the evolving state monopoly on legitimate violence. Annual Convention of the International Studies Association, Panel on Legitimacy and Violence: Globalisation and the Displacement of the State.

Leander, A. (2004a) *Eroding State Authority? Private Military Companies and the Legitimate Use of Force*. Rome: Centro Militare di Studi Strategici.

Leander, A. (2004b) Wars and the un-making of states: taking Tilly seriously in the contemporary world. In S. Guzzini and D. Jung (eds), *Copenhagen Peace Research: Conceptual Innovations and Contemporary Security Analysis*, London and New York: Routledge.

Leftwich, A. (2000) *States of Development*. Cambridge: Polity.

Liebes, T. and Katz, E. (1993) *The Export of Meaning: Cross-Cultural Readings of Dallas*. Cambridge: Polity.

Lindert, P. H. and Williamson, J. G. (2003) Does globalization make the world more unequal? In M. D. Bordo, A. M. Taylor and J. G. Williamson (eds), *Globalization in Historical Perspective*, Chicago: University of Chicago Press.

Lindzen, R S. (2006) There is no 'consensus' on global warming. *Examiner*, 12 July. At www.examiner.com/a-173632~There_is_no_consensus_on_global_warming.html.

Linklater, A. (1998) *The Transformation of Political Community*. Cambridge: Polity.

Lloyd, P. J. (1992) Regionalization and world trade. *OECD Economics Studies* 18 (Spring).

Locke, J. (1963) *Two Treatises of Government* (1690). Cambridge: Cambridge University Press.

Lomborg, B. (2004a) *The Skeptical Environmentalist: Measuring the State of the World*. Cambridge: Cambridge University Press.

Lomborg, B. (ed.) (2004b) *Global Crises, Global Solutions*. Cambridge: Cambridge University Press.

Long, P. (1995) The Harvard School of Liberal International Theory: the case for closure. *Millennium* 24(3).

Longin, F. and B. Solnik (1995) Is the correlation of international equity returns constant? 1960–1990. *Journal of International Money and Finance* 14: 3–26.

Lukasik, S. J., Goodman, S. E. and Longhurst, D. (2003) *Protecting*

References

Critical Infrastructures against Cyber-attack. Adelphi Paper 359. London: International Institute for Strategic Studies.

Luttwak, E. (1999) *Turbo-Capitalism.* New York: Basic Books.

MacIntyre, A. (1981) *After Virtue.* London: Duckworth.

MacIntyre, A. (1988) *Whose Justice? Which Rationality?* London: Duckworth.

Maddison, A. (2001) *The World Economy: A Millennial Perspective.* Paris: OECD Development Studies Centre.

Mann, M. (1986) *The Sources of Social Power,* vol. 1: *A History of Power from the Beginning to AD 1760.* Cambridge: Cambridge University Press.

Mann, M. (1987) Ruling strategies and citizenship. *Sociology* 21(3).

Mann, M. (1997) Has globalization ended the rise and rise of the nation-state? *Review of International Political Economy* 4(3).

Mann, M. (2001) Globalization after September 11th. *New Left Review* 12 (Nov.–Dec.): 51–72.

Mann, M. (2004) The first failed empire of the twenty-first century. In Held and Koenig-Archibugi 2004.

Massey, D. and Jess, P. (eds) (1995) *A Place in the World? Culture, Places and Globalization.* Oxford: Oxford University Press.

Mastanduno, M. (1999) A realist view: three images of the coming international order. In J. A. Hall and T. V. Paul (eds), *International Order and the Future of World Politics,* Cambridge: Cambridge University Press.

Mazlish, B. and Buultjens, R. (eds) (1993) *Conceptualizing Global History.* Boulder: Westview Press.

McCarthy, J. et al (eds) (2001) *Climate Change 2001: Impacts, Adaptation, and Vulnerability.* Cambridge: Cambridge University Press.

McGrew, A. G. (1992) Conceptualizing global politics. In McGrew et al. 1992.

McGrew, A. G. (ed.) (1997) *The Transformation of Democracy? Globalization and Territorial Democracy.* Cambridge: Polity.

McGrew, A. (2001) Making globalization work for the poor: the European contribution. Seminar paper, Swedish Ministry of Foreign Affairs.

McGrew, A. (2002) Between two worlds: Europe in a globalizing era. *Government and Opposition* 37(3) (Summer): 243–58.

McGrew, A. (2005) Globalization and global politics. In Baylis and Smith 2005.

McGrew, A. G. et al. (1992) *Global Politics.* Cambridge: Polity.

McLuhan, M. (1964) *Understanding Media: The Extension of Man.* London: Routledge and Kegan Paul.

References

McNeill, W. (1982) *The Pursuit of Power*. Oxford: Blackwell.

Mearsheimer, J. (1994) The false promise of international institutions. *International Organization* 19: 5–49.

Mearsheimer, J. (2001) *The Tragedy of Great Power Politics*. New York: Norton.

Meikle, J. (2005) Bill Gates gives $258m to world battle against malaria. *Guardian*, 31 Oct.

Meyrowitz, J. (1985) *No Sense of Place*. Oxford: Oxford University Press.

Milanovic, B. (2002a) True world income distribution, 1988 and 1993. *Economic Journal* 112: 51–92.

Milanovic, B. (2002b) Two faces of globalization. At www.worldbank. org/research (accessed Mar. 2005).

Milanovic, B. (2005) *Worlds Apart: Measuring International and Global Inequality* (Princeton: Princeton University Press).

Milanovic, B. (2006a) Why globalization is in trouble. *YaleGlobal Online*. At http://yaleglobal.yale.edu.

Milanovic, B. (2006b) Global income inequality. Working Paper, World Bank, Washington DC.

Miller, D. (1988) The ethical significance of nationality. *Ethics* 98(4).

Miller, D. (1992) The young and the restless in Trinidad: a case of the local and the global in mass consumption. In R. Silverstone and E. Hirsch (eds), *Consuming Technology*, London: Routledge.

Miller, D. (1995) *On Nationality*. Oxford: Oxford University Press.

Miller, D. (1999) Justice and inequality. In A. Hurrell and N. Woods (eds), *Inequality, Globalization and World Politics*, Oxford: Oxford University Press.

Milner, H. V. (1997) *Interests, Institutions and Information: Domestic Politics and International Relations*. Princeton: Princeton University Press.

Mitrany, D. (1975) The progress of international government (1932). In P. Taylor (ed.), *The Functional Theory of Politics*, London: LSE/Martin Robertson.

Mittleman, J. H. (2000) *The Globalization Syndrome*. Princeton: Princeton University Press.

Modelski, G. (1972) *Principles of World Politics*. New York: Free Press.

Moore, M. (2003) *A World without Walls: Freedom, Development, Free Trade and Global Governance*. Cambridge University Press.

Morgenthau, H. J. (1948) *Politics among Nations*. New York: Knopf.

Morse, E. (1976) *Modernization and the Transformation of International Relations*. New York: Free Press.

Moses, J. W. (1994) Abdication from national policy autonomy: what's left to leave? *Politics and Society* 22(2): 125–38.

257

Mosley, L. (2000) International financial markets and national welfare states. *International Organization* 54(4): 737–74.

Mosley, L. (2003) *Global Capital and National Governments.* Cambridge: Cambridge University Press.

Mueller, J. (1989) *Retreat from Doomsday: The Obsolescence of Major War.* New York: Basic Books.

Mueller, J. (2004) *The Remnants of War.* Ithaca: Cornell University Press.

Munck, R. (2002) *Globalisation and Labour.* London: Zed Press.

Murphy, C. N. (2000) Global governance: poorly done and poorly understood. *International Affairs* 76(4): 789–803.

Murray, I. (2006) Global warming FAQ: what every citizen needs to know about global warming. *Competitive Enterprise Institute* 106 (13 July). At www.cei.org/pdf/5430.pdf.

Naimi, M. (2002) Post-terror surprises. Sept., www.foreignpolicy.com/issue_september_2002/ml.html (accessed June 2003).

Neal, L. (1985) Integration of international capital markets. *Journal of Economic History* 45 (June).

Newman, D. (2006) The resilience of territorial conflict in an era of globalization. In M. Kahler and B. F. Walter (eds), *Territoriality and Conflict in an Era of Globalization,* Cambridge: Cambridge University Press.

Newman, E. (2001) Human security and constructivism. *International Studies Perspectives* 2(3): 239–51.

Nierop, T. (1994) *Systems and Regions in Global Politics.* London: John Wiley.

Norris, P. (2000) Global governance and cosmopolitan citizens. In J. S. Nye and J. D. Donahue (eds), *Governance in a Globalizing World,* Washington DC: Brookings Institution Press.

Nozick, R. (1974) *Anarchy, State and Utopia.* Oxford: Blackwell.

Nye, J. S. (1990) *Bound to Lead.* New York: Basic Books.

Nye, J. S. (2002) *The Paradox of American Power.* Oxford: Oxford University Press.

Nye, J. S. (2004) *Soft Power.* New York: Public Affairs.

O'Brien, R. (1992) *The End of Geography: Global Financial Integration.* London: Pinter.

O'Brien, R., Goetz, A. M. and Scholte, J. A. ((2000) *Contesting Global Governance: Multilateral Economic Institutions and Global Social Movements.* Cambridge: Cambridge University Press.

Obstfeld, M. and Taylor, A. M. (1998) The Great Depression as a watershed: international capital mobility over the long run. In M. D. Bordo, C. Goldin and E. White (eds), *The Defining Moment: The Great Depression and the American Economy in the Twentieth Century,* Chicago: University of Chicago Press.

References

Obstfeld, M. and Taylor, A. M. (2003) Globalization and capital markets. In Bordo, Taylor and Williamson 2003.

Obstfeld, M. and Taylor, A. M. (2004) *Global Capital Markets: Integration, Crisis and Growth*. Cambridge: Cambridge University Press.

Obstfeld, M., Sambaugh, J. C. and Taylor, A. M. (2003) The trilemma in world history: tradeoffs among exchange rates, monetary policies and capital mobility. Paper for conference, The Political Economy of Globalization, Trinity College Dublin.

OECD (1997) *Communications Outlook*. Paris: Organization for Economic Cooperation and Development.

OECD (2005) Aid rising sharply, according to latest OECD figures. At www.oecd.org/dac.

Offe, C. (1985) *Disorganized Capitalism*. Cambridge: Polity.

Ohmae, K. (1990) *The Borderless World*. London: Collins.

Ohmae, K. (1995) *The End of the Nation State*. New York: Free Press.

Olesen, T. (2005) *International Zapatismo: The Construction of Solidarity in the Age of Globalization*. London: Zed Press.

O'Neill, O. (1991) Transnational justice. In Held 1991.

O'Neill, O. (2001) Agents of justice. In T. W. Pogge (ed.), *Global Justice*, Oxford: Blackwell.

Oreskes, O. (2004) Beyond the ivory tower: the scientific consensus on climate change. *Science* 306 (5702). At www.sciencemag.org/cgi/content/full/306/5702/1686.

O'Rourke, K. (2001) Globalization and inequality: historical trends. Working Paper 8339, National Bureau of Economic Research, New York.

O'Rourke, K. H. and Williamson, J. G. (1999) *Globalization and History: The Evolution of the Nineteenth Century Atlantic Economy*. Cambridge, Mass.: MIT Press.

Parekh, B. (1989) Between holy text and moral word. *New Statesman*, 23 Mar.

Parker, G. (1988) *The Military Revolution*. Cambridge: Cambridge University Press.

Pauly, L. W. (1997) *Who Elected the Bankers?* New York: Cornell University Press.

Payne, A. (2003) Globalization and modes of regionalist governance. In D. Held and A. McGrew (eds), *The Global Transformations Reader*, 2nd edn, Cambridge: Polity.

Perlmutter, H. V. (1991) On the rocky road to the first global civilization. *Human Relations* 44(9).

Perraton, J. (2001) The global economy: myths and realities. *Cambridge Journal of Economics* 25(5).

References

Perraton, J., Goldblatt, D., Held, D. and McGrew, A. (1997) The globalization of economic activity. *New Political Economy* 2 (Spring).

Petersen, V. S. (2004) Plural processes, patterned connections. *Globalizations* 1(1): 50–68.

Petras, J. and Veltmeyer, H. (2001) *Globalization Unmasked: Imperialism in the 21st Century*. London: Zed Books.

Pieper, U. and Taylor, L. (1998) The revival of the liberal creed: the IMF, the World Bank and inequality in a globalized economy. In D. Baker, G. Epstein and R. Podin (eds), *Globalization and Progressive Economic Policy*, Cambridge: Cambridge University Press.

Piore, M. and Sabel, C. (1984) *The Second Industrial Divide*. New York: Basic Books.

Pogge, T. W. (2001) Priorities of global justice. In T. W. Pogge (ed.), *Global Justice*, Oxford: Blackwell.

Pogge, T. (2006) Why inequality matters. In Held and Kaya 2006.

Poggi, G. (1978) *The Development of the Modern State*. London: Hutchinson.

Porter, M. (1990) *The Competitive Advantage of Nations*. London: Macmillan.

Potter, D., Goldblatt, D., Kiloh, M. and Lewis, P. (eds) (1997) *Democratization*. Cambridge: Polity.

Reddy, S. G. and Pogge, T. W. (2003) How not to count the poor. At www.socialanalysis.org (accessed June 2005).

Rees, M. (2003) *Our Final Century*. New York: Arrow Books.

Reich, R. (1991) *The Work of Nations*. New York: Simon and Schuster.

Reinicke, W. (1999) The other world wide web: global public policy networks. *Foreign Policy* (Winter).

Rheingold, H. (1995) *The Virtual Community*. London: Mandarin.

Rieger, E. and Liebfried, S. (1998) Welfare limits to globalization. *Politics and Society* 26(3).

Rieger, E. and Liebfried, S. (2003) *The Limits to Globalization*. Cambridge: Cambridge University Press.

Rischard, J.-F. (2002) *High Noon*. New York: Basic Books.

Risse, T. (2000a) Let's argue: communicative action in world politics. *International Organization* 54(1): 1–40.

Risse, T. (2000b) Transnational actors, networks, and global governance. MS.

Roberts, S. M. (1998) Geo-governance in trade and finance and political geographies of dissent. In Herod, Tuathail and Roberts 1998.

Robertson, R. (1992) *Globalization: Social Theory and Global Culture*. London: Sage.

References

Robins, K. (1991) Tradition and translation. In J. Corner and S. Harvey (eds), *Enterprise and Heritage: Crosscurrents of National Politics*, London: Routledge.

Rodrik, D. (1997) *Has Globalization Gone Too Far?* Washington DC: Institute for International Economics.

Rodrik, D. (2001) The global governance of trade as if development really mattered. At www.undp.org/bdp.

Rodrik, D. (2005) Making globalization work for development. Ralph Miliband Lecture, London School of Economics, 18 Nov.

Rodrik, D. (2006) Industrial development: stylized facts and policies. Aug., at http://ksghome.harvard.edu/~drodrik/industrial%20development.pdf (accessed Nov. 2006).

Rosamond, B. (2003) Babylon and on? Globalization and international political economy. *Review of International Political Economy* 10(4): 661–71.

Rosenau, J. N. (1990) *Turbulence in World Politics*. Brighton: Harvester Wheatsheaf.

Rosenau, J. N. (1997) *Along the Domestic-Foreign Frontier*. Cambridge: Cambridge University Press.

Rosenau, J. N. (2000a) Change, complexity, and governance in globalizing space. In J. Pierre (ed.), *Debating Governance: Authority, Steering, and Democracy*, Oxford: Oxford University Press.

Rosenau, J. N. (2000b) Governance in a globalizing world. In Held and McGrew 2000.

Rosenau, J. N. (2002) Governance in a new global order. In Held and McGrew 2002b.

Rosenau, J. N. (2003) *Distant Proximities: Dynamics beyond Globalization*. Princeton: Princeton University Press.

Rosenberg, J. (2000) *The Follies of Globalization Theory*. London: Verso.

Rosenberg, J. (2005) Globalization theory: a post-mortem. *International Politics* 42(2): 2–74.

Rowthorn, R. and Wells, J. (1987) *De-industrialization and Foreign Trade*. Cambridge: Cambridge University Press.

Rudra, N. (2002) Globalization and the decline of the welfare state in less-developed countries. *International Organization* 56(2): 411–45.

Ruggie, J. (1993a) Territoriality and beyond: problematizing modernity in international relations. *International Organization* 41(1): 139–74.

Ruggie, J. (ed.) (1993b) *Multilateralism Matters*. New York: Columbia University Press.

Rugman, A. (2001) *The End of Globalization*. New York: Random House.

References

Rugman, A. M. (2005) Globalization and regional international production. In J. Ravenhill (ed.), *Global Political Economy*, Oxford: Oxford University Press.

Ruigrok, W. and Tulder, R. V. (1995) *The Logic of International Restructuring*. London: Routledge.

Rupert, M. and Solomon, S. (2005) *Globalization and International Political Economy*. New York: Rowman and Littlefield.

Russett, B. (1993) *Grasping the Democratic Peace: Principles for a Post-Cold War World*. Princeton: Princeton University Press.

Russett, B. and Oneal, J. (2001) *Triangulating Peace*. New York: Norton.

Sala-i-Martin, X. (2002) The disturbing 'rise' of global income inequality. Working Paper 8904 (Apr.), National Bureau of Economic Research, New York.

Sala-i-Martin, X. (2005) The world distribution of income. Draft paper, at www.columbia.edu/~xs23/papers/pdfs/World_Income_Distribution_QJE.pdf.

Sandel, M. (1996) *Democracy's Discontent*. Cambridge, Mass.: Harvard University Press.

Sandholtz, W. et al. (1992) *The Highest Stakes*. Oxford: Oxford University Press.

Sarkees, M., Wayman, F. and Singer, J. D. (2003) Inter-state, intra-state and extra-state war: a comprehensive look at their distribution over time, 1816–1997. *International Studies Quarterly* 47(1): 49–79.

Sassen, S. (1996) *Losing Control? Sovereignty in an Age of Globalization*. New York: Columbia University Press.

Sassen, S. (2006) *Territory, Authority, Rights: From Medieval to Global Assemblages*. Princeton: Princeton University Press.

Saul, J. R. (2005) *The Collapse of Globalism*. London: Atlantic Books.

Scharpf, F. (1991) *Crisis and Choice in European Social Democracy*. New York: Cornell University Press.

Scharpf, F. (1999) *Governing in Europe: Effective and Democratic?* Oxford: Oxford University Press.

Scheffler, S. (1999) Conceptions of cosmopolitanism. *Utilitas* 113: 255–76.

Schmidt, V. (2002) *The Futures of European Capitalism*. Oxford: Oxford University Press.

Scholte, J. A. (1993) *International Relations of Social Change*. Buckingham: Open University Press.

Scholte, J. A. (1997) Global capitalism and the state. *International Affairs* 73(3) (July).

Scholte, J. A. (2000a) Global civil society. In N. Woods (ed.), *The Political Economy of Globalization*, London: Macmillan.

References

Scholte, J. A. (2000b) *Globalization: A Critical Introduction*. London: Macmillan.

Scholte, J. A. (2005) *Globalization: A Critical Introduction*, 2nd edn. London: Macmillan.

Schwartz, H. (2001) Round up the usual suspects: globalization, domestic politics, and welfare state change. In P. Pierson (ed.), *The New Politics of the Welfare State*, Oxford: Oxford University Press.

Shah, A. (2006) Behind consumption and consumerism. At www.globalissues.org/TradeRelated/Consumption.asp.

Shaw, M. (1994) *Global Society and International Relations*. Cambridge: Polity.

Shaw, M. (1997) The state of globalization: towards a theory of state transformation. *Review of International Political Economy* 4(3).

Shaw, M. (2005) *The New Western Way of War*. Cambridge: Polity.

Shell, G. R. (1995) Trade legalism and international relations theory: an analysis of the WTO. *Duke Law Journal* 44(5).

Silver, B. J. (2003) *Forces of Labor: Workers' Movements and Globalization since 1870*. Cambridge: Cambridge University Press.

Silverstone, R. (2001) Finding a voice: minorities, media and the global commons. *Emergences* 11(1).

Sindharan, K. (1998) G-15 and South–South co-operation: promise and performance. *Third World Quarterly* 19(3): 357–73.

Singer, P. W. (2003) *Corporate Warriors: The Rise of the Privatized Military Industry*. Ithaca: Cornell University Press.

Singer, P. W. (2004) War, profits, and the vacuum of law: privatized military firms and international law. *Columbia Journal of Transnational Law* 42(2): 521–44.

SIPRI (Stockholm International Peace Research Institute) (2004) *SIPRI Yearbook 2004*. New York: Oxford University Press.

SIPRI (Stockholm International Peace Research Institute) (2005) *SIPRI Yearbook 2005*. New York: Oxford University Press.

SIPRI (Stockholm International Peace Research Institute) (2006) *SIPRI Yearbook 2006*. New York: Oxford University Press.

Sivard, R. L. (1991) *World Military and Social Expenditures*. Washington DC: World Priorities.

Skinner, Q. (1978) *The Foundations of Modern Political Thought*, vol. 2. Cambridge: Cambridge University Press.

Skinner, Q. (1989) The state. In T. Ball, J. Farr and R. L. Hanson (eds), *Political Innovation and Conceptual Change*, Cambridge: Cambridge University Press.

Sklair, L. (2001) *The Transnational Capitalist Class*. Oxford: Blackwell.

References

Sköns, H. and Wulf, H. (1994) The internationalization of the arms industry. *Annals of the American Academy of Political and Social Science* 535(1): 43–57.

Slater, D. (1995) Challenging Western visions of the global: the geopolitics of theory and North–South relations. *European Journal of Development Research* 7(2).

Slaughter, A.-M. (2000) Governing the global economy through government networks. In M. Byers (ed.), *The Role of Law in International Politics*, Oxford: Oxford University Press.

Slaughter, A.-M. (2004) *A New World Order*. Princeton: Princeton University Press.

Smith, A. D. (1986) *The Ethnic Origins of Nations*. Oxford: Blackwell.

Smith, A. D. (1990) Towards a global culture? In M. Featherstone (ed.), *Global Culture: Nationalism, Globalization and Modernity*, London: Sage.

Smith, A. D. (1995) *Nations and Nationalism in a Global Era*. Cambridge: Polity.

Smith, M. P. (2001) *Transnational Urbanism: Locating Globalization*. Oxford: Blackwell.

Smith, S. (1987) Reasons of state. In D. Held and C. Pollitt (eds), *New Forms of Democracy*, London: Sage.

Solana, J. (2003) The future of transatlantic relations. *Progressive Politics* 2(2).

Soros, G. (2006) *The Age of Fallibility: Consequences of the War on Terror*. New York: Public Affairs.

Sterling, R. W. (1974) *Macropolitics: International Relations in a Global Society*. New York: Knopf.

Stern, N. (2006) *The Economics of Climate Change: The Stern Review*. Cambridge: Cambridge University Press.

Stiglitz, J. P. (2005) The overselling of globalization. In M. M. Weinstein (ed.), *Globalization: What's New?* New York: Columbia University Press.

Strange, S. (1983) Cave! Hic dragones: a critique of regime analysis. In S. Krasner (ed.), *International Regimes*, Ithaca: Cornell University Press.

Strange, S. (1996) *The Retreat of the State*. Cambridge: Cambridge University Press.

Swank, D. (2002a) *Global Capital, Political Institutions, and Policy Change in Developed Welfare States*. Cambridge: Cambridge University Press.

Swank, D. (2002b) The transformation of tax policy in an era of internationalization. Conference on Interdependence, Diffusion, and Sovereignty, Yale University, 10–11 May, and annual meeting of the American Political Science Association, 29 Aug.–1 Sept., Boston.

References

Swank, D. (2003) Withering welfare? Globalization, political economic institutions and contemporary welfare states. In L. Weiss (ed.), *States in the Global Economy*, Cambridge: Cambridge University Press.

Tamir, Y. (1993) *Liberal Nationalism*. Princeton: Princeton University Press.

Tanzi, V. (2001) Globalization without a net. *Foreign Policy* 125.

Tarow, S. (2005) *The New Transnational Activism*. Cambridge: Cambridge University Press.

Taylor, A. M. (1996) Domestic saving and international capital flows reconsidered. Working Paper 5743, National Bureau of Economic Research, New York.

Taylor, P. J. (1995) Beyond containers: internationality, interstateness, interterritoriality. *Progress in Human Geography* 19(1): 1–15.

Teubner, G. (ed.) (1997) *Global Law without a State*. Aldershot: Dartmouth.

Therborn, G. (1977) The rule of capital and the rise of democracy. *New Left Review*, series I, no. 103.

Thomas, C. (1997) Poverty, development and hunger. In J. Baylis and S. Smith (eds), *The Globalization of World Politics*, Oxford: Oxford University Press.

Thomas, C. (2000) *Global Governance, Development and Human Security*. London: Pluto Press.

Thompson, G. (1998a) Globalization versus regionalism? *Journal of North African Studies* 3(2).

Thompson, G. (1998b) International competitiveness and globalization. In T. Baker and J. Köhler (eds), *International Competitiveness and Environmental Policies*, Brighton: Edward Elgar.

Thompson, G. (2006) The supranational regionalization of the international financial system. Paper prepared for the Garnet Conference: Global Financial and Monetary Governance, the EU, and Emerging Market Economies, 28–30 Sept., Amsterdam.

Thompson, G. and Allen, J. (1997) Think global and then think again: economic globalization in context. *Area* 29(3).

Thompson, J. (1994) *Mercenaries, Pirates and Sovereigns : State-Building and Extraterritorial Violence in Early Modern Europe*. Princeton: Princeton University Press.

Thompson, J. B. (1990) *Ideology and Modern Culture*. Cambridge: Polity.

Thompson, J. B. (1995) *The Media and Modernity*. Cambridge: Polity.

Thompson, J. B. (1998) Community identity and world citizenship. In Archibugi, Held and Köhler 1998.

Thompson, K. W. (1994) *Fathers of International Thought: The*

Legacy of Political Theory. Baton Rouge: Louisiana State University Press.

Tilly, C. (ed.) (1975) *The Formation of National States in Western Europe.* Princeton: Princeton University Press.

Tilly, C. (1990) *Coercion, Capital and European States AD990–1992.* Oxford: Blackwell.

Tilly, C. (2003) *The Politics of Collective Violence.* Cambridge: Cambridge University Press.

Tilly, C. (2004) *Contention and Democracy in Europe, 1650–2000.* Cambridge: Cambridge University Press.

Tomlinson, J. (2007) Globalization and cultural analysis. In D. Held and A. McGrew (eds), *Globalization Theory: Approaches and Controversies*, Cambridge: Polity.

Tormey, S. (2004) *Anticapitalism.* Oxford: OneWorld.

Tripathi, S. (2005) International regulation of multinational corporations. *Oxford Development Studies* 33(1): 117–31.

Turner, B. S. (1986) *Citizenship and Capitalism.* London: Allen and Unwin.

Tyson, L. (1991) They are not us: why American ownership still matters. *American Prospect* (Winter).

Ugarteche, O. (2000) *The False Dilemma – Globalization: Opportunity or Threat?* London: Zed Press.

UIA (Union of International Associations) (2000) *Yearbook of International Organizations*, vol. 1A. Brussels: Union of International Associations.

UIA (Union of International Associations) (2001) *Yearbook of International Organizations 2001/2002*, vol. 1B (Int–Z). Brussels: Union of International Associations.

UN (2005) General Assembly adopts 2006–2007 budget of $3.79 billion. Press release, United Nations, New York, 23 Dec. At www.un.org/News/Press/docs/2005/ga10442.doc.htm.

UN (2006) Growing share of UN resources in field operations. United Nations factsheet, at www.un.org/reform/investinginun/pdfs/factsheet.pdf.

UN High-Level Panel (2005) *A More Secure World.* UN High-Level Panel on Threats, Challenges and Change. At www.un.org/secureworld.

UNCTAD (1998a) *The Least Developed Countries 1998.* Geneva: UN Conference on Trade and Development.

UNCTAD (1998b) *Trade and Development Report 1998.* Geneva: UN Conference on Trade and Development.

UNCTAD (1998c) *World Investment Report 1998.* Geneva: UN Conference on Trade and Development.

References

UNCTAD (2001) *World Investment Report 2001*. Geneva: UN Conference on Trade and Development.

UNCTAD (2002) *World Investment Report 2002*. Geneva: UN Conference on Trade and Development.

UNCTAD (2003) *World Investment Report 2003*. Geneva: UN Conference on Trade and Development.

UNCTAD (2004a) *Development and Globalization: Facts and Figures*. Geneva: UN Conference on Trade and Development.

UNCTAD (2004b) *The New Geography of World Economic Relations*. Geneva: UN Conference on Trade and Development.

UNCTAD (2005) *Trade and Development Report 2005*. Geneva: UN Conference on Trade and Development.

UNCTAD (2006a) *Trade and Development Report 2006*. Geneva: UN Conference on Trade and Development.

UNCTAD (2006b) *World Investment Report 2006*. Geneva: UN Conference on Trade and Development.

UNDP (1997) *Human Development Report 1997*. New York: Oxford University Press and UN Development Programme.

UNDP (1998a) *Globalization and Liberalization*. New York: Oxford University Press and UN Development Programme.

UNDP (1998b) *Human Development Report 1998*. New York: Oxford University Press and UN Development Programme.

UNDP (1999) *Globalization with a Human Face: UN Human Development Report 1999*. New York: Oxford University Press and UN Development Programme.

UNDP (2001) *Human Development Report: Making Technology Work for Human Development*. New York: Oxford University Press and UN Development Programme.

UNDP (2006) *Human Development Report 2006*. New York: UN Development Programme.

UNESCO (1950) *World Communications Report*. Paris: United Nations Educational, Scientific and Cultural Organization.

UNESCO (1986) *International Flows of Selected Cultural Goods*. Paris: United Nations Educational, Scientific and Cultural Organization.

UNESCO (1989) *World Communications Report*. Paris: United Nations Educational, Scientific and Cultural Organization.

UNESCO Institute for Statistics (2005) International flows of selected cultural goods and services, 1994–2003: defining and capturing the flows of global cultural trade. Montreal: UNESCO Institute for Statistics. At www.uis.unesco.org/template/pdf/cscl/IntlFlows_EN.pdf (accessed Aug. 2006).

Urry, J. (2002) *Global Complexity*. Cambridge: Polity.

References

Van der Pijl, K. (1999) *Transnational Classes and International Relations*. London: Routledge.

Wade, R. (1990) *Governing the Market: Economic Theory and the Role of Government in East Asian Industrialization*. Princeton: Princeton University Press.

Wade, R. (2001a) Inequality of world incomes: what should be done? At www.openDemocracy.net.

Wade, R. (2001b) Winners and losers. *The Economist*, 28 April: 93–7.

Wade, R. (2004) Is globalization reducing poverty and inequality? *World Development* 32(4): 567–89.

Wade, R. (2006) Should we worry about income inequality? In Held and Kaya 2006.

Wade, R. and Wolf, M. (2002) Are global poverty and inequality getting worse? *Prospect* 72: 16–21.

Waldron, J. (1992) Minority cultures and the cosmopolitan alternative. *University of Michigan Journal of Law Reform* 25: 751–93.

Waldron, J. (1999) Minority cultures and the cosmopolitan alternative. In W. Kymlicka (ed.), *Minority Cultures*, Oxford: Blackwell.

Walker, R. B. J. (1994) *Inside/Outside*. Cambridge: Cambridge University Press.

Wallace, W. (1999) The sharing of sovereignty: the European paradox. *Political Studies* 47(3), special issue.

Wallerstein, I. (1974) *The Modern World System*. New York: Academic Press.

Wallerstein, I. (1983) *Historical Capitalism*. London: Verso.

Walters, A. (1993) *World Power and World Money*. Brighton: Harvester.

Waltz, K. (1979) *The Theory of International Politics*. New York: Addison-Wesley.

Walzer, M. (1983) *Spheres of Justice: A Defence of Pluralism and Equality*. Oxford: Martin Robertson.

Warnock, F. E. and Warnock, V. (2006) International capital flows and US interest rates. Working Paper, National Bureau of Economic Research, New York.

Watson, M. (2001) International capital mobility in an era of globalization. *Politics* 21(2).

Weiss, L. (1998) *State Capacity: Governing the Economy in a Global Era*. Cambridge: Polity.

Weiss, L. (2003) Is the state being transformed by globalisation? In L. Weiss (ed.), *States in the Global Economy*, Cambridge: Cambridge University Press.

Wheeler, N. J. (2000) *Saving Strangers*. Oxford: Oxford University Press.

References

Whitman, J. (2005) *The Limits of Global Governance*. London: Routledge.

Wight, M. (1986) *Power Politics*, 2nd edn. London: Penguin.

Williamson, J. (1990) *Latin American Adjustment: How Much has Happened?* Washington DC: Institute for International Economics.

Williamson, J. (1993) Democracy and the 'Washington Consensus'. *World Development*, 21(8).

Williamson, J. (2003) The Washington Consensus and beyond. *Economic and Political Weekly* 38(15).

WMO (2006) *World Migration Report 2005*. Geneva: World Migration Organization.

Wolf, M. (2001) The view from the limousine. *Financial Times*, 7 Nov.

Wolf, M. (2002) Countries still rule the world. *Financial Times*, 6 Feb.

Wolf, M. (2004) *Why Globalization Works*. New Haven: Yale University Press.

Wolf, M. (2006) Will globalization survive ? *World Economics* 6(4).

Wood, A. (1994) *North–South Trade, Employment and Inequality*. Oxford: Oxford University Press.

Wood, E. M. (2003) *Empire of Capital*. London: Verso.

Woods, N. (1999) Order, globalization and inequality in world politics. In A. Hurrell and N. Woods (eds), *Inequality, Globalization and World Politics*, Oxford: Oxford University Press.

Woods, N. (2005) The shifting politics of foreign aid. *International Affairs* 81(2): 393–409.

World Bank (1987) *World Development Report*. Washington DC: World Bank.

World Bank (2001a) *Poverty in the Age of Globalization*. Washington DC: World Bank.

World Bank (2001b) *World Development Indicators Database*. Washington DC: World Bank.

World Bank (2005) *Global Economic Prospects 2006*. Washington DC: World Bank.

World Bank (2006) *Global Economic Prospects 2007: Managing the Next Wave of Globalization*. Washington DC: World Bank.

Worldwatch Institute (2004) *State of the World 2004: Consumption by the Numbers*. Washington DC: Worldwatch Institute. At www.worldwatch.org.

Worldwatch Institute (2006) *Vital Signs 2006–2007*. Washington DC: Worldwatch Institute.

WTO (2001) *World Trade Report 2001*. Geneva: World Trade Organization.

WTO (2002) *World Trade Report 2002*. Geneva: World Trade Organization.

References

WTO (2003) *World Trade Report 2003*. Geneva: World Trade Organization.

WTO (2005) *World Trade Report 2005*. Geneva: World Trade Organization.

WTO (2006a) *International Trade Statistics*. Geneva: World Trade Organization.

WTO (2006b) *World Trade Report 2006*. Geneva: World Trade Organization.

Yergin, D. A. and Stanislaw, J. (1998) *The Commanding Heights*. New York: Simon and Schuster.

Young, O. (1972) The actors in world politics. In J. Rosenau, V. Davis and M. East (eds), *The Analysis of International Politics*, New York: Cornell University Press.

Zacher, M. (1992) The decaying pillars of the Westphalian temple. In J. N. Rosenau and O. E. Czempiel (eds), *Governance without Government*, Cambridge: Cambridge University Press.

Zevin, R. (1992) Are world financial markets more open? In T. Banuri and J. B. Schor (eds), *Financial Openness and National Autonomy*, Oxford: Oxford University Press.

Zürn, M. (1995) The challenge of globalization and individualization. In H.-H. Holm and G. Sorensen (eds), *Whose World Order?* Boulder: Westview Press.

Index

Index

Index

Index

Index